The Genes of Culture

Lance Strate
General Editor

Vol. 7

The Understanding Media Ecology series is part
of the Peter Lang Media and Communication list.
Every volume is peer reviewed and meets the highest
quality standards for content and production.

PETER LANG
New York • Bern • Berlin
Brussels • Vienna • Oxford • Warsaw

Christine L. Nystrom

The Genes of Culture

Towards a Theory of Symbols, Meaning, and Media, Volume 2

Edited by
Carolyn Wiebe and Susan Maushart

PETER LANG
New York • Bern • Berlin
Brussels • Vienna • Oxford • Warsaw

Library of Congress Cataloging-in-Publication Data provided for Volume 1

Names: Names: Nystrom, Christine L., author. | Wiebe, Carolyn, editor. |
Maushart, Susan, editor.
Title: The genes of culture: towards a theory of symbols, meaning, and media.
Volume 1 / Christine L. Nystrom; edited by Carolyn Wiebe
and Susan Maushart.
Description: New York: Peter Lang, [2021].
Series: Understanding media ecology; vol. 6
ISSN 2374-7676 (print) | ISSN 2374-7684 (online)
Includes bibliographical references.
Contents: v. 1
Identifiers: LCCN 2020005899 | ISBN 978-1-4331-7660-9 (v. 1; hardback)
ISBN 978-1-4331-7664-7 (v. 1; paperback) | ISBN 978-1-4331-7661-6 (v. 1; ebook pdf)
ISBN 978-1-4331-7662-3 (v. 1; epub) | ISBN 978-1-4331-7663-0 (v. 1; mobi)
Subjects: Culture. | Signs and symbols. | Technology—Social aspects.
Classification: LCC HM621 .N97 2021 | DDC 302.2—dc23
LC record available at https://lccn.loc.gov/2020005899
DOI 10.3726/b16789

Bibliographic information published by **Die Deutsche Nationalbibliothek**.
Die Deutsche Nationalbibliothek lists this publication in the "Deutsche
Nationalbibliografie"; detailed bibliographic data are available
on the Internet at http://dnb.d-nb.de/.

The genes of culture: towards a theory of symbols, meaning, and media. Volume 2 /
Christine L. Nystrom; edited by Carolyn Wiebe and Susan Maushart.
Understanding media ecology; vol. 7
ISBN 978-1-4331-8261-7 (v. 2; hardcover)
ISBN 978-1-4331-8262-4 (v. 2; paperback)
ISBN 978-1-4331-8263-1 (v. 2; ebook pdf)
ISBN 978-1-4331-8264-8 (v. 2; epub)
DOI 10.3726/b19431

© 2022 Peter Lang Publishing, Inc., New York
80 Broad Street, 5th floor, New York, NY 10004
www.peterlang.com

"Thinking again?" the Duchess asked, with another dig of her sharp little chin.

"I've a right to think," said Alice sharply, for she was beginning to feel a little worried.

"Just about as much right," said the Duchess, "as pigs have to fly …"

—*Alice's Adventures in Wonderland,* Chapter 9

About the Author

Born March 23, 1941, Christine Louise Nystrom received a B.A. in philosophy and English in 1962 from Washington Square College, New York University, and then an M.A. in language and communication in 1966 from Teachers College, Columbia University. In 1973 she earned the first Ph.D. in the field of Media Ecology. Her doctoral dissertation synthesized the scholarship of a diverse range of seminal thinkers to formulate a theoretical framework for the new discipline of Media Ecology. That dissertation, *Towards a Science of Media Ecology: The Formation of Integrated Conceptual Paradigms for the Study of Human Communication Systems*, remains an important text in the Media Ecology canon.

Nystrom joined Neil Postman in developing the Media Ecology program at NYU, and for some 30 years, she designed and taught courses that would give enduring shape and focus to the field. She served as executive editor of the journal *ETC: A Review of General Semantics* and directed the graduate program in Media Ecology. Together with colleagues Postman and Henry Perkinson, she created a vibrant intellectual community, inviting and supporting students to participate in transformative conversations about technology, self and society.

Table of Contents

Acknowledgments

First off, because "30 years as a teacher" does not adequately capture the impact Chris had on so many of us, we'd like to thank all of Chris's former students who encouraged us and shared their memories. (See the "Remembrances" section p. 229). Robert Albrecht, Missy Alexander, Mary Ann Allison, Susan Barnes, Eva Berger, Bob Blechman, Moshe Botwinick, Peggy Cassidy, Renee Chow, Brian Cogan, Sal Fallica, Peter Fallon, Stephanie Gibson, Michael Grabowski, Paul Levinson, David Linton, Joshua Meyrowitz, Casey Lum, William Petankas, Devon Powers, MJ Robinson, Maria Simpson, Jonathan Slater, Lance Strate, and Toni Urbano. And, most especially, we'd like to thank Chris's brother, Peter Nystrom. His kind words, remarkable patience and generosity certainly helped make this over-long task feel worthwhile.

For this volume specifically, we would like to acknowledge the remarkably efficient and cheerful assistance of Leah Edelman, outreach archivist at The Burke Library at Union Theological Seminary, in arranging access to the tape recordings of Chris's Australian lecture series. How those tapes ended up traveling from Perth, Western Australia to an archive at Columbia University in New York City is a long, unlikely bi-hemispheric tale for another day. For now, suffice it to say we are indebted too to the meticulous record-keeping of Chris's friend and fellow traveler, Christopher Morse, Professor Emeritus of Theology and Ethics at Union Seminary.

XII | THE GENES OF CULTURE

For the generous help of the kind one only asks of a sibling, Thomas Wiebe was of invaluable technical assistance. Other siblings—Margaret Wiebe and Frank Wiebe—read large swaths of these volumes. Their assurance that, yes, Chris's work is not only readable but of interest to people who neither study media nor work in education, was genuinely encouraging.

Finally, we'd like to acknowledge thanks to Margarethe Hubauer, and especially to Michael Sowa for the existence of and then generous permission to use that most joyous image, Koehler's pig.

Introduction

The two works that comprise this volume display two different sides of Christine Nystrom's scholarship. The first, *Human Symbolic Evolution: A Study of Tales, Tools, and Social Change*, is what we've fondly come to refer to as her magnum opus. Certainly, it was an ongoing project that reflects much of her life's work. It displays the enormous scope and highly abstracted perspective—the long view—with which she approached the field of human communication. And yet also evident, despite the broad strokes of history and philosophy, is the careful and critical attentiveness typical of her intellectual rigor. The second work, a series of lectures given at an Anglican education conference in 1989 in Perth, Australia, suggests the other side of Nystrom's work: contemporary social and *moral* criticism of notions of "development," "efficiency," and "progress" in a rampantly technological culture.

It was hard to decide which piece to put first. The lectures predate the final 1996 date we find on the various manuscripts of *Human Symbolic Evolution*. However, as close readers of Volume 1 of *The Genes of Culture* may detect, sections of the manuscript available to us were written at different points well before then. More to the point, the manuscript provides the groundwork for understanding and critically addressing the perspective offered in the lectures we have titled *Tales, Tools, Technopoly*. It is therefore logically, if not strictly chronologically, precedent.

Keep in mind, *Human Symbolic Evolution* frames the history of humanity as a story of the development of language, of symbol systems, of our ever-changing symbolic environments. The perspective Nystrom articulates—understanding media of communication within the framework of an ecology of mind—functioned as the foundational approach for the media program at New York University. Not surprisingly, large chunks of the manuscript were, and continued to be, widely assigned among graduate students.

These chapters are clearly part of what was originally conceptualized as a larger work; the prologue of volume 1 and the lectures give us a sense of where her tale was leading and what Nystrom intended to address. Studying the underlying patterns associated with large shifts in communications, she sees media not so much as agents of change, but as processes linked to solving the problems that inevitably arise out of prior stages of symbolic development—out of the fact that we communicate through symbol systems. Every "solution" adopted is itself necessarily flawed—and necessarily introduces further change. The result is a range of new challenges, which spark further change—and so on, ad infinitum. So long as humans survive, our history will continue to tell the story of new ways we try to solve the problems that arise out of our imperfect means of communicating.

Inadequacy and imperfection function therefore as both the engine of change and the inevitable result of change. When we deny that fallibility lies at the heart of what it means to be human and cling instead to the illusion of perfectibility, we risk falling prey to fanaticism—whether in a doomed pursuit of heaven on earth, or delusions of a master race, or dreams of some futuristic era of transhumanism arising out of the glory of new media technologies.

We can look at this notion of inexorable imperfection with a sense of gloom that we are destined to ongoing failure. Or we can embrace our fallibility, observing the human comedy of errors in good faith and with the optimism that things can in fact always be made better. While Nystrom embraced the latter perspective, she also recognized, with a sense of foreboding, the dismal possibility that humankind might be so strongly steeped in its own glories—the folly of our success, so to speak—as to lead us to our demise.

> We may in fact be perilously close to the end. It all depends on where we take the story from here. My race across the past and territories not my own is not spurred by confidence but by dread. If we cannot get a clear view of what our story has been, and where it stands, and how to correct its course, my mistakes in this matter will not matter much.

Her goal "to assess where we stand just now in the living tale of our species—and of our tools—and identify the problems we must solve if we do not wish to end it" must have seemed increasingly futile. Or, perhaps, after the retirement of their colleague Henry Perkinson, and then the death of her great friend and collaborator

Neil Postman, the pursuit simply became less of an adventure and more of a cross to bear.

Nystrom sought to deepen our understanding of the interaction of narrative and media so as to bring to our attention and help solve the problems arising out of our relationship to our new and ever-consuming technologies. Tools and technologies, she argues, give rise to and are shaped by narrative, which situates their use and foretells their purpose. And where Marx, for instance, tells a story about what Nystrom calls "tools of doing," of economics and the means of production, her focus stays squarely on "tools of knowing," on people and the means of *meaning*.

In *Tales, Tools, Technopoly*, we get an inkling of where Nystrom was probably going with her unfinished opus. Here, large swaths of history orient our attention to the central problems arising from the development of and changes in human communication. Oddly enough, because of our unique ability to represent, realize, and create "reality" through symbols, we need a way to control, structure, and contain the surfeit of information such representation provides. The Tale of Technopoly she introduces in these lectures is "the tale of technological progress with paradise to be regained, not in some misty hereafter, but here on earth, through the wonders of technology." The content of this tale is, in large measure, the celebration of consumerism. The activity through which that tale progresses is the process of turning human behavior into technique. In the 1980s, when Nystrom was writing this account, she called our attention to the way all behaviors were relegated to experts—whether in psychology, education, economics, surgery, politics—and made quantifiable. And, indeed, our experts continue to diagnose and quantify our activities so as to determine whether a child should be given a behavior modification drug, whether a patient can get insurance coverage, whether a candidate and will win elections and so on. But today, her arguments against the tyranny of experts are complicated by the fact that we have incorporated their tools into our technologies, thereby making the mechanics of quantification invisible. Today, we look to our phones to find out whether we've done enough exercise or slept soundly or—irony of ironies!—used our phones too much. We don't think about the premises upon which such tracking apps base their "scientific" output. Or even, simply, about how ridiculous it is that we might not be able to determine those things for ourselves.

Yet narrative has both form and content: its form has much to do with the media that carry it, which in turn gives shape to its content. The shifts in the forms through which narrative is given shape is perhaps the most problematic aspect of Nystrom's lectures and of Postman's later books and speeches. They both looked to the computer and saw the quantification of experience. They watched the rise of image-oriented stories and with them the decline of reading and the habits of mind associated with it. They saw with chilling clarity the increasing emphasis on speed, the deterioration of language, the absence of subtlety, complexity, ambiguity in our discourse and, in turn, in our thinking. Thus it is not merely that the stories conveyed through new media distract us from contemplating the problems arising out of our dependence upon our technologies. Today the technologies themselves orient us to distraction—so that we struggle to sit still with our thoughts, let alone to muster up the critical faculties we associate with analysis and problem-solving.

In their various discussions of Technopoly, both Nystrom and Postman knew they were giving short shrift to the potential benefits of new and developing technologies. Neither were advocates of "back to nature," or to orality (as the case may be), and Nystrom, in particular, resisted the nostalgia associated with an illusory Golden Age of print culture, where freedom and democracy and economic well-being reigned supreme. Both, however, were acutely aware of the selling power of new technologies—the glib boosterism, the tyranny of cheerfulness braying ceaselessly of improvement, speed, efficiency, productivity and, of course, profit. The way they saw it, new technologies did not need more or louder evangelists.

Both were aware of their own biases towards the written word. And they were also supremely aware of the limited capacity to fully appreciate all the potential consequences that developing technologies might bring. But, again, that was not the focus of their work.

They were committed instead to taking the longer view, the unfashionably darker perspective that would have us take stock of what was being put aside, left behind, forgotten.

For Nystrom and for Postman, the time had come for their human companions on this planet earth to look squarely at the problems brought on by the technologies they were using. These were large, moral, ecological concerns.

Anyone reading these pieces who is familiar with Nystrom's work will come across bits and pieces they've read before—in course notes, conference speeches, published articles. There is little that is remarkable about that. However, the crossover between her work and Postman's is. Certainly, her concerns with "narrative" overlap with his later publications and speeches (as in *End of Education*), as do her comments about problems and change (*Building a Bridge to the 18th Century*), and, most tellingly, her definition and explication of *Technopoly* (reiterated in his book of that name).

What deserves mention here is not who has the prior claim of authorship, but how closely and brilliantly—and how generously—they collaborated. Their intellectual camaraderie was a conversation in the very best sense of the word, by turns playful and pointed, inquisitive and declarative, tentative and audacious. It was a decades-long dialectic that brought out the best in each of them. And it has left an indelible intellectual mark on those of us who have had the privilege to listen in.

With all of this attention to her written work, it is easy to forget that Nystrom was, primarily, a teacher. For her, to work in education was to give—an act of social good; the intimation that one works for the betterment of all. For students, she was a ruthless critic, but this came out of a generosity that held us to flatteringly great expectations.

Her expectations for the field of Media Ecology helped promote an ethos of scholarship—an ethos that, alas, is rare in communication departments. For Nystrom, Media Ecology was not a sub-field of communications theory, but a meta-field that connected and explained ways of knowing—the function of symbol systems in the various categories of knowledge—from math and English to music and theology. As with Alfred North Whitehead and Susanne Langer, she saw the study of symbol systems as the dawning of a new age of philosophy, which gave rise to Media Ecology as the study of the means through which humans understood the world, created reality, and dreamed of the future.

> "In the main, this book is about our stories and why we tell them,
> and how they are related to our technologies and social change."

Nystrom writes these words in the undated prologue to *Narrative: The Ecology of Tales, Tools, and Social Change*—a piece found separately (indeed, saved from the recycling bin by her good friend and neighbor, Anne Garfinkel) from her other papers. Volume One opens with a major portion of that prologue because it provides such a wonderful introduction to her thinking about the way symbol systems and communication media give rise to meaning. But despite its original title, we are fairly certain this piece was intended to introduce the work that follows here: *Human Symbolic Evolution: A Study of Tales, Tools, and Social Change*—and that the title change points to the ways this major project emerged and developed.

The works presented in Volume One illustrate Nystrom's thinking about meaning and its relation to knowledge and information environments. As such, they provide the foundation for the ideas presented here. The present volume, however, suggests the further development of these ideas into a more fully organized conceptualization of meaning as both contained by, and arising through, narrative.

Intertwined here are two central themes regarding narrative. First, that different symbol systems and media give rise to different narrative forms and therefore, inevitably, to differences in meaning—influencing, for example, what gets attended to and valued, as well as what goes unseen or unremarked. But her second and equally resonant theme here concerns what Norbert Wiener called "the human use of human beings"—the conviction that ultimate responsibility for the narratives we live by lies beyond technology. That is, because human beings have choice, we carry the responsibility.

Nystrom's "tale of evolution" incorporates a description of the shift from the signalic mode of communication—which homo sapiens share with other animals— to the symbolic, which is to say language, mathematics, music, and so on. While this tale is also a great adventure—a tale of tools, discoveries and inventions— she reminds us that human beings, not symbol systems or technologies, are the storytellers. We are, perhaps, too easily fascinated with the action-adventure and consumed by a tale of technological progress and its promise of inevitable advancement. And thus we fail to pay attention to the fact we alone create and control the content of the stories we share, which are the means through which we perceive reality, and through which we conceive our future.

Nystrom asks us to remember, in other words, that we are not simply a manifestation of the technological means through which we communicate. Rather, we select which pictures to depict and which words to use. Hers is a crucial reminder: the stories we choose to tell—which are no less than the stuff of ideology, of culture, of mind itself—will ultimately shape the destiny of our species.

We include here a section of the original prologue, part of which was omitted from Volume One, that outlines specifically what Nystrom planned for this (unfinished) book. This provides a detailed introduction to the work that follows. Moreover, it outlines what she intended to do, which clearly links this project with the lectures on technopoly and narrative that form the second and final section of the present volume.

Carolyn Wiebe
Susan Maushart

Prologue

...This book begins with a view of humans as a species that has survived. And it starts from the premise that we have survived in the same way as have others who accompany us still on this whirling ball as it travels through space: not through the special favors of a benevolent Nature or laws bent this way or that to our advantage by an arbitrary god. We have survived, as others have, because our species has found ways to solve problems of adjustment to change. Some of the change is a result of natural laws and phenomena—like the climate—that seem to have little origin in our own behavior. By far the greater bulk, in human affairs, arises from our own tinkering—as, indeed, we now see occurring with even the climate. In either case, change is inevitable. And it presents us with a continuous set of problems—problems of adjustment to change. In that respect, our situation is no different from that of other beasts, and for millions of years our story was the same as theirs: those genetic variations that provided some creatures with better "solutions" to environmental problems enabled them to flourish; those that proved inadequate left others disadvantaged, and they died. Evolution, one might say, is the story of life's biological solutions to problems created by change. As biological creatures, we are part of that long tale. But not entirely.

For somewhere along the way, humans developed the capacity to invent, and through invention, adjust our environments to ourselves. History, one might say, is the story of humans' *technical* solutions to problems created by change. Sometimes our solutions involve new ways of doing, as when we establish a new form of government or modify our cultural habits to make new arrangements for the raising of children. Sometimes they involve new ways of thinking, as when we construct new criteria for judging what we call "facts." And sometimes they involve new material creations, like digging sticks, or wheels, or money, or computers. But whether they are new forms of economic and social organization, new methods of thinking, new tools of labor, or new media, human techniques and technologies are always *responses* to something, and that "something" is problems—problems that arise from change. No less than biological evolution, technical evolution is driven by the pressure of change and the requirement it imposes on living things: to adjust or die. It follows from this that our technologies must always lead back, at no matter what remove, to attempts of our species to solve problems of adjustment, and so survive. Thus the first premise of this tale leads to two rules for how it will unfold. The first is that it must always explain technologies as solutions to problems; the second, that those problems must always lead back to the struggle of our species to survive.

But that is not all. There are two more premises this story requires, or there would be no need for a tale. If human solutions were perfect, we would have invented once, and that would have been enough. History would be a tale of decreasing complexity, with precious little to explain. But it is not. So the second premise is this: that humans are not perfect, and neither are their solutions to problems of change. Every technique and technology, therefore, suffers from some inadequacies. These are, themselves, a source of additional problems, and require further change. This may be called "The Premise of Imperfection," and with the next, will give this story a peculiar twist.

The third and final premise we may call "The Premise of Ecology." It asks you to accept the view that all elements in a complex system (like human life) are interconnected, and in ways that we do not always see. Thus a new way of getting or doing or thinking or telling that solves some problem always itself *introduces* change, giving rise to new problems in places where we may least expect them. Let a man make a hoe to ease his planting, and it will change the surface of the earth and all that lives therein, sometimes to his sorrow. That much we have learned to see. But there is more to it than that. For the hoe also changes the shape of the hand that holds it, and the muscles that work the hand. And if a man hoes long enough, the frame that holds the muscles will start to shift and curve, until the hoe has bent the hoer to the shape its use requires. Thus the tools of labor change the world to which they are applied, but change the laborer as well. So it is with tools of knowing, too. They change the knower as well as the known. And both kinds of tools, in both ways, create new problems that require further change.

The Premise of Imperfection and the Premise of Ecology lead to a rule for this story that may make it seem somewhat strange. Humans are justly proud of all we have accomplished. And we tend, looking back along our past, to read it as the record of what we have achieved. That is perfectly understandable, and no doubt good for morale. The trouble is that it directs our attention to the wrong thing: to solutions, not problems. And this blinds us to the forces that drive the engine of change. The premises of *this* story lead to quite a different tale: a tale that focuses on problems, not solutions; on inadequacies, not success. It may not build morale, but it will give us a clearer view, I think, of how we have arrived at where we stand, and of what lies just ahead. The premises are, in face, so central to that end that I will ennoble them here by calling them laws—the Laws of Technical Change. They apply equally, I believe, to tools of doing and tools of knowing, techniques of production and techniques of communication. But because this book is more concerned with the latter, I will restate them here in the narrower case, as the Laws of Media Change.

The First Law is this: *Changes in communication techniques and technologies are attempts to solve information problems that threaten the ability of humans to survive.* This does not mean that our search for solutions is conscious and rational, or even that we are aware of what our problems are. New techniques and technologies may be hit upon in any number of ways, including by accident. But they will not be recognized as useful, or developed, or incorporated into the life of the group or culture unless they offer solutions to some important problem. Thus we have a corollary to the First Law—namely, that those media changes will survive, and succeed most widely, that most efficiently solve the most urgent information problems of the largest number of people.

The Second Law is this: *Every attempt to solve problems of information suffers from inadequacies. These inadequacies result in new problems, which are the impetus for further media change.*

The Third Law is this: *Every attempt to solve information problems itself introduces change into the state of our information, and thus presents additional problems which generate further change.*

Those, I propose are the laws. Like laws in any field, they are exceedingly simple. All the rest is complexity. But it is in complexity that all the interest lies, and through complexity, in the following chapters, that this tale will weave its way. For the guidance it may provide, here is its general plan. The book is composed of three sections. The object of the first is to refine the Laws of Media Change by examining, from the viewpoint they provide, four great developments in the history of human communication: the evolution of language, of writing systems, of printing, and of electronic information technologies. We shall be looking for two things in this part of the tale: the kinds of problems that arise in the ecology of information and the dynamics through which problems and "solutions" interact to fuel the engine of change. Whatever we may learn in the course of this tale will be summarized as a set of further laws and principles of change at the end of Part One. Part Two will tease out from the story of change one of its central threads—narrative—and examine in greater detail the role that narrative plays in ecologies of information at every level of human organization, from the life of an individual to the life of our species in the world. This part of the tale will conclude with a summary of what it reveals about the ecology of narratives and principles of narrative change. These will be used, in Part Three, to assess where we stand just now in the living tale of our species and our tools, and the problems we must solve if we do not wish to end it. The last chapter of Part III proposes some solutions to those problems. And at the end of this tale of our tale, I have added an Epilogue. In it you will find two stories of a different kind from what has gone before. They are works of pure imagination that treat of beginnings and ends. I offer them with no more serious purpose than this: in the hope that they might encourage you to work at constructing your own.

All that remains, then, is to begin. Only the greatest tales may start, "In the beginning..." and this tale is not that kind. It does start long ago, with talking beasts and other wondrous things only vaguely placed in the vast and dateless eons where no clocks tolled the time. And so I shall begin as my mother did, and her mother before, in their great unending tales: Once upon a time...

PART I

HUMAN SYMBOLIC EVOLUTION: A STUDY OF TALES, TOOLS AND SOCIAL CHANGE

(n.d., c. 1996). Excerpts from *Human Symbolic Evolution: A Study of Tales, Tools, and Social Change*. Unpublished manuscript.

CHAPTER ONE

Language: The Monkeys' Tale

Long ago, in a time before time as humans understand it, a creature like and yet unlike ourselves uttered a sound. And one of its companions, though it heard, gave no returning cry, nor by the least sign made response. And so it was, in silence and in stillness, that speech and all that is human began. For in that moment when nothing seemed to happen, something momentous came to pass: in a listening creature not yet human but far from ape, the cry of another called nothing into action. It called an idea of something into mind. A cry became, in that long stillness, not a signal for action, but a word.

What a lovely irony this is, and how hard for us to grasp: that the story of human speech begins with silence, not with sound. But so it must begin, or we shall never understand how we humans diverged from all the other calling, crying, chattering beasts. Nothing is more clear than this: that we are not distinguished from our fellows on this planet by our capacity to communicate by sounds. Whales sing, monkeys howl and chatter, birds call, even cicadas chitter to one another in the tall grass of summer. The world was not silent before we came, and it would not long be silent were we gone. No. The wonder of human speech does not lie in its sounds, various and elegant though they be. The center of speech lies elsewhere, in the *word*. A word does not happen on the lips, or at the ear, or in the air between. It is not a sound, but a use a mind makes of sound. A word is something that happens nowhere else in all the world but in the mind of its maker. And it happens inaudibly, invisibly.

In fact, a mind does not require, to make a word, any sound at all. I am making words as I sit here in silence at my desk. And you, I hope, are making words of these marks as you sit in a silence of your own. But the words are not here, on the page. They are something you do with the marks in your mind. If you should fall into a doze, and the book slides to the floor, and an aimless ant wanders across its pages, the ant will encounter no words—merely alterations of light and dark. And if your infant daughter, pursuing the ant, should track it across the open book, there will be no words to slow her down. Even a visitor who understands no English, stooping to retrieve the book, will find no words on these pages, though he may recognize the distinctive patterns of print, and know that their purpose is to evoke words, and may even call the patterns "words" in his own tongue. Unhappily for us, we do the same in ours: call these distinctive shapes of light and dark, and the sounds that we make, "words."

So language often works great mischief in our thought, confounding two quite different things by calling them the same. In the present case, there can be no greater mischief than this: to let our thought run blithely down the path our habits of naming provide and arrive again at the wrong conclusion—that words and the sounds or scribbles that evoke them are the same. They are not. *Anything* can be a word, to a mind that makes it so. A flicker of light. A movement of the hand. A puff of smoke. Even silences may serve a mind as words, if they are set off in patterned ways from a surround of noise. It may be, in the end, that this will be the key to languages in the sea. Humans have for decades sought to understand the meaning in dolphins' sounds. Might it be that, in the great and noisy sea, it is not the sounds they make that carry meaning, but the silences bracketed by the sounds? Only our bias towards thinking of words as sounds obscures the rich potential of a language based on patterned silences. Perhaps that is why the dolphin seems to laugh.

Certainly that is why our efforts to assess the language capacities of our nearest evolutionary cousins, the chimpanzees and great apes, were misdirected for decades. Since language in humans is primarily codified in speech, and speech (we reasoned) is centered in sounds, then the great apes' capacity for language must be assessed by their ability, with training, to talk. Or so we thought. But the apes could not be made to talk. Even in circumstances carefully designed to replicate the environments and experiences of human infancy and childhood, the best and brightest of our cousins produced nothing approximating intelligible human sounds. And this fact posed a considerable problem for almost everyone interested in the origins of language and mind. For if the apes displayed no ability to produce the sounds of speech, then how could those sounds have been shaped, over the course of evolution, into human language? Where would human language, and mind, have come from? For some, the answer was plain enough: they were the special gifts of God to man, His separate creation, not rooted in anything that came before. If it were not so, why did the apes show not the least inclination to speak?

Only in the middle of this century did the answer to that question, and the error in our reasoning about language, come clear. The apes do not "talk" because they lack (at the least) the complex physiology—the positions of pharynx, larynx, lips, teeth, and tongue—that permits the articulation of the sounds humans make in speech. But this does not necessarily mean they lack the capacity for *language*. For speech sounds are only one of the many codes in which the complex mental activity that is language is given expression. The sign languages of the deaf, to take the most obvious example, are another—although our confusion of language with speech sounds made it far from "obvious" until fairly recently, with the cruel result that the deaf have been made to suffer not only the loss of hearing, but also the terrible calumny that they are mentally deficient as well.

The realization that language is not the same thing as making sounds changes the questions we need to ask about the development of human mind and language, not only as it happens in the present but as it unfolded in the long past as well. Studies of the language capacities of the chimps and great apes, for example, no longer ask whether they can be brought to speak, but whether they can perform the complex linguistic operations—the activities of *mind*—that human children do. And evidence bearing on this question is sought, not in the sounds they can learn and use, but in their learning and use of American Sign Language. Can the apes learn language, in this sense? The question is important for all kinds of reasons: for what it can tell us about learning, and about language, and about minds—theirs and our own. More than that, it is compelling, for humans have a desperate longing to make contact, it seems, with intelligences different from our own.

The answer is hotly debated still, because the evidence is far from perfect and everything hinges, to boot, on what one takes "use language" to mean. Happily for us, we will not need to enter that debate here—at least, not so far as it concerns what individual apes *might* do, in the extraordinary circumstances created for them by human experimenters. The object of our inquiry here is not to explain what might have been or yet might be among some apes in peculiar circumstances. It is to account for what was and is the case in human history and experience, as it concerns the development of communication and tools, mind and society. For that purpose, the most compelling fact about the great apes' and chimpanzees' capacity for language is this: while it now seems likely that these, our nearest cousins, have at least some rudimentary potential for using signs as words and thus creating language, *they never did*. And as a species they do not do so today. But humans do. On these facts there is no debate at all. Every physiologically normal human infant raised in the company of its own kind learns language. Quickly. Apparently without effort. Certainly without systematic training. Why does our species do this? Why did it ever? More to the point, why is it that the apes, apparently so near, did not? These are the questions that will concern us here, for in their answers we may find the keys to the pattern on which the complex tapestry of the human tale is woven.

But another question must come first. What is it, exactly, that we humans did, and do, that no other species, to our knowledge, does? To answer, we must return again to the beginning. And in the beginning, of course, was the word. Humans became human, in all the ways that concern us here, because at some point in the time before recorded time we made sounds serve a new function on this planet. Or rather, a new set of functions, for that is what a word is: not a thing, but a set of uses to which we put sensory stimuli like sounds, or movements, or patterns of light and dark. Specifically, a word is a use of such stimuli to store and organize experience in memory, to retrieve it from memory, to connect it to something in present experience, and to evoke in another a similar set of memories and connections— *without necessarily triggering in oneself or the other an automatic behavioral response*. A word is, in short, a use of some sign to bring something into mind, not a reaction into behavior. It is a use of a sound or a mark or a gesture or, yes, even a significant silence, to summon thought about, not action towards, something; to trigger not a reflex, but reflection. That is the critical difference between sounds-as-words and sounds-as-signals, between human speech and birds' calls, wolves' howls, and monkeys' cries. In humans, sounds and other signs allow us to represent the world to ourselves internally and operate upon it there, without the risk of action. A word splits off, in a way we do not fully comprehend, stimulus from response.

All of this is easy enough to say, but it is not so easy to understand. Part of the difficulty comes from the fact that in humans, sounds do not *always* function as words. The telephone shrilled on my desk a moment ago, and my hand leapt to the receiver. I did not think *about* telephones, and interruptions, and who that might be, and whether or not I wished to answer. My hand acted on its own, so to speak, without the intervention of thought. I responded to the sound as a signal—with a conditioned response—not to the sound as a word. To confuse matters even more, we often make the same response to "speech" sounds. If I say "Ruth," to my sister, who sits across the room engrossed in a book, she will raise her head—as you will turn yours, without thinking, if you hear your name called from behind as you walk in the street, or duck if someone shouts, "Look out!" The sounds have the patterns of what we call "words," but not their functions. They have operated for you, and for my sister, as signals—triggers of conditioned reflexes—just as surely as the wild chimp's "danger" bark serves as a trigger, in the rest of the tribe, for a reflexive leap to the trees. When we respond to sounds (or other signs) as signals, we are not different from any other creature that uses calls or grunts, gestures or growls, to trigger learned or innate response. With this exception: *that we have a choice, and they do not.* And on that exception hangs all the difference between us and our fellows on this earth. When the telephone rang, I *might* have thought, and as a consequence modified my response. I know this, for on many occasions I have. When I say the sound "Ruth" to my sister, she *might* have thought, "What *about* Ruth?" (as she would do if she overheard me say the same sound in conversation with another), or "What does she want now?" and made no response at all. You *could* use the sounds "Look out!" as an opportunity to reflect on the variety of circumstances in which those sounds might be uttered, and the different kinds of responses appropriate to each.

We are rarely conscious of making a choice between reflexive and reflective response, between signal and word. We are barely aware that the option is there at all. Certainly, we do not understand how we make the choice between one mode of response and the other, or what factors constrain our choosing. But in humans, the choice is always there. It is even reflected, some evidence suggests, in two different pathways through the brain which incoming signals may travel. One channels them to the limbic system, the seat of those responses we recognize as feelings of anger, physical desire, and fear, and of the chemical and motor reactions they trigger; another, to the neocortex, the center of memory and thought, whence they *may* be routed on to the centers of speech or movement (for verbal or physical response), or simply stored.

In no other species, so far as we know, does this option exist. Except, perhaps, in the chimps and great apes, where the neurological potential for choice may be present, but the option was never exercised. And now, I think, we are in a position to ask again that most intriguing of questions: Why not?

The answer is so simple that it sounds at first like no answer at all. The creatures that survive today as the chimps and great apes did not develop the capacity for reflective response to signs—for response to signs to words—because they did not need to. They could survive quite well without that option. We need look no further for proof than to the simple fact that they survive without it to this day.

To make this observation useful, I must ask you to think about the process of evolution in a somewhat unusual way. For complex social and historical reasons we have come, most of us, to sum up evolutionary change in the useful catch-phrase, "The survival of the fittest." By this we mean, quite rightly, that in the competition among members of a species for the always-limited resources of an environment, those individuals better able to obtain adequate food, defend themselves against predators, secure access to many and healthy mates, are more likely than the less "fit" to produce many offspring and thus pass on, through their genes, those characteristics that made them stronger, more competent, and so on. In this way, nature "selects" and perpetuates those genetic variations (for there is always variation among the members of a species) that give some individuals an edge over others in the struggle for environmental dominance and survival. The strong, as we like to say, survive.

All that is well and good, so far as it goes. Like many clichés, "the survival of the fittest" is true enough, as a reading of evolution, in what it says. It is in the part left out that the error lies. Most of us, I would guess, if we think of the *weak* at all, think that they die. As a colleague of mine likes to put it, in evolution, nature does not so much favor the strong as eliminate the weak. But he is wrong. Not entirely, of course—for certainly in the competition for dominance of an ecological niche, many of the weaker members of a species die. But many do not. They are driven, instead, to the fringes of the territories their stronger brothers and sisters hold, where the terrain is somewhat different, and their native foods less abundant, and the chances for survival less favorable. There, on the outskirts of their earlier habitats, they lead a fugitive existence. And there, it often happens, the genetic quirks that provided no advantage in the environment of their birth may turn out to be of unexpected value in coping with the new. What was weakness in one set of circumstances may become, when circumstances change, a strength. And now, of course, the other side of evolution, "the survival of the fittest," comes into play—but the meaning of "fit" has changed. Given world enough, and mates enough, and time, a new set of traits, suited to the new environment, will come to predominate among the outcasts of the older species, and a new subspecies, inhabiting a different environmental niche, will have been born.

What I have outlined for you here is a view of evolution that stands "survival of the fittest," in its usual meaning, on its head. The strongest members of a species survive, true enough. But the result of their success is adaptation to an environment and perpetuation of the same traits, not change. The impetus to evolution—to diversification, "progress," and change—comes from the weak, not the strong. In reflecting on our own species, we humans have pinned on ourselves more than one self-congratulatory sobriquet to indicate our nearness to, but critical difference from, our evolutionary forebears. Thus we have called ourselves by turns, "Man: The Upright Ape," "The Tool-Using Ape," "The Talking Ape," "The Thoughtful Ape," and even (in some desperation) "The Naked Ape." I should like to suggest another title, not very flattering but quite consistent with the view of evolution I have just set forth. So far as our origins are concerned, no label suits us better, I think, than "Man: The Incompetent Ape." I very much doubt that this title will gain much currency. Nobody likes to think that he is the descendant of a loser—although a little humility about the roots of our elevated position in nature's hierarchy might do us all some good.

My purpose in conferring on us this dubious distinction is neither to insult our present status nor to advance our moral education. The title is apt because it is the best explanation I can think of to account for the development of language, tools, and culture among humans, but not among the species we left behind, and which survive without them to this day. At the center of this explanation lies a notion I will call "The Principle of Progressive Inadequacy," and it goes like this. The development of the unique capacities that characterize humans today—tool-making, reflective thought, elaborated languages—is a result of various inadequacies that left some of our forebears disadvantaged in the competition to maintain a secure foothold in a contested environmental niche. Time and again, the inadequate members of the species and subspecies that led to us were forced to the outskirts of the environments dominated by their more competent brothers and sisters, and there, new circumstances made their inadequacies and other genetic variations among the "losers" advantageous. Over the slow centuries, natural selection fostered the perpetuation of such newly useful characteristics among the population, until the emerging subspecies achieved the state of successful interdependence with its environment that we call "adaptation." But again, the competition for resources would drive the less competent to the outskirts of the ecological niche, where the cycle of change would recur—until at last those characteristics were established in one fugitive population that allowed it so to modify its environment and itself, through tools, language, and social behavior, that the process of physical evolution slowed to a point where, in *homo sapiens*, it became almost invisible.

Of course, one need not claim that competition between and within species is the only lever that sets evolutionary change in motion. The same process may be triggered by environmental changes that leave the previously disadvantaged in favored positions. But even then, the same principle is at work: change originates in inadequacy, not strength. The strong survive, but the weak move on. If not, they die.

Perhaps an example or two will help to illustrate how the process of evolution-through-inadequacy might have worked. Consider, for example, the opposable thumb and the upright stance—two characteristics that distinguish modern humans from all the other primates and played a vital role in the evolution of our kind. In jungle terrain, where the survival of our earliest ancestors would have depended on rapid flight to and through the thick canopy of forest branches, a long thumb that juts out at an angle from the rest of the hand would be a distinct liability. As any gymnast can tell you, the best grip for swinging on a bar, or catching it in flight, is the grip that presses the thumb flat against the side of the other fingers. Any other position of the thumb interferes with the hard downward slap on the target bar required to catch it, and increases the risk that thumb and wrist will be sprained, if not broken. Successful and rapid "flight" also requires relatively long arms and torso, but a compact body from the pelvis down.

Now, among the tree-dwelling apes of the Miocene were some with shorter arms and torsos, and greater length from the pelvis down. And in some, genetic variation provided a longer thumb that did not always lie flat in the plane of the fingers, but sometimes swiveled around. In others, the fearsome canine teeth—the major weapons of attack and the dominant feature of threat display—were smaller than their siblings'. For no two apes are exactly the same. Any one of these accidents of birth would have left a forest ape so under-endowed less able to protect itself—to fight or to flee. And its disadvantage would have become more acute as the leafy forest canopies began to shrink and the competition for a secure niche in the trees became more keen. In that competition, most of the losers no doubt died. But others would have been driven to a marginal existence, not in the safety of the trees, but on the far more dangerous forest floor. There the strongest of the swingers and the larger-toothed fighters would have come to hold the safest territories, closest to the trees, while the weaker were driven progressively farther afield, to the outskirts, the edges of clearings, and ultimately to the tall grasses of the savanna.

Over the course of that long forced march outward from the safety and lush vegetation of the trees, the troublesome rotated thumb, the shortened forelimbs and torso, the smaller canine teeth would have come to serve the "losers" well. For in place of the riper fruits of jungle and forest—now in the hands of the strong—the less competent apes would need to subsist on the smaller and tougher roots, nuts, and seeds of dryer grasses and trees. For the fine work of separating seeds and nuts from grass and gravel, a thumb that can pinch the forefinger is a useful instrument indeed. And molars can grind and pulverize tough objects more efficiently if the jaws can move from side to side without the restrictions imposed by large and overhanging canine teeth. And the redistribution of body weight and center of gravity that shorter and lighter forelimbs and torso provide makes it easier to maintain balance on two feet, raising the head above the tall grasses for a clearer view of opportunity or danger—and freeing the hands for continuous picking, grasping, holding, gesturing. Over the long centuries, such newly advantageous characteristics would enhance the survival of the "weak" until they had, themselves, become the "strong" in their new environment, and a new link in the chain that leads to us would have been forged.

It is a long way indeed from an upright, open-handed creature with grinding jaws to *homo sapiens*, and the processes of change are far more complex than I have sketched in these few sentences. Simplification inevitably distorts, and the most grievous distortion in this simple account is that it hides the interactions of changed environment, diet, jaws, posture, and hands with brain, mind, and social behavior. One of the most critical of those interactions concerns the co-evolution of body and brain, without which we would never have traveled the long, long road to tools and speech. The key point here is that the operations required to maintain balance on two feet, to pinch the tip of forefinger against the tip of thumb, to grind food and move it back in the throat for swallowing are more complex than the operations required for simpler tasks. In particular, they require finer muscle control and greater coordination of information from different sensory systems. Eye and hand must work together, for example, to separate small objects and pick out one from others, and finer visual and tactile discriminations must be made than in grasping large objects in the palm.

More important even than this, new environments place new demands on memory—of which new things are edible and which are not, and where they may be found, and what new movements and sounds reveal the approach of predators not known in the forest canopies, and what new responses are required, away from the safety of the trees. Every movement outward from a familiar environment to a new, in short, requires that more information be acquired, stored, and retrieved. Every such movement also requires that finer distinctions be made between one pattern of sensory data and another, and simultaneously, that similarities in such patterns be somehow identified. Finally, every such movement from the familiar to the new requires greater variability in response to information of different kinds. And all of this requires increased size and complexity of the brain—especially, of the neocortex, where information processing of this kind occurs and memory is stored.

And now we are very close, not in evolutionary time but in principle, to understanding how and why our hominid ancestors arrived at last at the word. And why the apes of the jungles and forests did not. Consider what a species at home in the trees would need, in the way of information and response, to survive. I do not mean what *every* species needs—to coordinate its motor activity, identify its food, mark its territory, and the like—but what a species of this particular kind, in jungle or forest habitat, would require. What kinds of threats does it encounter, and what sorts of warnings and responses are necessary to survive?

In fact, life in the treetops is relatively secure for those competent there— at least so far as predators are concerned. The major danger to the tree-dwelling monkey is the snake. Forest apes, who spend more of their time on the ground, confront a larger variety of threats—from, for example, the carnivores of the cat family, and other species of apes (which do, it turns out, enjoy a bit of meat when it can be easily obtained). Still, the types of predators on forest monkeys and apes are limited, and only a handful of different responses is required. Non-climbing predators may be avoided by a timely leap to the trees, snakes by rapid flight through the branches, and marauding baboons driven off by a group attack. Since the types of danger and the responses required are few and invariant, the number of different warning signals needed is small and choices among responses to each are unnecessary. In fact, any delay between warning signal and response would reduce an individual's chances of survival. Thus, natural selection would favor those monkeys and apes in which the connection between signal and response is instantaneous and invariant—in a word, reflexive.

But predators are not the only threat to tree and forest-dwelling apes. In fact, since they are so well-defended in that respect, the major danger to their survival lies elsewhere: in the competition, and therefore aggression, among themselves. For all kinds of reasons connected to their survival, primates must live in groups, and the cohesion of the group must be maintained if the individuals are to survive. If the competition among the members for food and mates is allowed to go unchecked, if the group is continually at war within itself, the band will die. The means of controlling competition and aggression among the higher apes is the establishment of complex "hierarchies of dominance," systems of rules for who must give way to whom in situations normally marked by competition. The status of different members of the group is worked out in the early squabbles among the juveniles, whose tussles and chases are sufficient to establish who is stronger than whom but not to inflict serious injury. And the hierarchy so constructed is maintained in adulthood by the exchange of signs associated with aggression and submission, threat and appeasement. Because these signs have their origins in the physical encounters of which they are reminders, and because the use of sounds is dangerous to a band of apes on the forest floor, the signals that regulate social behavior are for the most part gestural, not vocal.

As Jane Goodall and other students of modern apes and chimps in the wild have documented, the dominance and affiliative relations among the members of a band are both precise and complex. Still, the signals that regulate those relations are small in number, and the responses they call forth are both rapid and fixed. After all, the young chimp that does not respond instantly and appropriately to an older male's threat display would not long survive. Thus, in the social as well as the alarm communications of tree and forest dwellers, natural selection favors the reflexive response.

But now consider the survival needs of a band that dwells, not near the safety of the trees, but out on the open savanna. The predators they face are more varied than those in the forests, and so are their patterns of stalk and attack. Since they cannot be easily dodged, in the open, by a leap to the trees, more information and more *precise* information about the nature, position, and movements of predators is needed, and more variation in response. In the forests, he who hesitates is lost. On the savannas, she who bolts is lost. Thus natural selection would favor, among the hominids of the plains, development not only of a larger and more complex set of warning signals, but a fractional delay of response in which choices (of escape routes, for example) might be made.

The dangers of open country also require a change in the eating habits of savanna dwellers. Forest apes consume their food where they find it, as most creatures do. But the risk of exposure while feeding makes that a perilous course for a grasslands species ill-equipped to fight and slow to flee. Survival would favor those who could delay the normal response to food until it could be brought to a better-defended location for sharing out and consumption. And this is an important interruption in the link between stimulus and response.

As Richard Leakey and others have suggested, changes in the foraging and eating habits of savanna dwellers, and the more stringent requirements for defense in the open, would also foster more intense cooperation among the members of hominid bands and a more complex social structure—including, at some point, a division of labor between those best equipped to forage and scavenge farther afield (most likely the stronger males) and those tied closer to a better-defended central site (females with young). The greater the complexity of social arrangements and diversification of roles, the larger the number of signals required to preserve the social order, regulate aggression, and maintain affiliative bonds. And the greater the resulting discrimination and variation in response, favoring again the interposition of delay.

It is impossible to reflect for long on the situation of ape-like creatures in open terrain without confronting again and again the problem of defense. On the face of it, it seems highly unlikely that a creature so vulnerable should survive at all. It was not massive in build or tough of hide. It carried no shell or quills, gave off no hideous scent. Its canine teeth were relatively small, and its hands devoid of claws. It could not cover large distances at tremendous bursts of speed, and the savanna provides few places for a creature of such size to hide. It is slow to reproduce, as these things go, and gives birth to only one offspring at a time, so its numbers do not increase rapidly enough to afford great losses. Its young are born physically immature and remain helpless and vulnerable for years. And the slow rate at which it reproduces means that natural selection would require long years to distribute through the population the characteristics that help it to survive. How would such disadvantaged creatures, in a setting so perilous, live long enough to become strong?

The answer is clear. They would not have made it to the open plains at all if they had not found, on the long trek from the forest floor, weapons. And they found them in the same coordination of eye and hand, the same picking and grasping motion, that their new diet favored—there, and in the availability of stones and hardened lumps of clay in the sunbaked clearings outside the canopy of trees. Modern monkeys can throw things, and do. And they rapidly improve in force and accuracy with systematic practice. In jungle terrain and dense forest, of course, they do not practice, because there is little need. A missile will not travel very far before it is deflected by branches, vines, and leaves, and flight among the branches is a surer means of defense, so long as the trees are at hand and one is a competent swinger. Besides, force and accuracy in throwing require a firm stance on two feet and excellent balance. And, of course, hands freed from the demands of locomotion. Throwing things is an occasional, not a routine activity among monkeys and apes, because they do not much need it to survive.

But incompetent swingers, denizens of clearings, do. And their upright stance, superior height, opposable thumb, eye-hand coordination would all work together to make them forceful hurlers. And a barrage of missiles is a fearsome, if not always lethal, defense. That is, it *can* be—if the objects thrown are of the right shape and hardness. A handful of leaves, or a ripe banana, is scarcely a lethal missile. So it would not be enough for clearing-dwellers to become fine throwers. They would need to make finer distinctions among throwable objects, as well, and learn which are more effective, and somehow store the visual and tactile patterns of "good for throwing" in memory to serve as models to guide the searching hand and eye when a new threat arose. And all these complex processes are precursors to the word.

But they are also precursors to the making of a tool. Tools begin, not with the construction of something new, but with the selection and use of natural objects for special functions—like rocks for defensive throwing. Some species of contemporary monkeys use natural objects in this way, and some have gone the next step as well—modifying a found object to serve a particular use. Some monkeys, for example, strip protruding leaves from slender twigs so that the naked stem may be poked into a termite hole to withdraw a tasty meal. But this performance lacks the critical feature that is essential for the development of tools—and of language, as well. Having finished its meal, the termite-fishing monkey leaves the termite mound *and throws the twig away*. The significance of this act lies in what it tells us about the monkey's mind: namely, that the stick, the termite hole, and the satisfaction of hunger are all of a piece. The stick is not conceptualized as a separate object, but merely as one aspect of the complex event in which it plays a part. The termite mound is another aspect of the whole, and hunger and its satisfaction a third. They are behaviorally and cognitively integrated or fused in such a way that they operate together or not at all. When hunger is satisfied, the monkey loses interest in the termites and the stick. In the presence of hunger but no termite mound, a twig is merely part of the backdrop of scrub and trees, not an object of attention at all. They are all part of the same event, and have no independent cognitive or behavioral significance.

The twig-using monkey cannot separate the twig from the specific context of action in which it is embedded. Therefore, it cannot imagine it in another context. In this critical sense, the twig is not a "tool" at all. It is merely a part of a specific set of circumstances—an element in a single behavioral routine. For convenience, we may call this kind of modification and use of a naturally occurring object a "proto-tool."

And now we have come to a critical point in our understanding of the relationship between tools and language. The difference between a proto-tool and a tool is precisely analogous, cognitively and behaviorally, to the difference between a signal and a word. Like a proto-tool, a signal is not separated, in the mind of its user, from the entire set of events in which it occurs. It is *part* of those events, just as the twig, to the termite-fishing monkey, is part of the complex "hunger-termite-hole-stem-eat" event, and it has no independent significance apart from the complete and specific set of circumstances in which it is heard or seen. The alarm bark of a chimp, to others who hear it, is simply the auditory part of the "on-the-ground-leap-for-the-trees-swing-away" event. It does not "mean" danger, or predator, or anything else except that complete behavioral routine in those circumstances. It "means" the whole activity, including the response. And it is never separated from the whole activity, never disembedded from the specific complex of circumstances and behavior in which it occurs.

But a word, or a tool, is. The distinguishing feature of words and tools is that sounds or gestures or objects (in the case of tools) are split off from the behavioral contexts in which they originally occur. And this separation makes it possible to use the sound or gesture or object in a different context, even to a different end. More important even than this, it eventually makes the sound or object notable in itself, apart from any particular context in which it is used. It becomes a separate object of perception, interest, contemplation. And that is the beginning of a word, of a tool, of thought.

It is easy enough to imagine how a rock or stout tree limb may have become detached from the original context of its use, in our ancestors' migration outward from the trees, and thus developed into the first genuine tool. It is even easier to imagine why the termite-fisher's twig did not. Twigs and stems are plentiful in the vicinity of termite mounds. They are part of the same ecology. A hungry monkey, chancing on a termite hole, has all it needs ready to hand. To hold onto the twig, once hunger is satisfied, would therefore provide no advantage—particularly in a creature that needs its hands for locomotion, and needs them empty for a rapid leap to the trees when danger nears. But the situation is different for a bipedal creature farther out on the open plains. Savanna terrain is largely open grassland, in which outcroppings of rocks and trees only occasionally appear. A foraging ape in the tall grasses can hardly be sure, when a predator appears, that a missile for throwing will lie ready to hand. Survival would favor those who, through happenstance and reinforcement, learned to hold on to a rock or tree limb as they moved from place to place. Certainly, those bands of hominids that established their central dwellings near lakeshores and other clearings where rocks and rubble abounded stood a better chance than others, in the long nights of the hunters, to survive.

The carrying of a rock from such a stockpile into the field on foraging expeditions is a long step toward splitting it off, perceptually and behaviorally, from a fixed set of environmental and behavioral wholes, toward coming to see it as a useful thing-in-itself, an object, a tool. It is also a long step toward an idea of the future—an idea that begins in behavior that is not a response to some physically present set of conditions, but is associated instead with conditions that *might* arise. What is most important about such a behavioral change is not that it represents "planning ahead," as we might think of it, but that it leads to what we might call "conditionality" —to responding to things and events not as they are, but as they *might be*. "Conditionality" is the ability to call to mind a set of circumstances different from those given by immediate sensory data. And it is *that* ability that permits us to imagine alternative futures, see the potential in objects and events, choose among courses of action.

Conditionality is essential to the development of tools, for it allows one to see, in a rock or a branch or a clean-picked bone, not how the object looks, but how it *might* look, and how it might be made to look. Without conditionality—the ability to represent to oneself an alternative set of affairs and guide one's behavior in the present by that imagined alternative—the systematic practice of modifying found objects, of transforming the shape of a rock by striking off an edge, for example, would not arise.

Conditionality plays a central role, too, in the evolution of the word. To bring an alternative set of circumstances to mind and hold them there, to regulate one's behavior by those circumstances rather than by response to present sensory data, requires new ways of storing and retrieving information, new ways of representing it to oneself. And it also requires, of course, the repression or separation of response from sensory signal.

It is impossible to say precisely how vocal sounds came to serve as means to index the storage of information in memory, to retrieve it, and to represent it in mind without overt response. We may guess that the process occurred in much the same way as the process through which rocks and naked bones became tools— and almost certainly at the same time. But for a clearer view of how it may have unfolded, we must turn away for a while from the sunbaked savannas of our past and direct our attention much closer to home: to the lives of our children, as they make their own momentous journey from wordless infancy to speech. For that journey will have much to tell us, I think, about the longer path our ancestors trod.

CHAPTER TWO

The Children's Tale

What goes on in the minds of very young children as they move from infant cries, through wordless babbling, and come at last to speech? If they could only tell us, or we could remember, how much simpler the task of understanding ourselves would be. But they cannot, and neither can we. So we must take the less certain course, reasoning from what we observe to what must be going on inside. But this is a course fraught with peril, and unless we are very careful, we shall quickly fall into a snare that has trapped some very great explorers of language and mind. That snare is woven of two assumptions. The first is that the linguistic productions of young children are a direct reflection of the workings of their minds. And the second is that the ways in which children understand language are the same as the ways we understand it as adults.

These assumptions are so deeply and widely held that we are scarcely aware of making them. They seem, in fact, no more than common sense. It is common sense, for example, to suppose that since children use single words first, and link them together in complex structures only later, and come to such "causal" utterances as "Since..." and "As a result..." very late indeed, their mental processes must begin with noticing parts which are gradually built up into complex wholes, with such sophisticated notions as causality occurring only after the simpler relations have been noticed and named. And it is also common sense to suppose that since children use what we call "nouns" first and verbs only later, they must attend first to objects and only later to their dynamic relations. But in both these suppositions, common sense is wrong—so wrong, in fact, that we would do better to stand it on its head to get a more accurate view of the matter.

The relationship between children's speech and their cognitive processes is not at all direct. Quite the opposite. While their *utterances* proceed from the simple to the complex, building up sounds into words, words into phrases into sentences, their cognitive processes are moving, so to speak, in the other direction—breaking down complex perceptual, behavioral, and social wholes into parts. In a sentence, that is what language learning is: a process of breaking apart experiential wholes, labeling their pieces, and reassembling them again in a different form, in the code that we call language.

That is a very abstract idea. Perhaps it will be clearer if we start thinking, not about language, but about an infant's situation in the world it enters, and even before. What is its experience like, in the weeks before birth and just after? It does not take long to say, because for the preborn and the newborn, there is only one experience: sensation. At first, before we "quicken" in the womb, even sensation is seamless and undifferentiated, for the brain and neurological system are not yet developed enough to distinguish signals arising from the movements of muscles from those that originate at the "surface" of the developing fetus—at lips, eyes, and skin. When at last those systems are differentiated and we "wake" in the womb, the long process of sensory-motor learning begins. This is a process in which we learn to use sensations arising in different parts of our bodies to adjust our position and relieve distress. It begins before birth and continues long after—in fact, throughout our lives. If you step on a cracked piece of pavement, for example, and your ankle begins to turn, the information from your muscles (registering as pain) will trigger an instantaneous response in which you shift other muscles to take the weight off your foot, preventing a sprain. If you set yourself the task of learning to shoot an arrow through the center of a target, you will correlate sensations from a variety of sources—eyes, skin, and various sets of muscles—to produce a more and more accurate result. Like the developing fetus in the womb, you do not "know" what muscles you are adjusting, or how it is all done. The result—relief of pressure and pain, the arrow striking closer to home—is all you need to govern the rest.

But there is one great difference between your experience and that of the baby in the womb or newly born. You know where "you" end and "the world" begins. That is, you know that part of your sensation comes from inside you and part from outside, from "it." But the preborn and the newborn do not. Before birth and for some time after, there is no line between "inner" and "outer," between "me" and "not me," between "I" and "it." In the infant's experience, it is all one—just different sensations arising from vaguely different parts of itself. But it soon begins to learn

THE CHILDREN'S TALE | 21

that different sensations "go together" and relieve different kinds of distress. It flails its arm, and the sensory experience of that movement "goes with" a diminished sensation of discomfort that originates, perhaps, in too much pressure on the skin of the elbow. It cries, and the sensation produced by its vocal cords and muscles "goes with" the sounds it hears and a change at lips, mouth, and stomach as it is fed. Thus the infant learns, as all sensory creatures do, to modify different parts of its own behavior to bring about differences in other parts of its experience. And part of what it learns to modify is its production of sounds, because these are tied very closely, in the early days of life, to vital changes in its sensations of wellbeing. *We* know, of course, that those changes are the results of the response of adults to the infant's cries. But the baby does not. It only "knows" that it can change its world in consistent ways by varying its sounds. And this, we might say, is the infant's earliest "linguistic theory"—not, of course, in the sense of a conscious belief or statement about the world, but in the sense of a rule that regulates learning and behavior. If we could put such a rule into words, it would go something like this: "I am the world. My world changes when I change my sounds. My sounds change the world."

But why emphasize sounds this way in the infant's perceptual theory of the world? After all, the neonate also experiences the world as visual sensation, and touch and smell, and changes in these sensations also "go with" changes in its sense of distress or well-being. True enough. And in fact the infant is learning, in the early weeks of life, to correlate different patterns of auditory, visual, tactile, and olfactory sensation with changes in its "internal" state. Thus one set of tones and smells and patterns of light and dark (that the baby will much later learn to call "Mama") goes with the sensations of the nipple at its lips, and milk in its mouth, and softness under its fists, and all of these go with the easing of distress that is hunger. But there is something peculiar about the *sounds* in the infant's world that sets them apart from the visual and tactile sensations they go with. When the baby moves its eyes or turns its head, its visual experience changes. Things appear and disappear. When it moves its arms or kicks its legs, its tactile experience changes. And since "the world," to the infant, is nothing more than the sensations it experiences, it does in fact "change the world" by moving its head and body, shifting and focusing its eyes.

Of course, some of the sounds in the baby's world cannot be made to go away. They come, they go, they vary in pitch and loudness and other qualities that have no consistent connections with the baby's sensation of its own muscles—because they are not, in fact, made by the baby but by others. And because sounds carry over distance, the infant experiences them before the other sensations to which they are connected. For those reasons, and because of their vital connection with the baby's sense of well-being or distress, sounds come to assume a special role, a more central role, in the complex wholes that are an infant's experiential world. Sounds become not just one part but the *key* part of all the rest that goes with them.

While all this is going on in the first six weeks or so of the newborn's life, other significant physiological changes are taking place. The baby's control over the muscles of lips and tongue increases, and the base of the tongue and larynx begin to descend into the throat, enlarging the pharynx. As a result, the infant can produce a greater variety of sounds, including vowels, and with greater control. Because of the central role of sounds in the early weeks of life, the baby attends with great interest to its own productions, cooing, gurgling, and lalling for long stretches at a time, even when alone.

The infant at the babbling stage is rarely alone, and in the presence of others it begins unconsciously to match its sounds and their rhythms (as well as its non-vocal expressions and movements) to theirs. This process is wonderfully helped along by parents and older children in the baby's environment who, themselves delighting in the infant's approach to human sounds, gladly repeat such longed-for combinations as "Ma-ma" and "Da-da" and "Baby" with endless patience—and no small measure of diverting visual display and comforting physical contact. To the infant, such sounds, repeated over and again, are part of the whole sensory experience in which they occur. So too are the various configurations of shapes, colors, and shadows that infants learn to discriminate as distinct faces and expressions. They are bound up with all the other sensory changes, "internal" and "external," the baby experiences in their presence. And since such repeated patterns of images and sounds are experienced as parts of more complex wholes, they evoke in the infant the whole set of experiences and responses to which they are connected. In effect, that is what a sound such as "Mama" or the configuration of features we call "a smile" *means* to the infant who hears or sees it: the entire set of "inner" and "outer" sensory experiences it is connected to.

Similarly, when the baby at last produces sounds approximating those that others around it long to hear, it identifies those sounds with all the changes in experience that accompany them. From the infant's point of view, something done with its lips and tongue and breath goes together with a particular set of pleasing changes in its visual, auditory, and tactile experience, and these go together with feelings of wellbeing. The sound it produces and hears is merely the audible part of that complex whole, and the whole is what the sound "means."

We come to a critical point in the understanding of language and how it works. To grasp it, you must keep in mind that when the infant begins to produce babbling sounds, around the sixth week of life, it cannot yet clearly distinguish sounds it produces from sounds produced "elsewhere." Its own sounds and others' register alike, so to speak, at its ear. *We* know that it is the sounds others make that "go with" the changes in well-being the baby experiences, but the baby does not. In its experience, the source of origin of the sounds is not yet distinguished and is therefore irrelevant. It is the sounds themselves that "go with" the feelings that accompany them, and the sounds themselves, therefore, that evoke those feelings. Thus when the baby replicates parental sounds that "go with" feelings of well-being, *its own sounds, no less than others', evoke those feelings in itself.* That is why the baby repeats, alone in its crib, the coos and oohs and aahs, the inflections and rhythms and at last the syllabic combinations, of the speech that has been used to it: because the sounds call up in itself the same feelings of well-being that go with those sounds when adults use them.

In effect, the baby is learning to "condition" its own responses by reproducing in itself the state of affairs originally brought about by others in their relation to the baby. This is the process that G. H. Mead called, long ago, "internalizing the other," and it underlies, in various transformations, all the "higher" functions of language: the internal representation of experience, reflective thought, and the communication of ideas.

All that is very far in the future for the six- to eight-week-old, who does not even grasp as yet that there *are* "others" and a world that is not part of itself. Before the infant can arrive at language and thought, it must arrive at the word. And this requires several major changes in its perceptual and behavioral "theory" of the world: the separation of "I" from "it," the separation of "self" from "others," and the separation of sounds from response.

These separations, interconnected though they are, occur in somewhat different stages during the first eighteen months or so of the baby's life, and it is important to understand how—not just because this is the personal "tale" of each and every one of us, but because it contains the clues to much that is puzzling about the evolution of our species, about human thought and behavior, and about our precarious state in the world today. The most important clue is this: that our first experience of the world as biological creatures, our first awareness, is awareness of an undifferentiated whole. The second is this: that the differentiation of experience into "parts" occurs only gradually, and never completely. That is, there are aspects of our experience—some of our perceptual experiences, for example—that are *never* fully differentiated, never broken into pieces, but continue to work as wholes, as "gestalts," as psychologists would say. Thus "unities" persist alongside fragmented experiences, and are no less part of our "sense" of the world and ourselves than are the distinctions we have learned to make. Third, every step in the process of splitting experience into different parts requires a corresponding process: the development of some structure for bringing the parts into relationships—for correlating them and making them work together. And these new "coordinating" structures give rise, in human experience, to different kinds of awareness and different kinds of learning. And finally, these processes occur interactively at all levels of human functioning—the neurological, perceptual, behavioral, and social—and are in fact both "causes" and "effects" of neurological, perceptual, behavioral, and social experiences.

Such grand statements as these are about as far removed from the baby in its crib as the baby is from language. So let us return to the infant—or rather, to *you*, since this is not the tale of some alien and miscellaneous "it," but an account of your own experience, and mine, at a time we remember only vaguely, in nameless longings and our dreams.

When last we looked in, you were two or three months old, oooh-ing and aaaah-ing merrily in your crib, attending with interest to the sounds and the pleasant feelings evoked by them, and getting the sensation of them in your chest, throat, and head. What can we say about you and what you have done so far in your short life? Well, that would depend, of course, on who is doing the talking.

A neurologist, stroking his beard, would tell us that your nervous system is by now differentiated into a "proprioceptive" system that carries information about your "interior" (for example, the movement of your muscles, the contractions of your stomach) and an "exteroceptive" system that carries information from your skin, eyes, ears, and other nerve endings sensitive to things like pressure. He would also report that you are now able to distinguish the two kinds of sensations these systems give rise to, and to "locate," in a diffuse way, the different parts of your awareness they come from. And he might add that information from the various "exteroceptors" is beginning to be differentiated, so that "vision" and "sound" and "smell" are now perceived as discrete experiences.

A cognitive psychologist standing over your crib, her clipboard in hand, would tell us that you have been learning to correlate information from your ears, eyes, and skin with information from your muscles, and therefore to achieve better control over your movements and vocal productions. She might also add that you are learning to distinguish two classes of sounds: those that go with sensations from your own vocal chords (i.e. "your own") and those that don't, and that the world you experience is beginning to divide, therefore, into "things I control" and "things I don't." A social psychologist might say that you have "internalized others" and are using their sounds, which you can produce yourself, to condition your own responses. A psychiatrist, of course, would say "What do *you* think?"—but pressed to comment might observe that you are still "all ego," meaning that you do not yet distinguish "the world" from yourself, or "I" from "Thou." Your mother would tell us that you're adorable and *very* smart—starting to talk, already!—and that no matter what all those bigshots have to say, you know the difference between her and everyone else.

They would all be right, of course. And of course they would all be wrong. You are not "just" a brain and nervous system, or a set of behavioral learnings, or a microcosm of social relations, or an "ego," or the apple of your mother's eye. You are a very complex little whole yourself, and the particular way in which your genetic predispositions, prenatal experience, and physical and social encounters with the world are interrelated makes you unique in all the world. And you're very, very busy, at three months, in trying to sort things out and put them together again in new ways. If we were to ask *you* what your experience is like, and you could answer, you'd probably say that things (or rather, *you*) are getting curiouser and curiouser every day, and nothing's quite as simple as it first seemed.

It is just as well that you cannot anticipate what lies ahead, because your world is going to change even more radically in the next nine to twelve months, and your behavioral hypothesis that the world is all connected, and connected to you, is going to work less and less well, with some frustrating and frightening results. As you spend less time in the soft and responsive environment of infancy, where things move if you touch them, yield when you press against them, you will encounter a world more and more resistant to your behavior and commands. Not only will sounds persist when you have no sensation of making them, but playpen bars and chairs and walls will continue to block your way even when you "disappear" them by closing your eyes or looking away. The floor will come up and strike you from behind when your eyes and feet tell you it's somewhere else. Nothing will work the way you've come to expect it to, and at first that will drive you to wails of frustration and rage. But after a time you'll revise your initial "theory" and divide the world into two: things you change by your own behavior and things you don't.

But even that is too simple, because you'll discover along the way that your cries continue to produce a kind of change. Those things that are hard, and don't move, and don't make sounds may not be in your control, but those that are soft, and do move, and have certain smells and shapes and make sounds of a certain kind—those are responsive to your cries, and when you "produce" them by crying, things get better. Thus it will seem to you that while some of the world, like tables and chairs and floors, is "not me," the rest of it—like the patterns associated with the sound "Mama"—is connected to you and governed by your cries. But alas, this theory, too, cannot long endure. As you grow less perilously dependent on your parents' immediate response (from their point of view), they will respond with less alacrity and dependability. And it will happen more and more, as you approach twelve months and fifteen, that the particularly comforting response associated with "Mama" will not follow at all, no matter how you cry, for Mama will not be there to hear you. Thus you will learn to your distress that Mama, no less than tables and floors and playpen bars, is independent of you, at least in part; that she, like them, is in some way not you, but "other."

What a frightening and enraging time it must be for an infant, this period when its first "theory" of the world is coming apart and nothing is working quite the way it used to. We should not be surprised that the baby shrieks with frustration and clings with new fear as "'it" and "others" move out of the infant's control, and "the world" becomes a separate and unpredictable place. What should surprise us is the relative equanimity of most toddlers as they move through this passage, which makes those of mid-adult life pale by comparison. What enables them to go on when all bets are off and the world spins out of control?

The answer, of course, is that the child's world does not in fact spin out of control all at once. There are, after all, regularities in the behavior of "things" and regularities in the behavior of people, and even if it turns out that more of your experience is due to "them" and less to you, the world is manageable if you can figure out those regularities and how to control them. Happily for most of us, we had already learned, by the time our world divided into "me" and "it" and "others," one of the keys to putting it back together. We had learned to attend to sounds, and how to make and shape them with some dexterity. And that sounds are tied in a very powerful way to everything else in our experience. When we become aware that there is a world outside ourselves, and others who are separate from us, our early "linguistic hypothesis"—"my sounds change the world"—is not rejected but revised. In its modified form, the new hypothesis goes something like this: Sounds change the world. Their sounds change my world. When I make the same sounds, I can change the world in the same way.

Thus infants enter, between babbling and language, a transitional stage in which they develop what might be called "signalic speech." In effect, they learn to use speech sounds, not to name things, but to bring about the events, and the responses from others, with which those sounds are linked. When the baby first says "juice," for example, it does not mean what we mean. The sound, for the child, is not a noun, not a name for a thing. It is instead a command, meaning something like, "Let there now happen all those things that happen when Mama makes this sound, and that result in my thirst being satisfied." And the baby understands the words of others in the same way—not as names, but as the audible parts of complex acts. When you say to a one-year-old, "Where's baby's nose?" and the infant touches it, she does not yet know that "nose" is that nub on her face. To the baby, the sounds mean "Do that activity," and "Where is baby's ear?" means "Do that other activity."

Now, in limited circumstances, signalic speech works quite well, and by eighteen months or so, the baby will have learned a "vocabulary," not of words, but of some twenty or so speech signals which suffice to "command" those events most central to its needs. But much is changing in the baby's life during that time, and by the age of two, the child will find its signals quite inadequate to manage the increasing complexity of its physical and social world. As the baby encounters a greater variety of foods and drinks, for example, its early needs differentiate into more complex *wants*, and into preferences for slightly different "events" hard to command through a limited set of signals. This is not a problem so long as the child is in the company of adults who have learned to "read," through hundreds of shared experiences in many different contexts, subtle differences in the baby's vocal and non-vocal signals, and can therefore respond appropriately.

But by eighteen months or so, the toddler finds herself more and more in the company of others who do not share such a history of mutual experience—baby sitters, visiting aunts and uncles—and they frequently fail to produce the specific "event" the baby thinks its signal is connected to. And even parents, for their own good reasons, often fail to respond as expected. By now, of course, the child has learned that sounds by themselves do not produce events, but require the presence of others. And it more and more happens that when "juice" is commanded to happen, others are elsewhere. So the toddler patters off in search, repeating "juice... juice... juice," maintaining in himself the expectancy of the event which is to follow. Sometimes it does, and sometimes (grownups being busy folk) it doesn't. From the child's point of view, this must be frustrating and enraging. From ours, it is a critically important step in the acquisition of language. The act of using a sound to maintain an inner expectancy outside the presence of the situation or object "connected" to that sound is the beginning of the use of sound to summon and maintain an *idea*. It is the beginning of a word. All that is required to complete the process is one thing more: the detachment of sound from any response. Here too, the separation of adults and children from the same immediate context plays a vital role, for it is being in the same physical setting with the child—seeing what it sees, hearing what it hears—that provides adults with the information they need to understand the child's signals and respond appropriately. When contexts are not shared, when the child comes from one room and the adult is in another, that information is not available. The child's speech signals are therefore ambiguous, and the responses of adults more likely to be wrong. Decontextualized signals, in short, don't work.

But there are other reasons, too, why signalic speech fails. The principle that governs the child's early learning is that one sound "goes with" one and only one set of events, one response. But as the toddler spends more time with more adults in a wider variety of contexts, she discovers a baffling inconsistency that makes signalic learning all but impossible. For adults in fact use many different sounds for what to the child are the "same" events—for example, "cup" and "mug" and "glass" and "juice" and "drink" for what the child conceives as a *single* behavioral whole. And they use the *same* sound, like "water," in situations the child experiences as quite *different* events, like drinking, bathing, and playing at the sink. Thus it becomes more and more difficult for the child to connect specific sounds with specific situations, to produce the "correct" response itself and to command the desired response in others.

At somewhere between eighteen months and two years, these mounting problems with signalic speech converge to bring about a kind of "paradigm crisis" in the child's behavioral understanding of speech sounds and how they work. The toddler's early "linguistic hypothesis" ——that sounds *cause* situations to change in expected ways—breaks down, and another comes to take its place: that sounds she and others use do not necessarily bring about change, but are somehow connected to the different parts of experiences, and can be used to indicate those parts without causing the experiences to happen. That is, a sound can be used either to command an event or merely to *name* it. And the naming of it can bring the idea of it into mind without bringing the event itself to pass. Thus the child arrives, at last, at a rudimentary behavioral understanding and use of words in their two different functions: to command things and events and relationships, to alter their state and bring about an expected end; and to *name* things and events and relationships so that they may be thought of, and used to express thought and to know the thought of others. The first of these "understandings" is acquired by children long before the second, but it is the second that is essential to the development of true language, mind, and thought. We have no more illuminating and poignant account of the difference and its significance, or of the moment of transition from one stage of understanding to the next, than in Helen Keller's account of what happened to her at the well in the garden, with her teacher Annie Sullivan, on the day she first grasped the significance of a word. Her story is worth retelling here, not only because it is one of the few first hand accounts we have of that tremendous event, but also because the experiences that led to it reflect, in crucible, the precipitating factors in the "paradigm crisis" that all children pass through on their way to language.

Annie Sullivan's letters to her friend, Mrs. Sophie C. Hopkins, provide the context. Sullivan has been teaching the deaf and blind seven-year-old finger-spelling for several weeks, and finds Helen quick to imitate the gestures but frustratingly inconsistent (from Sullivan's point of view) in her use of them. Helen has learned to sign "c-a-k-e" when she wants cake, and "d-o-1-1" when she wants her new doll, but she uses the signs "m-u-g" and "w-a t-e-r" interchangeably for the drinking activity which she pantomimes. On the morning of the critical day, Sullivan again tries to teach Helen the difference between "mug" and "water." But since they "mean" the same thing to the child—the whole activity of drinking— she cannot understand what is wanted of her, and the session ends in frustration. Abandoning this effort, Sullivan undertakes a different lesson. Giving Helen two different dolls, which are for the child two quite different "events," she tries to teach Helen to make for them the *same* sign. This is so incomprehensible to the child that she flies into a rage, and that session, too, is abandoned. Shortly after, according to Sullivan, Helen asks for the sign for bathing (or washing), and Sullivan gives her "w-a-t-e-r," the same sign she had earlier tried to teach the child in connection with drinking. It is in the context of these confusing and frustrating events that teacher and child seek the calm and comfort of the garden. But here is Helen's own account of the day:

> One day, while I was playing with my new doll, Miss Sullivan put my big rag doll into my lap also, spelled "d-o-1-1" and tried to make me understand that "d-o-1-1" applied to both. Earlier in the day we had had a tussle over the words "m-u-g" and "w-a-t-e-r." Miss Sullivan had tried to impress it upon me that "m-u-g" is *mug* and "w-a-t-e-r" is *water*, but I had persisted in confounding the two. In despair she had dropped the subject for the time, only to renew it at the first opportunity. I became impatient at her repeated attempts and, seizing the new doll, I dashed it upon the floor. I was keenly delighted when I felt the fragments of the broken doll at my feet.... I felt my teacher sweep the fragments to one side of the hearth, and I had a sense of satisfaction that the cause of my discomfort was removed. She brought me my hat, and I knew I was going out into the warm sunshine. This thought, if a wordless sensation may be called a thought, made me hop and skip with pleasure.

> We walked down the path to the well-house, attracted by the fragrance of the honeysuckle with which it was covered. Someone was drawing water and my teacher placed my hand under the spout. As the cool stream gushed over one hand she spelled into the other the word *water*, first slowly, then rapidly. I stood still, my whole attention fixed on the motion of her fingers. Suddenly I felt a misty consciousness as of something forgotten—a thrill of returning thought; and somehow the mystery of language was revealed to me. I knew then that "w-a-t-e-r" meant the wonderful cool something that was flowing over my hand. That living word awakened my soul, gave it light, hope, joy, set it free! There were barriers still, it is true, but barriers that could in time be swept away.

> I left the well-house eager to learn. Everything had a name, and each name gave birth to a new thought. As we returned to the house every object which I touched seemed to quiver with life. That was because I saw everything with the strange, new sight that had come to me....

I learned a great many new words that day.

Helen Keller, *The Story of My Life*, pp. 36–37.

Annie Sullivan's letter recording the same events is more specific on the last point. "All the way back to the house she was highly excited," she writes, "and learned the name of every object she touched, so that in a few hours she had added thirty new words to her vocabulary." And nineteen days later, Sullivan writes: "Helen knows the meaning of more than a hundred words now, and learns new ones daily without the slightest suspicion that she is performing a most difficult feat." (p. 373)

There is no direct evidence to indicate that normal children's acquisition of the idea of words as *names* is as abrupt or dramatic as Helen's. But two observations do suggest that many children experience some sort of crisis in their early understanding of how words function, and a relatively sudden revolution of language learning around a new principle. One is the oft-noted change in temperament of toddlers around the age of 24 months (the "terrible twos"), when temper tantrums and other apparently unprovoked expressions of fear, despair, and rage suggest a sudden and thorough collapse of the child's unconscious paradigm for how things work. And the other is the great jump in vocabulary, the sudden flurry of naming, that follows shortly after. But whether the process is sudden or gradual, the outcome is the same: a perceptual and behavioral reorganization of the world in which sounds come to be understood as attached to autonomous, fragmented "pieces" of the world "out there," rather than to complex responses, activities, and relationships in which the child plays the regulating role. And so it happens that children come, at last, to the use of sounds, not as signals to command response and bring about complex events, but as ways to parse experience, indicate this or that "piece" of it, store it in memory and summon it to mind, think about it and communicate thought to others. They arrive, in short, at the word.

What a little thing a word is, and how awesome its power. Through the agency of the word, the human child gains access to a world that lies beyond the senses, that is not subject to the laws of physical space and biological time. Through this little thing, the idea of a name, we acquire the capacity to imagine and plan, to think and revise our thinking, to subordinate reflex and reaction to reflection and reason. It is no wonder that we rejoice with Helen Keller in the moment when the mystery of language is revealed, and that poets sing of the word as a new dawn in creation.

Except... except that it is nowhere near that simple. And here I must confess that in my own account of how children arrive at the word, I have made the process rather too tidy. I have written as though, in the moment we grasp that words are *names* we abandon our earlier "theory" that they are parts of complex events, with the power to call those events into being. But that is not the case. The new linguistic "paradigm" is added to the old, but does not replace it. Our primordial behavioral theory remains in place alongside the new, or perhaps "below" it—a muted, nearly invisible "subtext" to the rational, analytic, logical understanding of names as arbitrary, detached "tags" to call things by. The word "call" itself reveals, in fact, the persistence of the early "theory" of sounds alongside the new, for to "call" something means both to refer to it and to summon or bring it, to make it happen.

It is the "subtext" of words, our initial behavioral learning that sounds are part of and therefore summon experiences, that accounts for the magic that attaches to names and naming, to words. I do not refer here only to ancient or "primitive" beliefs that gods and demons, for example, may be summoned and controlled by the saying of their names, or to the belief of young children that saying wicked things will bring to pass what is spoken. I mean equally the dozens of ways, gross and subtle, in which the most rational and semantically sophisticated of us respond to words as though they are somehow connected in nature to the things and events they represent. It is worth reminding ourselves, in this connection, that one of America's largest and most powerful enterprises, the advertising industry, stakes billions of dollars every year on the susceptibility of adults and children alike to the magical power of names.

It is not my intention here to catalogue the countless ways in which humans have come to grief through our confusion of names with things, of "reality" with our ways of representing it, of the signalic with the symbolic functions of words. Hundreds of fine books have already been written on that subject, and thousands of hours spent on efforts to straighten us out on this business of words, and on the attainment of pure reason which many believe is the destiny of our kind. The fact that such efforts have not been notable for their success tells us something of critical importance about the human estate—something that no amount of optimism, no zeal in instruction, can overcome. It is not because we are stupid, or recalcitrant, or poorly informed that we cling to the assumptions of our prelinguistic infancy. We do so because those are the assumptions, the perceptual hypotheses, the ways of knowing and learning of sensate biological creatures. And we do not leave off biology when we acquire mind. That is the peculiar nature of humans, our unique gift and our doom: that inside the fragile envelope of human skin are housed two different ways of experiencing, feeling, knowing, and learning, two creatures and two "realities" given in quite different ways, not one. As creatures of skin and sensation, blood and bone, we know the world much as our forebears do: as a complex and seamless whole. And we learn as they do: through imitation, and trial and error, and conditioned response. And we survive as those closest to us in evolution survive: by responding to a part of something—a sound, a smell, a pattern of light—as though it were the whole. Sensory-motor learning, signalic learning, conditioned learning—these are not "stages" we pass through once and then have done. They are our ways of knowing and learning as creatures of biology; they operate and preserve us throughout our lives. And though we may wish to forget it, and hide from the fact at our peril, we are nine-tenths creatures of biology still, and shall be so long as our species survives.

But we are also creatures of the word. And through the word, we know and feel and experience a different world from the world given to our senses: a world not of wholes but of pieces, not of reactions but of ideas. Through words we can take apart, in mind, what biology gives our senses whole. We say "a cup," and can think of "a cup" as if it were an autonomous entity in the world, though none of us has ever seen, or will a "cup" that is not part of some larger whole: cup-in-the-hand, or cup-onthe-desk, or cup-on-the-shelf. And the same is true for the hand, the desk, and the shelf. Each is connected, in our sensory world, to something more. But through names we can cut the connections and reshuffle nature at will: take the horns from a goat and the mane from a lion, the head of a man and the legs of a horse, and imagine a creature to vex our dreams to nightmare. Or bend steel to the shape of the wing of a bird, and fly. With words we can take a moment from time and pin it to a page, bind it in leather, and imprison it for the ages on some dusty shelf. Or send the sounds of a living breath across the infinite spaces where no creature of flesh and bone will ever survive. Through the word we outlast death itself—deceiving death, as the poet says. Except that part of us is not deceived. And there is the bitter irony, the agony of the word. For through words we make a world our senses cannot enter, a place biology cannot even understand. And words, for all their power, cannot encompass what biology understands.

Language *represents* experience, or parts of it; it does *not* replicate it. Indeed, that is where the power of language lies: in the fact that it is a code, not a replica of the world as we know it biologically. That is why words can construct a universe we cannot hear or see or touch, why they call to mind times that do not exist to our senses—the "future" and the "past"—and invent "things," like cups and tables, unicorns and gargoyles, that nature has never produced. Because language is a *code*, it operates according to rules that are not the rules of our creaturely experience, of our sensorymotor-biochemical world. And that world cannot be made to fit within the structure and rules of language.

What an exquisite irony this is, and what pathetic creatures we. What we most deeply and unshakably feel, what fifty million years of biology tell us and the experience of our senses daily confirms, the "knowledge" that we act on every time we move, every time we breathe—that everything in the universe is a complex and interdependent *one*—we cannot think or express in words, cannot tell each other to ease our separation and loneliness. The harder we try, the more words we use, and the more words we use, the more finely we segment and partition the wholeness we want to convey, and the more inextricably we are caught up in the rules for combining words—which are not at all the same as the biological "rules" through which our sense of connectedness was given. And so the more we talk, the farther we get from what we wanted to say. It is no wonder that language drives humans in two directions at once: to a desperate need to express and communicate our experience in words, and to an equally desperate need to recover experience by escaping words. Perhaps that is why humans received, with the gift of language, another that is ours alone: the gift of tears.

These are weighty matters, and though they are central in any account of the human tale, and lie at the very core of this one, we need not dwell upon them here. It is enough to understand, for the moment, that in arriving at the idea of *names*, children solve one set of problems, but in the same articulate breath create another. The problem names solve is the inadequacy of signals and signalic learning to accommodate the increasingly complex needs and wants of the two year old encountering an expanding and more diverse world. To make the fine distinctions between one whole experience and others that differ in increasingly subtle ways, more and more signals are required, to the point where they become unreadable to unfamiliar others, especially as others spend less time in shared physical contexts with the child. Names solve this problem by providing a way to break down complex wholes into a relatively smaller number of "parts" important to the child (and her culture), and to indicate them with precision in a wide variety of different contexts, whether others and the "things" named are present or not. But having taken the world apart, names pose a new problem: how to reconstruct it again. For language has as its object the representation and regulation of experience, and experience does not consist merely of a collection of parts—of "me" and "you" and various "its." Human experience consists of *relationships* among you and me and it, and to serve any function at all, language must somehow reconstruct the interdependencies severed by names, must somehow resurrect the wholes of experience, not just its parts.

It does so—or rather, we do so—through the complex system of rules for naming and asserting relationships that we call "grammar." Grammar permits us to indicate not only *what* "parts" of the world chopped into names are to be reassembled—me and car and Mama or shoes and doll and Papa—but in what sorts of relationships: giving or taking, holding or breaking, loving or hating, and so on. Grammar is a set of instructions for how words must be ordered and modified, how sounds must be strung together, to represent and regulate subtly different "wholes" of experience. Through our knowledge of the rules of grammar, we can use a relatively small number of sounds and names over and over again, in slightly different combinations, to represent, recall, and command an infinitely larger set of experiences and ideas. That is the great triumph of language: it is a marvelously efficient and compact code for storing and transforming, retrieving and communicating an enormous diversity of experience and ideas.

But the key to its success—its efficiency as a code—is also the source of its inadequacies. *For a code, to be efficient, cannot be as complex as what it codifies.* If it were, it would serve no useful function. The relationships indicated by grammar—not just English grammar but *any* grammar—are not, in the end, the same as the relationships we experience as creatures of biology. Just as names make independent "entities" of "things" we have never experienced as autonomous units, so grammar reassembles them in configurations that do not match the sensory world. "It is raining," we say. But *what* is raining? There is no "doer of the action" that performs the activity of "raining." We say "It" because the rules of English grammar require that our sentences have subjects, even if we must make them up. We say, "The boy kissed the girl goodnight"—as though the "action" is all *his* doing. Our eyes would tell us something quite different. But language requires us to make one sound at a time, one word at a time, to string the named pieces of experience out like clothes on a line, according to rules of order that are quite different from the "rules" of biology. Grammar is a device for reassembling the coded "bits" of experience in a new form—a temporal, sequential form. It is a way of recounting experience over time, of *telling* it. Grammar is, in short, primitive narrative, and every sentence a tiny story about how what "things" go together, or ought to. When I was a child, my teachers told me that every such story, every sentence, is a "complete thought." Ah, if only it were so—what a different place the world would be! What makes it go round, for humans, at least, is not the completeness but the *incompleteness* of sentences, the inability of any code to represent fully or even adequately the complexity, diversity, and integration of what it codifies. Sentences cannot hold the entirety of the human experience, of what we sense, perceive, "know" biologically, behaviorally, and socially. Mathematics cannot hold it. Even art cannot hold it. They are all systems of representation, and every such system both leaves something out and *transforms* experience by trying to recapture it according to a different set of rules.

It is the peculiar fate of our species to live in the gap between the world as given biologically and the world as constructed in non-biological codes, between the world as experienced and the world as told. It is the peculiar need of our species to negotiate that gap, to try without ceasing, even in our sleep, to make the world as we sense it and the world as we represent it one, unified, whole. And it is the peculiar grief of our species, but also the perpetual force that drives us on, that the gap can never be closed.

For the world of our creaturely experience and the world of words are not independent of each other. They are joined in one body, one mind, and each transforms the other in a continuous cycle of change. Think back to how children come to language, as I have told that tale. It is the complexity and diversity of their biological and social world that drives them to a new means of regulating it—to a new code for managing the interdependencies on which their survival depends. That code, in turn, allows them to do new things—to carry an idea of something out of the immediate context that suggested it and express a want or need, via a word, to someone in a different context. Thus names expand the physical and social contexts in which the child can function. But single words are not adequate, by themselves, to provide listeners with the information supplied by the context the child left behind. And so children must learn to supply the missing context in another form, by elaborating on names, modifying single words, linking them to verbs—in short, to make up for the absence of physical co-presence by supplying a new kind of context: the expanded linguistic context that is grammar. But grammar, in its turn, allows one to "see" new kinds of relationships in one's world, to imagine new separations and re-combinations of both "things" and people. And what grammar allows the mind to think, the mind is quick to direct the hand to do, or at least to try. Thus the new means of coding experience "feeds back," so to speak, into the world experienced—enlarging, transforming, and complicating the physical and social world. And that is not the end of it, for the new complexities of the world transformed by grammatical thought and the physical operations it suggests must now be represented in a still more elaborate code, with rules for connecting one sentence to another, for example, in larger units of discourse. And those rules, again, allow us to think and "see" in still newer ways: to weave experiences together in new patterns, to explain, to articulate "cause," to work out contingencies ("if... then"), to reason deductively. And so it goes.

We are engaged continually in elaborating our codes to represent our social and biological experience, and in transforming our biological and social experience along the lines our codes suggest. But the gap between codes and experience can never be closed, for whenever we divide our experience into units and reassemble it according to rules of order, something is left out. "All grammars leak," the linguists say. All sentences leak. All logics leak. All theories leak. All narratives leak. Leaks, and the compelling need to plug them, to recoup elsewhere and otherwise what our means of representing human experience in codes leaves out—that is the price we pay for being human, for being a species neither wholly biologic nor wholly symbolic. We can escape it only by escaping language itself—or by shedding our biological nature. Indeed, that is one way to read our present situation in the West: as the struggle of a people to escape the pain of the human condition by two different routes. One is to retreat from language, from consciousness itself, through drugs, alcohol, and even self-inflicted death. The other is the effort to transmute ourselves—or our minds, at least—into machines like computers, and so have done with biology. Perhaps that is, in the end, the destiny of our species, if we survive our present anguish: to give birth to something so new, so foreign that no biological creature can even imagine it—a variety of "intelligence" that is not connected to what we understand by "life."

But it is far too early in this tale to treat of ends. It is time, instead, to circle round again, after this long detour, to our beginnings. What does a child's learning of language teach us about how language may have evolved?

CHAPTER THREE

From Signal to Speech

If language is as peculiar and problematic as I have painted it, then why would it ever have arisen? And more to the point, why does it everywhere survive? The answers, I think, are the same whether we ask those questions about our infants' struggle toward the word or about our species' longer journey to the same end. *Language arises because certain kinds of changes in social and physical experience render signalic learning and communication inadequate to store and retrieve new information and to regulate the interactions among creatures dependent on each other for survival.* In our children, three factors in particular lead to the breakdown of what I have called "signalic speech." One is the movement out of the restricted and responsive environments of infancy into a set of less predictable, more demanding physical environments, and the corresponding "complication" of the child's problems, wants, and needs—all of which require some measure of adult cooperation for their satisfaction. A second factor is the expansion of the child's social world to include a growing number of others who are relative strangers, in the sense that they have not been participants in the long history of shared experience that makes the child's signals "readable" to those who have lived with her from birth. And the third factor is the increasing separation of child and adults in physical space, a decline in the amount of time they spend in shared sensory contexts, and a corresponding loss of the clarifying information context provides for otherwise ambiguous signals.

No doubt the same factors played the central role in the breakdown of signalic communication among our ancient ancestors and favored the development of that alternate form of coding and communicating that survives as human speech.

We shall never know for certain what crisis precipitated the ancestral equivalent of Helen Keller's epiphany at the well and gave rise to the first use of a sound as a word. We may guess that the moment happened, not once, but many times, among different bands of early hominids, in somewhat different circumstances and at different times. And we may even sketch, in imagination, the long chain of events that made such moments necessary if our species was to survive. It would have begun, as the journey of our children toward the word begins, with the movement of hominid bands out of the relatively warm and stable environments of the East African "cradle" and into new and more challenging terrains, some one and a half million years ago. We cannot say with certainty what set our ancestors to wandering, not only west and north and south on the African continent but into Europe and Asia as well. But it is likely that two factors played an important role: increasing population density, as "homo erectus" mastered the skills necessary to survive, and a set of far-reaching climatic changes that would render the "cradle" no longer so hospitable. For around 1.5 million years ago, the gradual cooling of the earth's surface that would result in the great Ice Age of the Pleistocene was already underway. In the lands south of the equator, the lakes and forests and savannas began to shrink, and the deserts to grow, as the climate turned cooler and more arid. And in the northern latitudes the polar ice began to creep down over previously temperate lands.

We must not imagine that the Ice Age of the Pleistocene (1.8 million to 10,000 years ago) was an era of uniformly intense cold in the northern hemisphere and desert dryness in the south. It was, instead, a 1.8 million-year era of climate fluctuations in which long periods of glaciation alternated with shorter periods of milder, wetter conditions, in a set of ten or more cycles. Thus our hominid ancestors experienced, in their gradual spread across Africa, Europe, and Asia, a wide variety of different environmental conditions, requiring different skills, new learning, and varying social arrangements.

Some have reasoned that the migration of our hominid ancestors away from the lakeshores and savannas of their East African cradle could not have been accomplished without language as a means of storing and passing on skills and information—indeed, that the complexity of food-gathering and social life even on the savannas argues for a very early evolution of speech. But I do not think it likely. Gestures and vocal signals function quite well among relatively small bands in a stable environment where survival needs can be met through a limited set of routinized activities—even if those activities require divisions of labor and such forms of cooperation as scavenging and even hunting imply. Lions frequently use complex team strategies in bringing down their prey, and the dwarf mongoose manages a complex social life—including shared "babysitting" arrangements and cooperative strategies for attack and defense—without language. The simplicity and slow development of tools before the movement outward from the East African cradle also suggests that signals and imitation served for a very long time as adequate means of learning and preserving the skills necessary for survival. And recent computer-assisted projections backward of the evolutionary development of the physiology required for the shaping of sounds into those of human speech suggest that the savanna period is far too early for vocal control of sounds precise enough to serve as words.

The long, slow migration of our ancestors outward during the early Pleistocene, however, would have had several major consequences for communication. One, of course, would be the continuous expansion, within any band, of the "vocabulary" of signals required to cope with novel physical environments and the changing survival needs and social structures to which they would give rise. And another would be the increasing differentiation of groups, both physically and socially, as their spread into quite different environments favored different diets, competencies, and social arrangements. It is impossible to say what modifications in brain physiology and neurology may have occurred during the million or so years in which our ancestors spread through Africa and into northern Europe and Asia, and what alternate means of acquiring, storing, and communicating information may have emerged in that time, proved inadequate, and failed to survive. Brains are soft tissue, and synaptic structures leave no "tracks" on bone for archaeologists to find. We do know that adjustment to different environments fostered the evolution of quite different physical types, and that as late as 70,000 years ago, at least two different species of "Homo" still inhabited northern Europe. We should not be surprised, then, that the wandering of hominid bands into different environments during the mild interglacial cycles would foster different social arrangements and with them, different patterns of vocal signals among widely separated bands.

During periods of intense glaciation, however, the habitable regions of the continents would shrink, driving the widespread bands and tribes into closer proximity—and closer interaction. For the climatic change would affect not only the extent of habitable terrain, but also the types and sources of food. Large game—too large for two or three hunters to bring down—would prove a more reliable and efficient source of energy than vegetables and smaller game in climates of either increasing cold or spreading drought. But large game would also require more inter-group cooperation and planning to locate, track, and kill. Thus our ancestors would arrive at the second of those conditions that, among children, stress signalic speech to the breaking point: dependence for survival needs on others who have not been participants in the history of shared experience that makes signals intelligible to intimates and therefore effective means of predicting and regulating response. In other words, just as in children, so among our forebears the behavioral "hypothesis" that sounds are connected to and therefore "cause" events would break down in interactions with other tribes who used and responded to the same sounds differently, or not at all.

At the same time, we may imagine that periods of glaciation and drought would drive the food-suppliers of the ancient bands farther afield from central bases in their search for game—farther than a simple "come-to-me" call would suffice to produce the manpower needed once quarry was sighted. As in toddlers whose needs arise in one room when help is in another, so in the case of our ancestors would such separations from others give rise to two consequences. One would be the need to repeat to oneself, over the course of the journey for help, the sound associated with the response required—a process that separates signals from the context of activity in which they are embedded and gives rise to the use of sound to keep *in mind* some state of affairs. And the second would be the inadequacy of signals to specify clearly enough, in the absence of information provided by shared context, the specific response required. In short, the increasing separation of band members from contexts of immediately shared activity would at the same time render one function of sounds—as signals—increasingly unreliable, and reinforce a new function: their use to maintain an expectation in mind, to represent a state of affairs outside the immediate context of its occurrence. And that is the beginning of sound as symbol, as word, as speech.

Thus we may trace, in the expansion and diversification of our ancestors' environmental and social experience during the million-and-a-half year period of deglaciation and reglaciation, the emergence of the same critical factors that precipitate the breakdown of signalic learning and communication in the lives of our own young. And we find in the same period, but especially toward its end, increasing evidence of a new way of "seeing," of that abstractive capacity to extract an object from the context of its original function or a sound from the context of immediate activity, that is the correlate and hallmark of the word. Somewhere during the long cold nights of the middle Pleistocene (around 500,000 years ago), for example, our ancestors learned to control and maintain fire, and put it to new uses—as in cooking. The archaeological evidence reveals a steady diversification and systematization of stone tools, including tools to make other tools. The hardships of climate suggest that some adaptation of animal skins for clothing would have been required for survival. And more important perhaps than any of these, as indications of a new turn of mind, are the first traces, around 300,000 years ago, of collections of significantly shaped natural objects, of carvings on bones and stones, of materials that may have been used in drawing, and of ritual. The significance of such objects and the activities they suggest is that all of them reflect increasing use of materials, not so much to control and alter physical experience directly, but to *represent* it. And that, again, is the critical difference between the use of sounds as signals and the use of sounds as words.

But we must be careful not to slip into either/or language and interpretation here, in considering how our ancestors may have used and understood signs even 100,000 years ago. There are good reasons for supposing that our species passed through an extremely long period of physical, social, and cognitive development before the "command" and "reference" functions of signs were clearly differentiated, and that for the most of that period—indeed, perhaps until the widespread use of reading and writing—signs functioned simultaneously to represent and, *through representation*, to control that which was represented.

To the modern, highly literate mind, the notion that a name, a drawing, even a dramatic representation of some experience, as in theater or ritual, has any direct connection in nature to what it represents strikes us as peculiar. And the consequence of that notion—the belief that by representing something we somehow *affect* what is named, or drawn, or reenacted—strikes us as patently absurd. We find such notions laughable because most of the words and images and vestigial rituals we encounter, as people of print and tele-technologies, are very far removed indeed from the contexts of cooperative social action in which we live from moment to moment, day to day. Consider the words on this page, for example. Is there anything you expect to *do* about them? And if so, when? Tomorrow? Next year? Whose cooperation would you need, if any, to carry out the activity they represent? And would that activity have any immediate consequences for your survival? Of course not. In a literate world, we are accustomed to dealing with representations many, many steps removed, in space and time, from any specific action-response. And the attenuation of the connection between sign and activity signified diminishes our sense that they are in any way "naturally" or "causally" connected.

When our ancestors first began to use signs to represent in one context what they had experienced in another, however, matters were radically different. The earliest representations that survive on stone and bone, and the much later drawings on the cave walls at Lascaux and Altamira, are of things and events intimately connected to the survival of the group and closely tied to its cooperative activities. They have a response-connection far more immediate and urgent than any we can conceive, and thus a power connection, a "causal" connection, a "summoning" and "controlling" function that we moderns are only faintly aware of in our own responses to pictures of people and events with whom we are closely and deeply involved.

Yet we may find even in ourselves, after some hundred thousand years of symbolic development, strong traces of the ambiguous attitude toward representations that must have characterized our ancestors' early use and understanding of visual and vocal signs. To grasp what I mean, put down this book for a moment and look in your wallet, or around your home, for a photograph of someone near and dear—your son or daughter, mother or father, husband or wife. Now take a pin or a pencil, or even your fingernail, and scratch out the eyes. If you are like most of the students I have asked to do that—not to *think* about doing it, but actually to *do* it—you will find all kinds of "good reasons" not to, the most common being that it would destroy the photograph, and it's the only one you have. But try to be honest. If you had fifty copies, or a hundred, would you find the task any less repugnant? If so, you may congratulate yourself on having achieved a separation from the human past, and the psychodynamics of signs, that most of us (myself included) must shamefacedly admit we have not yet attained. For most of us, no matter how educated, would feel at the least a distinct queasiness about "harming" the photograph of someone we love. But why? We "know" perfectly well, you and I, that a photograph is merely a chemically-treated piece of paper, and that the image on it is not connected by physical bonds to the person the image represents. And yet, deep down, we feel that somehow, just maybe, it is; that our action on the photograph may harm, not just the photograph, but the person as well. As my students say, "Better safe than sorry."

If we modern folk, after 500 years of literacy and 70,000 of speech, are still of two minds about the connection between signs and what they represent, are still moved by the "power connection" between pictures and their objects, words and what they name, how much more deeply that connection must have been felt in a world where vocal and visual signs were more intimately and urgently embedded in the immediate experience and activities of the group. For it is a principle universally observed that the closer the connection in time, space, and regularity of occurrence between any sign and the activity that "goes with" it, the more we assume a causal relation between the two, and the more likely we are to invest the sign with a "magical" power to control what it represents. And the converse is also true: the greater the "distance" between some sign and the activity associated with it, the less we interpret the sign as signal or command, and the more as a symbol with purely referential meaning.

To elevate these observations to a general rule and give it a fancy name, we may say that the history of human communication and mind is largely the story of the "progressive de-contextualization" of signs—of the increasing separation of signs from the responses with which they were originally linked in time, in space, in contexts of physical co-presence and cooperative activity, and in regularity of response by others who share the same history of experience. And along with this process, of necessity, goes another that we may call, for the sake of balance if not euphony, "progressive *recontextualization*": the supplying of lost contextual information *by other means*, which are usually other signs. For once a sign is removed from the contexts of shared activity in the same sensory field—when people are separated from each other in space so that one cannot see, hear, smell, experience what the other does—the sign becomes ambiguous, and the response uncertain. The simple solution, of course, is to bring the other to where you are with a call. This is what young children do, of course (and the lazy, or those in positions of superior power), until they have been taught otherwise. But what if the other cannot hear you, or cannot or will not come? Then you must somehow bring the context to them. Our children, born into a ready-made world of words, learn to do this by elaborating speech along the lines already available to them in their culture's grammar. They re-contextualize their vocal signs by means of other vocal signs.

But how would one re-contextualize a vocal sign in a world where grammar is not yet "invented"? How supply the missing visual context, action context, to evoke the needed response? How else but through that facility already well-developed in the "higher" mammals, and particularly in the chimps and great apes: the gift of imitation, of gestural and postural reenactment. And surely this is the means our ancestors used to elaborate the "meaning" of their vocal signs. With one very important difference from the imitations practiced by their predecessors. In all the higher mammals, imitation serves the functions of skill-learning and practice. The cubs of a lioness, the kittens of a cat, the young females in a tribe of baboons imitate the activities of their elders, of their own kind, and thus learn what is required of them to survive. But the need of a hominid game-spotter, for example, returning to camp for help, is *response*-centered, not practice-centered. And to produce the needed response would require the reenactment, not of his *own* behavior in the distant setting, but of what he saw. It would require him, in short, to enact something not himself, to be at the same time himself and something "other"—like a bear, or a mastodon, or a stag. And that is a major step toward the idea of representation, the idea of a symbol. For a symbol is both what it is (an oddly shaped piece of rock, for example) and something other (the child-swollen woman it looks like, or the idea of such a woman).

It is quite likely that such forms of enactment, originally tied to pragmatic needs for immediate and specific cooperative response to events at a distance, underlie the development of ritual, although the connection is by no means direct. Ritual, after all, is not mere enactment. It is repeated, stylized enactment, and the response it summons is a repeated, stylized response that does not immediately "go anywhere," that does not at once "spill over" into action on the larger world. The response ritual summons, in fact, is not a "literal" response but itself an enactment, a stylized version of the group's past and future responses to the "real" events the ritual enacts. Thus ritual is a bridge, an interim stage between acting out something to produce an immediate response (as we might do to summon a police officer to the scene of an accident, in a land where no one speaks our tongue) and "pure" drama, which does not summon a behavioral response at all, but only the ideas and feelings associated with such a response. (We may experience fear and anger in response to the actions of an evil character in a play, for example, but we do not rush the stage to drive him off, either during the performance or after.) The "content" of primitive ritual—reenactments of the hunt, for example—lies very close to the life experiences of the group, and its enactment is not much separated in time from the "real" activities it represents. Men may not actually fling their spears as an antler-clad companion charges at them around the fire, but they will have made that response to the movement of a stag the day before and the day before that, and they will again tomorrow. And the precision of their response will make a real, not a pretended, difference. Thus ritual enactment *does* affect, though at a slight remove, the outcome of the events enacted. Because of this intimacy and regularity in the connection between enacted and "real" experiences, early ritual lies in that vast grey area where signs function simultaneously to represent *and* command or control what is represented. And that is why ritual is always, always, imbued with "magical" power.

Indeed, ritual, along with all forms of "magic," is our best evidence that the "symbolic" or "representative" functions of signs developed gradually out of their "signalic" or "command" functions, that it took a very long time for the two functions to be separated, and that they remain closely linked below the threshold of our conscious, rational understanding of symbols even today.

But ritual is more than a symptom of a state of cognitive affairs, now or in the history of our species. It has also played a vital role in changing and accelerating our symbolic and social development. For whatever its origins, ritual represents an important step forward in the separation of enactment and response. In effect, it provides a means to represent some set of events that has happened or is going to happen somewhere else, or in a slightly different time (yesterday, tomorrow), and to enact responses to those events without the risks of "real" immediate consequences. Thus ritual provides a new and safer context for the rehearsal and practice of the group's cooperative activities and for the training, without risk, of its young. It provides, in short, a means of passing on acquired information and skills symbolically.

The young played a special role in what might be called the "developmental consequences" of ritual. For they would be, from infancy, observers of, if not active participants in, enactments of events whose real counterparts they had as yet no experience of and would not share for years to come. (I assume here that children would not participate in the "real" hunts that ritual enactments might have represented). The young would also, of course, be quick to imitate their elders in play, where their mock rituals would have no consequences at all. In children, then, as in others, like women, for whom many ritual enactments would *not* have been closely tied to real activities with real consequences (like hunting), the sense of a causal connection between enactment, vocal sign, and "real" event would have been less powerful, and the use of a sign to *represent* without changing things, more familiar. Thus it may well have been among the interactions of these two groups, women and children, that the first use of signs to refer without commanding—the first use of words—arose.

Ritual may also have played a central role in the elaboration of vocal signs that led, over centuries, to grammar. Three of the characteristics of ritual, in particular, suggest this connection. The first is that, as enactment, ritual does not merely represent "things," as the antlers of a stag or the claws of a bear, being parts of the larger wholes, might represent them. Enactment is dynamic: it represents things in the contexts of their interactions, and its focus is on their changing *relations* over the time of the events enacted. In this sense ritual is, like grammar, primitive narrative. Or perhaps more accurately: if grammar is primitive narrative, then ritual is primitive grammar. Second, ritual is not dumb-show, silent pantomime. It develops out of the need to re-contextualize vocal signs, and in a vocalizing species it would inevitably be accompanied by sounds.

Finally, the essence of ritual is repetition, *stylized* repetition: repetition in which variation in the sounds, gestures, actions, and their relationships is kept to the absolute minimum that is possible, given different performers, to achieve. Ritual repetition, in a word, is precise. It *must* be precise, because the assumed causal connection between the ritual enactment and the real-life events it enacts is based on repeated correspondences between the two, and a causal connection "means" that a change in the enactment will produce a change in what it enacts. That is why precision is a fundamental, a necessary characteristic of all forms of magic, "black" or "white." Make an error in the drawing of a pentagram, set down the candles slightly wrong, intone the names of the spirits you call in a different order, and you are likely to get more than you bargained for—or nothing at all. Change the words of the Mass to a different tongue, change the garb of the priests, let a woman conduct the rites when one never did before, and you will have schism in the church. The violence of reaction of even the mildest congregation to something as "simple" as a change in the order of service tells us there is more behind their feeling than nostalgia or the "comfort" of tradition. And it is not hatred of English, or of women, or of the color blue that convulses the church when it tries to change its rituals. Charge the orthodox, if you will, with an ancient turn of mind, but do not insult them with trivialities. Their rites are rites of power, of *summoning*, not remembrance. And all their power lies in doing things as they were done the first time they produced their consequences. *Precisely*. Alter anything about the ritual and you will alter its consequences. Sloppy ritual, in a word, doesn't *work*.

In primitive ritual, then, we have a focus on dynamic relations, coupled with the use of sounds, and precise pairings between sounds and acts, repeated over and over in a context charged with power and urgently connected to the life of the group. We have the ideal conditions, in short, for the learning of vocal signs for relations, and that is the raw material of grammar. All that was needed was one step more, one more pressure on the attenuated connection between vocal sign and behavioral response, one more removal of sounds from the context even of ritual action, to separate the "command" from the "reference" function of sounds and push us over into names, words, speech. What circumstances would have provided that push?

But perhaps that is the wrong way to put the question. I have suggested that between 100,000 and 50,000 years ago, as representation and ritual intensified, there were already some—like women and children—whose exclusion from the ritually reenacted activities of the group would have weakened the "causal" connection between sign and act. Among such groups, the tendency to use and respond to signs as signals, as commands, would have been weaker, and to use them as names, as references, stronger. But in an action-centered context, such tendencies—with the delay between sign and response they imply—would surely have been perceived as *dis*advantages, as weaknesses and liabilities, not strengths. For repeated delays in responding to the signals of others, and variations in response, make one seem unpredictable, unreliable, and therefore dangerous in situations that demand immediate and invariable cooperation. That is why children are regarded as socially "dangerous" even today. Not yet fully "conditioned," their responses are unpredictable. In contemporary social situations, where our survival is hardly at stake, the consequences are merely embarrassing. In physical situations, like a hunt, where everything might hinge on immediate and reliable response to signals, the consequences would be deadly—not only to the child but to the group. And so the children would be left, with the women, behind. Perhaps the ancient charge against women, too—that they are unpredictable, wayward, "flighty"—has its origins in their tendency, developed earlier than men's, to respond to signs with variance and delay, to process them as symbols, not commands.

What circumstances, then, would have turned the "symbolic tendency" to advantage, from weakness to strength, and so promoted its development and spread?

The answer may lie, again, in the environmental changes of the mid-Pleistocene—particularly, in the relatively long and mild interglacial periods from 128,000 to 75,000 and 55,000 to 35,000 years ago. In those warmer periods, the ice withdrew, the arid regions grew lush with water, and the peoples of the earth wandered again. Meat-eaters now, they followed the game—some as ceaseless nomads, some in seasonal migrations tuned to the advance and retreat of the sun. And as they wandered, they faced new challenges, new hazards, new demands, for different environments pose new problems of shelter, defense, terrain. They placed new demands on learning, too—of the signs and habits of different creatures and how they are best hunted; of what roots and stalks and berries are edible, and where and when they may be found and how prepared; of which materials will harden in fire, and which new ones will chip or bend. Most of all, the wandering life places new demands on memory, for new knowledge and skills are of short use if they cannot be recalled. Perhaps these demands were greatest on those who experienced the greatest seasonal change, for those who could not preserve knowledge, from spring to spring, of how the streams flashed into flood, and where the birds nested, and when which tubers grew, would not long survive. Neither would those whose own knowledge was great, but who lacked the means to pass it on to their young. For a group or a species that cannot transmit survival information to its offspring may last for a generation or two, but then it will die.

This, then, was the set of problems that turned the "symbolic tendency" to advantage and intensified it: the need of nomadic people to preserve somehow, over periods of time as long as a year and through all the intervening change, memory of a set of natural signs and their related activities in places far away; and the need to preserve and communicate a rapidly expanding body of acquired knowledge and skills to the young. Among those already practiced in enactments of events in which they were not directly involved—children, certainly, and women, perhaps—such means of representing the activities of progressively more distant times and places would have come quite naturally, especially with the expansion of time for leisure and play. And children, finding such activities pleasurable, might soon have learned, as children do, to "summon" these enactments with the vocal signs to which they were "attached." Thus it well may be, strange though it seems, that in the history of our species it was the children who taught their elders the uses of a word. For the child's vocal sign would "call for," in others, an enactment that was itself a representation, a memory—an enactment that the adults being busy, might not choose just then to perform. But the sound would serve to call the enactment, and therefore the memory of the activities it represented, to mind. Thus vocal signs might come to function, through the agency of children, as means both to preserve and retrieve information from memory, without the intervening step of enactment. And that is the first function—meaning, the *survival* function—of words.

It would be hard to overstate the survival advantage that words would give those ancient groups that arrived at them. To see why, consider the alternate means available to acquire, store, and transmit a continually expanding body of skills and knowledge to the young—namely, through signalic learning, with its reliance on imitation and reinforcement through repeated enactments, like ritual. This is, in fact, one of the major ways in which we humans learn today, and have learned (as I have tried to show) through most of our long history. Why, then, should such means have proved inadequate, some 75,000–50,000 years ago??

Consider. It is easy enough to imagine that in cave days, as learning increased, there would have been some in each group whose long life and repeated experience at certain tasks (like the gathering of herbs) would have made them especially "wise"—living repositories of specialized acquired skills. And these might, in turn, have apprenticed one or two among the young, and through repeated enactments and reinforcement, trained them in the same activities. Specialization and apprenticeship are, after all, time-honored solutions to rapid increases in knowledge. But among groups that are relatively small, this is a dangerous route to go. Learning through repeated doing, without the agency of symbols, is painfully slow; it requires close and continued contact between teacher and learner in a one-to-one relationship; it works poorly, if at all, outside the presence of the materials with which the skills must be learned; and it requires the full engagement of the teacher and learner. One cannot learn by doing while the body and hands are occupied with something else. And in a small group, there is always the danger that old age or accident will carry the teacher off before one-tenth of what needs to be passed on has been learned, depriving the group of a significant part of its "memory" and survival-enhancing skills. No doubt just such catastrophes often befell those in whom the "symbolic tendency" had not been sufficiently developed to foster the use of words. And such groups, if they survived at all, would fall farther and farther behind.

It is not enough, then, for small groups to "store" their acquired learning in the lives of different members and pass it on to their offspring one at a time. When life is short and perilous, knowledge must be disseminated throughout the group, so that "redundancy" will preserve it though several members die. What better means to serve that end than *group* enactments, repeated and precise, of the activities and skills survival required? That, indeed, was one function of ritual, and the evidence suggests that all our ancestors who still survived at around 70,000 BCE— including our Neanderthal cousins and the Early Modern Human newcomers with whom they interbred—practiced ritual enactments during the long cold of the Pleistocene winters between 100,000 and 50,000 BCE.

But in the end, ritual without words must fail in the face of continuous expansion and change. For ritual is, by its very nature, conservative, inflexible, resistant to change. It preserves what is known, but does not accommodate much variation or easily incorporate the new. It is surrounded, to boot, with awe and power—never performed casually, at the drop of a hat—and it requires, like any enactment, the full bodily engagement of its participants. It is, therefore, like drama, confined in place and time, not portable or immediate enough to store and trigger memory "in the field." But most of all, ritual is keyed, like Proust's madeleines, to remembrance of things past. And those forced to rely on ritual and reenactment alone would soon find themselves with outworn skills, unable to adjust to change.

There may be another reason, more potent even than these, that rendered signalic learning and communication inadequate to cope with the demands that new environmental and social conditions placed on our ancestors around 70,000–50,000 BCE. Though it has never to my knowledge been demonstrated, there is reason to believe that signalic means of learning and storing acquired skills require increases in brain mass and configurations of skull shape that symbolic processes do not. If this is indeed the case, then natural selection would favor, in a species whose survival depended on its capacity for signalic learning and "recall," the evolution of progressively larger brains—and of the skulls that confine and limit them. This is in fact the pattern we see from the earliest of our hominid ancestors to Neanderthal, whose skull was considerably larger than our own.

There is an upper limit to the size and shape of the skull that can pass the pelvic bones of a female in childbirth, and the female pelvic structure is itself limited by evolutionary and ecological factors—among them, the skeletal design required to walk upright. Eventually, then, a trait initially advantageous to a signalic learning species—larger and larger skulls to accommodate larger and larger brains to accommodate more and more acquired responses—might turn to disadvantage, even disaster, as females died in childbirth, straining to deliver their over-large young. Thus it may be that the alternate route to learning and storing information in words—a continuing reliance on an ever-increasing body of signalic responses—would prove not just inadequate but ultimately deadly to a species that followed it too far.

Perhaps this is what happened to Neanderthal, our large-skulled, differently-shaped cousin in the evolutionary tree. The evidence is that somewhere during the long Ice Age of the Pleistocene—perhaps around 75,000 BCE—his path and that of our own immediate ancestor, Early Modern Human, diverged. Both had come as far as ritual—or so the archaeological evidence suggests. And until about 50,000

BCE, both survived. But then Neanderthal disappeared, a victim, perhaps, of the "signalic solution" to the demands on memory of environmental expansion and change, or subsumed by interbreeding with the more successful creatures who had learned, along the line, to speak. The evidence is too sketchy to say for sure. Perhaps in the face of uncertainty it is best to let poetry have the final say. Two paths diverged in a wood, and we, we took the path less traveled by. And that has made all the difference. For from about 40,000 years ago on, as the sudden explosion in tools, invention, and art leaves no doubt, the history of the human condition has been the history of a species that *speaks*.

I have elsewhere[1] proposed a law that says, "Behind every instance of widespread communication change, there is some pressing problem." And a corollary that said: "The more urgent the problem, the more rapid and thorough the change." The shift from signals to symbols, from buzzes and howls and, yes, even gestures, to words, language, speech, is a communication revolution of the first order, both in time and magnitude. Behind it, then, we should find a problem of the first magnitude—a species problem, not just the problem of an individual or tribe. And of course, we do. To take the longest possible evolutionary view, language, we might say, was the ultimate solution of a very weak species, in a sequence of novel and perilous environments, to the problem of preserving, updating, and transmitting survival-enhancing information to its young and thus keeping itself alive and adaptive to change.

In the simpler forms of life, which produce enormous numbers of young in rapid successions of generations, DNA (with the help of natural selection) is a medium adequate to that task. In the more complex forms, DNA must be supplemented by structures for storing and transmitting *acquired* information. Where a species inhabits an environment stably over long periods of time, so that the number of "routines" it needs to acquire is relatively small, signalic means of learning and communication are adequate, given enough offspring and a short enough reproductive cycle to let DNA and natural selection do their part.

However, our ancestors were neither strong nor swift nor rapid reproducers. They had neither the luxury of time nor the margin for error that DNA by itself requires to keep a species alive and adaptive in the face of change. Nor could they establish that secure niche in a stable environment that restricts signalic learning and communication to a manageable handful of complex routines. Driven time and again by competition and ecological change into new environments with demands for new social arrangements, new adaptations of materials into tools,

---

1 See "Narrative: The Ecology of Tales, Tools and Social Change," in *Nystrom 2020, The Genes of Culture: Towards a Theory of Symbols, Meaning and Media*, Volume 1.

new cooperative strategies and skills, they required ever larger and more complex systems of signals to regulate group interactions and trigger learned responses over intervening distance and time. And every elaboration of social structure, tools, skills, and signals itself changed the social, material, and "symbolic" environments, fostering further diversification, movement outward, and change. Until signalic means of regulating cooperative activity, and of learning, storing, and transmitting acquired skills to the young, could no longer accommodate the complexities of past, present, and future experience, nor the skulls of infants grow any larger to accommodate brains massive enough for more.

Our species needed, in short, a non-biological way to code and communicate information, in a form more subject to rapid revision, and less perishable, than DNA, more flexible and efficient than signals. Language is the best solution to that problem our species has yet produced. That is why it has survived, everywhere, as our primary communication technique.

It is not a perfect solution, as we shall see. Nor did it make our earlier solutions go away. We humans are the walking repositories, or better, the stewards, of all the achievements of living things since the struggle to live and multiply began. We carry within us the triumph of the gene, the DNA "response" to the command, "Go on." And the signalic structures for which generations of creatures died so that some could learn. And overlaid on these, the achievement of some three million years of perilous journeying outward from the savannas of our past: the gift of language, reason, and mind. None of these is idle in our own struggle to survive; none a mere vestige of a long-vanished world. Each plays a vital role still in shaping who we are, as persons and a species; in governing how and what we know and learn; in transforming the present and constructing the future we will bequeath to our own young.

I said in speaking of children and words that we live, we humans, in two different worlds. But that is not quite true. We live in three: a physical, material world, represented in us by the gene; a social world of desperate dependencies we rely on to survive, moderated and governed largely by signals; and a symbolic world—the world of language and reason, poetry and science, ideology and art—that elaborates and transforms the others. They are not independent worlds, the material, the social, and the symbolic. A change in any one feeds back and forward on the others to which it is inextricably tied, in a continuous, convoluted, open-ended loop of change. They are not entirely congruent worlds, either. Our genes, our signals, and our symbols bid us march to the sound of different drums, issue different orders to be carried out in different ways, drive us in different directions at once, so that we rarely know precisely what we want or need, or how to achieve it, or why. No wonder we humans are mostly dizzy and confused, that we despair at our loss of the whole, that the gift of our past seems more often burden than bequest, more bane than boon. But willing or no, we are its stewards. And it is an awesome heritage.

CHAPTER FOUR

Language and the Birth of Self

And when the woman saw that the tree was good for food, and that it was pleasant to the eyes, and a tree to be desired to make one wise, she took of the fruit thereof, and did eat, and gave also unto her husband with her; and he did eat.

And the eyes of them both were opened, and they knew that they were naked.

Genesis 3:6–7

Of all the consequences of the monumental act of disobedience that is language, none is more poignant than this: that in failing to respond to the sign of another as command, we sever the tie that binds us each to each and become conscious of our difference—of the "other"-ness of the other and, in the same breath, of our interdependence. We become, in a word, self-aware, self-conscious. And after that, nothing is ever the same. The gates of Eden—the garden of harmoniousness one-ness—close behind us and we find ourselves outside, naked and vulnerable in a perilous world.

The tale of the Fall is an ancient one, but as an account of language and its consequences, it is remarkably apt. If you read the full account closely, you will see that it is not names, with their power to command, that lead directly to the disobedient act. It is a notion, insinuated in Eve's ear by the serpent, "most subtil" (and limber tongued) of beasts, that a word—here, God's—might not have one invariable consequence, but some alternative outcome. And if different consequences of a word are possible, so are different responses. One may, therefore—must, in fact—choose. It is the idea of choice among possible responses, and Eve's exercise of that choice, that leads her in the Biblical tale to wisdom—with all its world-changing consequences.

I say that this account is apt because it is in fact the power to choose among alternative responses to signs, and to hold in mind different possible consequences, that distinguishes the symbolic behavior of humans from the signalic behavior of beasts and gives us, in place of conditioned reflexes, reflective thought, "wisdom," and mind. But the Genesis tale is also apt in specifying what follows. Hard on the heels of the primordial leap to language, three things happen. First, Adam and Eve's eyes are opened and they see themselves in a new way: they become "self" conscious. Second, they invent—sewing fig leaves into aprons in the world's first "technical" act. And third, Adam offers, in response to God, the world's first explanation—the first connected account of himself, and his relation to Eve, and their joint relation to a part of their world, the Tree, in an act. He formulates, in a word, the world's first narrative. It is inadequate, of course. So Paradise is lost, and the long human story begins.

Self-consciousness, tools, and narrative. What strange consequences of language to single out for note in such an ancient tale of human origins. And none is stranger than the first. No sooner have they tasted of the fruit forbidden, we are told, then Adam and Eve become visible to themselves in a new way, from some new point of view, as though they are transported in a flash to some vantage point outside themselves from which they can see themselves, their own bodies, as objects. On *why* this should be—why language gives us the capacity for self-awareness, self-reflection—and on why it is so important that it takes first place of mention in the account of human beginnings, Genesis is silent. But more contemporary tale-tellers, happily, are not. One of the most insightful and original of these, the American philosopher and social psychologist George Herbert Mead, provided in the early decades of the 20th century an account of the relation between language, the self, and human society so penetrating and compelling that its echoes still reverberate in a half-dozen fields of social and humanistic inquiry today. For that reason, and because no telling of the human tale can proceed very far without accounting for this most central fact—that we are aware of ourselves, of our own inner lives, and are able to reflect on our own existence—I provide here a very compressed retelling of Mead's account.

It is easiest to grasp, I think, if we begin by reflecting again on what it is that children are doing as they learn to understand the speech of others and to speak themselves. In brief, they are learning to correlate one part of a complex event, its audible part (like the sound "juice"), with all that goes with that sound—including, of course, the changes in feelings of well-being that accompany it. To put it some-what differently, the child stores in memory, as a linked pair, the sound and the complex of events and feelings that go with it, so that the repetition of the sound "summons" the memory and feelings of the whole event. Thus the speech part of an event comes to stand for or evoke the larger whole, and the whole, from the child's point of view, is what the sound means—both when others make it and when the child herself produces it.

Now, it is important to remember that speech sounds only occur, in the child's early experience, in the context of interactions with others. And it is in fact those others, like mothers and fathers and older siblings, who bring about the events and changes in feeling the baby experiences in connection with speech sounds. Thus what the child is learning—incorporating into memory and feeling as her "own" meaning of speech sounds—is in fact the behavior of others with those sounds: what others do, with what consequences for her, when they make such sounds and how they respond to her when she makes them. So begins, in in-fancy, the process Mead called "internalizing the other": incorporating into one's internal world, via speech sounds, the responses of others and evoking in oneself, by producing those sounds, the responses others originally made. And it is through this process that the child continually constructs and modifies the meanings of speech sounds: by internalizing the responses of others to them. In effect, a meaning is a prediction, on the basis of past experience with others, their sounds, and their consequences—all internalized in memory—about how others will respond to a word. Throughout the early years of life, the child hones those predictions by testing them in dozens of different interactions with a growing va-riety of others, as her social world expands, and by refining and generalizing the "internalized other" accordingly.

Several years ago, I sat chatting over coffee with my sister and a friend while my young nephew, a toddler of some thirteen months, played on the floor nearby. As I looked idly on, an electrical outlet on the baseboard across the room caught his eye, and he made his way toward it at a rapid crawl. About a foot from it, he turned his head to us, slowed his movement toward the outlet to a creeping side-ways sidle, and, index finger extended to touch (but eyes fixed firmly in the op-posite direction—on us), began to pipe, "Hot? Hot? Hot?" (He had learned "Hot! Don't touch!" in connection with the kitchen stove, and my sister, in one of those lapses of educational diligence attributable to parental weariness, had slipped into using "Hot!"' to him as a reliable shorthand for "Dangerous" and "Don't touch.") As we watched him inch imperceptibly closer to the outlet, all the while looking at us and repeating, "Hot? Hot?", Ruth said to me wearily, "He knows. He's just testing me." But wet baby-fingers and electrical outlets are a combination it is best not to ignore, so I crossed the room and swept Peter up, saying firmly (Heaven help me!), "Yes, hot! Don't touch! No!" (What a hash that must have been to his linguistic sensibilities—especially the combination of "Yes" and "No." But he survived it somehow and learned, as all toddlers do, how to use "No!"—over and over and over again.)

The point is that my sister was right: the baby *was* testing, but not quite in the sense I think she meant—as a battle of wills. He was testing a quite complicated set of predictions about the responses of others to his own behavior, and to the sound "Hot," and about the applications of those responses to a particular situation—that is, involving an electrical outlet, not an oven. And from my response he learned not only that his predictions about the response-meaning of "Hot" and "Don't touch" and "No" were correct, and all related, but that the responses could be generalized to others *not* his mother.

Much the same process of testing linguistic predictions arrived at by internalizing and generalizing the responses of others underlies children's wearisome repetition of words, usually with a questioning inflection, once they have arrived at the idea of names and reference. Nothing can be more trying to the patience of adults riding in a car with a two-year-old, and attempting to converse among themselves, than the child's insistent piping: "Bus, Mommy? Bus? Bus? Bus?" "Yes, dear, that's a bus." "Car, Mommy? Car? Car? Car, Mommy?" "Yes, dear. Car." It is true enough, as parents will say, that toddlers do this to "get attention." But they are also acquiring a great deal more: not only a vocabulary, but a knowledge of the responses of others to themselves, and to words, and to the world, that will lead them, ultimately, to self-awareness and reflective thought.

How this occurs is illuminated by something else I saw my young nephew do, several days after his "experiment" with the electrical outlet. Again he sat on the floor, now surrounded by a variety of plastic toys which he picked up and shortly discarded, one after the other. A short distance away gleamed the bright, sharp steel of a pair of sewing shears, dropped by his mother when she rose to answer the phone. Their glitter amid the rubble of plastic and cloth toys caught his eye, and he made for them at top speed. But as he began to reach for them I heard him say, not very loud and not inquiringly, but softly and quite definitely, "Hot. Hot. Hot." And he withdrew his hand. He did not lose interest in the scissors, you understand. Everything about his behavior indicated that he maintained a lively curiosity about them, and a strong impulse to touch. But each time his hand went out, his own soft "Hot... hot... hot" restrained it, until I went over, placed him back among the safer toys, and put the scissors away.

Now, there is nothing very exceptional about this little incident. Any parent or doting aunt can describe dozens like it, and will, usually to point out how quickly an unattended toddler can get hold of what he shouldn't. But what is more remarkable is how often, as in this case, children *can* get hold of things they shouldn't, but *don't*—even when there is no adult to intervene. My nephew's behavior suggests one reason why. As Mead would put it, Peter used the sound "Hot" to call up in himself the response of others to him, certain objects, and his action, and used that "internalized other" to modify his own behavior. In other words, children become, through the agency of words they say to themselves, *self*-conditioning: capable of governing their own action, before they initiate or complete it, by calling to mind the response of others, codified and triggered by a word. It is as though they, as though *we*, carry about within us not one "self," but two: a spontaneous, impulsive self that generates action—that reaches, for example, for the scissors—and another, an internalized "other" evoked by words, that responds to our action before we make it and sometimes (at least) stops or modifies it.

And now we are quite close to understanding what it means to say that through language, we become *self*-conscious. To be conscious of yourself, reflective about yourself, aware of your own existence as an object and interested in it, implies that somehow you can step outside yourself, observe yourself from a point of view not your own. We know that we do this, that we are both actors and audiences for our own behavior. But we also know that we do not leave our own bodies, that actor and audience inhabit the same skin. It must be, then, that the "audience" for whom we act, the observer who sometimes applauds, sometimes hisses and boos, is simply another part of ourselves, an "other" whose responses we have learned through social interactions mediated by language, and who is called up by every use, audible or silent, of a word. And it is through this "other" that we become aware of, capable of reflecting critically on, actions that originate in different parts of ourselves.

I do not mean to imply, in all of this, that the thirteen-month child, or the three-year-old, or even the child of six is aware of these processes, or of himself, in the same way as an adult. Self-consciousness is a many-layered phenomenon; its levels are, in theory, infinite—meaning that we may be conscious not only of our bodies or behavior, but aware of our consciousness of them, then reflective on the fact that we are aware of our consciousness, then interested in the process through which we reflect on the fact that we are aware of our consciousness, and so on. And self-consciousness also extends, at each "level," in many different dimensions, so that we may be aware of our bodies, or our behavior, or our thoughts, feelings, and motives, or of our memories, or of our statements and theories about our memories and feelings and motives or any component of them, at different moments. Thus even adults will vary in the way they are self-conscious and, since self-consciousness is tied to language and social experience, cultures will vary as well.

We have only begun, in recent decades, to explore the vast terrain encompassed by the term "self-consciousness," and it is far too early to offer here more than a handful of generalizations about how it may develop either in children or in the history of cultures and of our species as a whole. At this point in our tale, however, a handful of generalizations will suffice. The most important is that self-consciousness, and therefore the self as an object of interest and concern, arises through interactions with others who are "internalized" and called up through the agency of language. Thus language, from an evolutionary point of view, not only solves a problem of information by providing an efficient means of coding, retrieving, and passing it on, but *changes the state of our information* by adding to it a vast new domain. Before the advent of the word, our forebears were, like all the other creatures on this planet, conscious of and responsive to the world outside their skins. Through language, we humans became conscious of ourselves and our existence, conscious of the world within. And this in turn generates, as we shall see in a bit, a new set of information problems that add fuel to the process of change.

Second, as Mead pointed out, language is the means through which "society," as a "generalized other," becomes incorporated in the "self" of each of its members. This is not to say that each of us internalizes precisely the same social world. Children come into the world different from each other in gross and subtle ways, and interact with very different others who respond to them in different ways. Thus the particular responses on which the child generalizes the "other" are always unique in some features, and no two of us grow up with exactly the same conception of society or self. Nonetheless, within the same language community there is enough similarity in the responses of others to children's linguistic productions that what is generalized allows us to share enough meaning to be mutually intelligible. As a general rule, the smaller the number of others with whom children interact, and the more consistently those others respond to the children in their charge (and to objects and one another), the greater will be the similarity in the "generalized other" that children internalize and the larger the field of meanings they will share. Conversely, the greater the number of others with whom children interact, and the more divergent the responses of adult others to the children in their charge, the greater will be the differences among the children and the less meaning they will share. In other words, small and cohesive societies characterized by great consistency in the responses of adults to children will tend to produce children more like one another in their responses to the world and to themselves than will large and diverse societies with considerable differences in child-rearing practices.

Third, even in small and tightly cohesive societies, the "self" of the individual is never a seamless, undifferentiated unity but a composite of at least two "parts": a set of largely biological needs and impulses, experientially and socially elaborated into a larger and more diverse set of preferences or wants, and a learned social self or generalized other that restrains and governs biological impulses and wants *but is no less forcefully felt as "one's own," with another set of equally and often more powerful wants.* Depending on the character of the society and its arrangements for satisfying both sets of wants, the two "parts" of the self interact with varying degrees of tension. To take a simple example: if a society instills in its children a strong prohibition against urinating in public, so that the very idea figures in the nightmares of the young, but then fails to provide adequate public toilet facilities, the biologic and social self will inevitably conflict in moments of tension so agonizing as to be unendurable. But in societies where either that prohibition is not inculcated in the young or it is, but with ample alternate means of securing "privacy," there will be little tension between the social and biologic "selves," at least on that issue. In the more "repressive" cultures of the West, where industrialization and urbanization have fostered intense conflict between the social and biologic "selves" of their people, distressing internal tension is more or less a norm, and may often be experienced as an internal dialogue between the two different "voices" of the self. To take a trivial example, which I choose because it has been interrupting these weighty reflections for some minutes now: On my desk sits a little bag of chocolates given to me by an acquaintance this morning ("and which you should have known better than to leave right there in plain sight, hamster-brain," comments my social self— hereafter "SS"), and it occasions this internal dialogue.

Biologic Self:	I want candy. Gimme.
SS:	No. Don't want it. Bad for me.
BS:	I'm hungry. Gimme.
SS:	No. It'll ruin my appetite, give me pimples, make cavities, I'll have to go to the dentist, he'll drill, it'll hurt. Don't want it.
BS:	Tastes good. I want it.
SS:	Makes me fat and ugly. Don't want it.
BS:	Ymmmmmmm. I want candy.
SS:	*I* want to be thin and beautiful and healthy.
BS:	Will feel so good if I eat it.
SS:	Will feel rotten if I eat it.
Mediator Self/Meta-Self:	Oh, for Godssake, eat the damned candy and get on with it.
(SS:	Erase that! Shouldn't swear!)

(I just ate the candy. It made me feel great. And it made me feel rotten.)

My point here is that, as the complications of living in large and diverse groups require more stringent social controls on impulse, the tensions between the biologic and learned social selves become more frequent and distressing. As they do, we give more attention to them and, since those tensions are located, via the internalization of others, *inside* us, we become more attentive to our inner lives. Thus the heightening of self-consciousness and the development of introspection in both individuals and societies in general is very much a function of the particular restrictions that the requirements of group living in different circumstances impose on impulse. Self-consciousness, in short, is made *possible* by language, but develops in different ways and to different degrees according to the social and material conditions of group life in a given place and time. We should not be surprised, therefore, to find that individuals and cultures vary both in the ways they are self-conscious and the particular problems of self they experience. Indeed, some recent scholarship on the history of consciousness is beginning to reinterpret the experience of cultures present and past from that point of view.

The little sample of the "dialogue of selves" I reported above—The Great Candy Debate, we might call it—also suggests two or three other generalizations worth developing here for the light they may shed on the unfolding of this tale later on. You may have noticed, for example, the sudden appearance of a new "voice" at the end of the dialogue—the voice which in fact ended it. I called it "Mediator Self" or "Meta-Self," to mean a self that observes the others and settles their competing claims. But where did *that* come from? From later social learning, of course—about the futility of endless debates and the need for action. More specifically, I suspect, the irritated "Get on with it!" came from my anxious professional self, watching the precious moments of a Sabbatical slip away while "I" dither over candy instead of writing. The point, as you will know if you listen to your own "voices," is that in highly complex societies like those of the industrialized West, where people function in dozens of different kinds of social structures and relate to different communities of others quite differently, the "self" is more a conglomerate than a partnership, and the internal conversation more of a parliament of competing voices than a dialogue. If you are at all like me, you may have, overlaid on your "biological" self and the self developed in your earliest interactions with parents and siblings, selves acquired through your transactions with female friends, and male friends, and sexual intimates, and fellow joggers, and baseball fans, and churchgoers, and teachers, and co-workers. And you may have, beyond these, a homemaker self, a parent self, a consumer self, a community-worker self, a political-action self—to name just a few. You may be accustomed to calling these "roles," to distinguish them from the thread of consistency and memory that runs through them all. My point in calling them "selves" is to emphasize that they are quite different parts of "you," of "me." Whatever we call them, these dimensions of the self, "they" see the world and respond to it in quite different ways: use language differently, talk about different things in different words and different tones of voice, use different standards of judgment and different kinds of reasoning, bring different kinds of facts to bear on issues and decisions, even dress differently, choose foods differently, and feel differently about the same things. I don't know about you, but I don't dress the same way (or want to), talk the same way, think the same way, even walk the same way or choose the same foods when I'm at a ballgame and when I attend a concert. I do not reason in the same way when I argue with my sister as I do when I argue with my colleagues. I feel one way about "the homeless" as a political activist, and a different way as a shelter volunteer, and still a different way as a homemaker trying to get my Saturday chores done without being hassled every fifty steps for my spare change.

Of course there is some consistency among our various "selves"; if there were not, we should be quite mad. But on many issues they are in serious conflict, and even when not, their competing claims on our attention, energy, money, and above all, time, engage us in wearing internal conflicts about what "I" want—or, more accurately, which "I"'s wants are going to be satisfied in the limited time available between, say, Friday evening and Monday morning. When those conflicts become intolerable, as they seem to do with increasing frequency among the middle class in American culture, we may turn to "self-help" books of popular psychology or to therapists—frequently with the result that *another* "self," another "voice," is added to the internal colloquy. It is no wonder that educated Americans are so fiercely self-preoccupied, so haunted and confused by the questions, "Who am I?" and "What do I want?" We have so many "I"s to choose among.

That, in fact, is the point to which I have said all this: not to bemoan the complexities of modern life, but to suggest that a major factor in the development of self-consciousness, culturally and historically, is the diversity of communities of others with whom the members of a society may engage, and the differentiation of vocabulary, interests, activities, values, and ways of knowing among those communities. To put it more plainly, we experience greater conflict among our "selves," and therefore become more "self"-conscious, when we have internalized a variety of others who are quite different *from each other* in their responses to the world. And we are more likely to experience such widely different others, when our culture segregates human activity and knowledge into different domains, each with its own concerns, vocabulary, ways of thinking and valuing, places and structures in which activity and social interaction take place, and rules for social and intellectual conduct. The more a culture divides up human knowledge and activity—separates "religion" from "school," "school" from "play," "play" from "work," "work" from "art," "art" from "science"—the more specialized and divergent these "discourse communities" (as Mead called them) become, and the more divergent the "selves" we acquire as we move back and forth among them in the process of growing up. This means that increasing specialization of knowledge and differentiation of roles in the history of cultures is a major factor not only in how societies will conduct their public affairs, but in how their members will experience their "internal" affairs—their "selves"—as well. It also means that self-consciousness is affected historically and culturally by the means of communication available in a culture and how they are used. To understand why, we must return for a moment to the processes through which children expand their social and language learning.

Social psychologists have divided these processes into two somewhat different kinds, sometimes called "primary" and "secondary" processes. In the preceding pages, I have focused almost entirely on children's "primary" learning: learning that results from their direct interactions with social others and the material world. Learning of this kind—through direct experience—is "primary" in at least three senses of the word. It occurs first in the physiological development of the child, beginning while the infant is still in the womb. It lays down a set of initial "world theories" or generalizations through which later learning is filtered and modified. And it is a more potent form of learning than any other. As a child, I once put my finger into a very low-power light socket, despite all parental injunctions. Once was enough. To this day I cannot bring myself even to replace a burned-out fuse.

As that experience suggests, primary learning, for all its potency and efficiency, has distinct disadvantages from the point of view of both individual and species survival. Fortunately for us, nature has endowed us, over the long course of evolution, with capacities to learn through means less risky than direct experience. Children have eyes and ears as well as skin and muscles, and these "distance receptors" allow them to learn not only through contact and active engagement, but through observation of the interactions of others, and of others with objects, and of objects with objects. And these "secondary" observations, no less than direct experience, are incorporated into our predictions about the consequences of objects and actions and speech sounds. They become, in short, part of the "generalized other" that allows us to reflect on and modify our own behavior: part of the self. Thus the complexity of the self depends not only on the variety of others whose responses we experience directly, but also on the diversity of others whose behavior is accessible to us indirectly—whom we experience vicariously, so to say. And the extent to which we can experience others vicariously depends, of course, on the means available in a culture to *represent* human behavior for our observation and learning.

Ritual reenactment of the activities of a tribe's ancestors, preserved over time by countless repetitions, is probably the earliest way in which others distant in time were made accessible to generations who could have no direct experience of them. Ritual provides, in other words, a means of vicarious interaction—symbolic interaction—with a community of others removed in time and place from one's own. Such symbolic interactions allow the past not merely to be recalled, but to be incorporated into the living present, as part of the "other" internalized in the self. Later forms of drama and, later still, dramatic recitations, served similar functions among the peoples of the world and still do today—not only among tribal cultures but wherever theater and ritual survive.

But dramatic enactment is not the only means through which we may encounter others of different places and times and incorporate them into our "selves." Among literate peoples, books, journals, and magazines are passports to worlds far removed from our immediate experience. Through them we may become silent but vitally active participants in dozens of different communities of others, some long vanished from the earth but accessible still through the agency of the printed word. For many of today's nominal readers, of course, books are dead and dusty things, and the people one meets in them no more than curious relics who spoke and thought in antique ways. But if one belongs to a living community in which books and those who people them are referred to and discussed, incorporated into conversation as a matter of routine, then the voices of those who speak through print become living voices, and their language, values, and ways of thinking may be assimilated to one's own. It is no mere convention of scholarship that people long dead are referred to, in the conversation and writing of academics, in the present tense, not the past. "But Plato argues...," I will say to a colleague in a lunchtime debate, or "Freud says...," or "Mead believes...,"—as though these are living participants in the conversation who have simply stepped away. Robert Maynard Hutchins once referred to the ongoing interaction of the voices of the past, represented in books, with living voices as "The Great Conversation" in which we are all, or can be, participants. And that "conversation" does not only take place "out there," between the covers of books or between soup and dessert at the noontide table. It also takes place "in here"—in the internal dialogues among our various "selves," to whom, through the preservation of the word in writing, a "Freud," a "Socrates," a "Mead" may be added. Thus through books, magazines, journals, the peoples of reading cultures acquire the capacity to see themselves from a large variety of different points of view, and to give increasingly diverse meanings to their own behavior, the behavior of others, and their experiences of the material world.

Nor are books the end of the matter. As technologies proliferate for recording and representing human behavior in various forms—as radio voices, in film and video images, in computer symbols—the communities of others to whom we have access become ever more various. And so do our opportunities for choice among the varieties of others we may symbolically engage. And people *will* choose differently: some to enter, via books, communities peopled by the likes of Socrates, Nietzsche, and Freud, or Galileo, Newton, and Einstein, or the characters of Tolstoi, Steinbeck, Joyce; others to share the company, via television, radio, film, and fan magazines, of rock stars and pop celebrities; still others may prefer the community whose language, values, tastes, and meanings are represented in the pages of stockbrokers' newsletters and magazines of gracious living. As a people's choices of symbolic others with whom to engage proliferate and diverge, so will the social worlds they experience through media and the "selves" they develop. Thus the realm of *shared* meanings, *shared* values, *shared* ways of thinking and assessing the world and one's own behavior may shrink until even people who share the same physical territory—a town, a city, a country—may find that they have very little in common. So changes in communication may make strangers of neighbors, and heighten the sense of the uniqueness, the autonomy, the aching aloneness of the individual self.

"O wad some power the giftie gie us, To see oursel's as ithers see us!" Like many a wish, this one of Robert Burns's is fraught with irony. Given or stolen, blessing or curse, the capacity to "see ourselves as others see us"—to be conscious of ourselves and reflective on our own behavior and situation in the world—has long been ours. It arose along with language and, like language and other means of communication, has developed differently in different times and places throughout the long course of human history, as the conditions of social and material life have changed, with consequences we are only beginning to understand and an ultimate end we can none of us foresee. Among the blessings self-consciousness has bestowed on us are our abilities to reason, to imagine alternative courses of action and their likely consequences, and to restrain our own impulses—to be self-governing. Not the least of the virtues that come in its wake are human empathy, charity, and the capacities for self-improvement and moral choice. But for every blessing of self-consciousness there is a corresponding curse, for each of its virtues, a vice: overweening self adoration, searing hatred of the self, the too-great terror of the final loss of self-consciousness in personal death.

Beyond these, self-consciousness poses a problem that daily becomes more urgent for our species as a whole. We live in a world where our own technologies and their by-products create conditions that threaten us all. Our hope for survival depends on cooperative action among peoples of many and widely different tribes, nations, cultures—vastly different communities of discourse, characterized by different languages, different ways of thinking, valuing, and judging thought and behavior, different kinds of consciousness, different conceptions of world and self, resulting from different histories of material, social, and symbolic experience.

In the U.S., the diversity of peoples, the fragmentation and specialization of knowledge and activities, and the proliferation of media for representing diverse others have led to a rapid decline in shared meanings and values and a growing sense of incoherence in both public and private life. If even within a single nation the social self is so fragmented and differentiated that the "public"—meaning the realm of shared concerns, meanings, and agreements about goals and problem-solving strategies—has all but disappeared, what hope do we have of attaining a *world* public coherent enough to address *world* problems? Through what means can coherence be constructed in a world of increasing differentiation and complexity?

CHAPTER FIVE

Narrative

In the beginning God created the heaven and the earth.

And the earth was without form, and void; and darkness was upon the face of the deep. And the Spirit of God moved upon the face of the waters.

And God said, Let there be light: and there was light.

Genesis 1:1–3

In the beginning, the ancient tale of Genesis tells us, God spoke, and the world began. In the beginning, says the still more ancient tale of the Walbiri, the Pintupi, the Bororo, the Taimanni, the Ancestors called the world into being through song. Throughout the world's primordial tales it runs, this theme: that in the beginning, at the very source of the beginning, is the word. The same idea is woven into the very fabric of language. In dozens of different tongues across the globe, dozens of different words for speaking, for telling, for singing, for saying can be traced back to roots that also have the meaning of calling forth, bringing to be, making, creating. Thus did our remote ancestors, closer in time to the origins of speech than we, express their awe of the word and an insight that we, inured by millennia of talk and centuries more of writing, have all but forgotten. They understood, our ancestors did, in a way that we do not, that language did more than record and express the human world. It created the world as humans know it.

In saying this, I am not speaking metaphorically or poetically. But I do not speak as a solipsist, either. There is a material world outside our skins, outside our minds, and it goes its way at least in part independent of us and our language, even of our consciousness of it. Things happen in that world, and other things, things without language, like trees and flowers and even the simplest of animals, respond. But that is not the world as humans experience it. The world as we know it has a past, because language permits us to codify experience and store it and call it to mind again in memory. And it has a future, because language allows us to model, through words and their grammatical relations, what has not yet happened. The world as humans know it is not simply the world of sense data, of material facts. It is the world of possibilities, of contingencies, of potentialities, because language permits us to take experience apart and reassemble it in mind, not as it is, but as it might be.

Yes, there is a material world outside our consciousness, our memory, our knowledge, even our imagination of it. But that is not the world in which we humans experience ourselves most intensely to *be*. We live in the material world, but we locate our sense of being elsewhere: not in the world we inhabit, but in the world that inhabits us—the world represented within, where self and consciousness and "I" are born and live and die. That world, too—the world where we experience our own experience—is called into being through language.

And even that is not the end of it, of the world-making power of the word. By giving us the capacity to see things not as they are, but as they might be, language transforms and by transforming creates a new material world. The act that makes of fig leaves an apron to cover one's shame does not compare in mystery to the process that brings the fig leaves themselves to life, but it is an act of new creation just the same. And the weaving of leaves into garments is only the rudest beginning of the language-inspired transformation of the natural world. What worlds we may create, or destroy, before we humans are done speaking we cannot foresee. Through our capacity to represent and imagine, we have already transformed the atom and are tinkering with the gene. The heavens themselves are filled with man-made lights, and though we have not done it yet, we may one day soon make for ourselves, or of ourselves, a new black hole, or a star. It is no wonder our ancestors were awed by the creative and destructive power of the word. They could not foresee its more recent consequences, of course, but the language and literature they have passed on to us reveal how deeply they felt the scope and scale of word-fostered change.

We have experienced in our own time something of the power of changes in ways of coding, storing, and communicating information to change the human world. And we have expressed our own awe at the enormous force in such changes by creating new phrases, metaphors for violent upheaval, as in "the knowledge explosion" or "the communications revolution" and its myriad attendant social "revolutions." The kind of change set in motion by the evolution of language itself was neither so violent nor so sudden as such modern metaphors imply. The transformations of the material, social, and psychological world that accompanied the development of speech mounted up gradually over the long course of centuries, of millennia, in a slow swell, a building wave, not a volcano of change. New tools led to better ways of doing, and these to improvements in the conditions of life, better ways of nurturing and sustaining it. Thus populations grew; bands divided and moved apart, spreading into larger territories, encountering new conditions, developing more diversified tools and techniques and different combinations of sounds to name and remember them by and pass them on. Social organization grew more complex, with groups linked in larger, looser structures for purposes of mating and economic exchange: families diverged and linked in bands, bands separated and linked in tribes, tribes separated and linked in clans, all interwoven by invisible networks of kinship and reciprocal obligations—relationships requiring, as did tools and techniques and the new flora and fauna of expanding habitats, new words to distinguish and name and remember them by, and new sentences to represent their connections. And all this occurred in the context of a younger, less stable natural world, where the ice still grew and retreated, new rivers formed and diverged, earthquakes and the drift of continents thrust new mountains up, altering climate and the configurations and resources of the land. Thus even peoples with a foothold of generations in some favored clime might be set to wandering again, driven not by restlessness but need. And each such movement from the familiar to the unknown would have required new learning, new language, new tools.

It must have happened, too, not once but many times, that tribes originally of common blood and language, common clan, would separate or, with new rivers or mountains rising between, lose contact with their kin and pursue, over the long centuries, a separate language and cultural evolution until, when some new wandering brought them into contact again, they met as strangers, not remembered friends. With each such encounter with difference, the sense of tribal definition, tribal identity, tribal consciousness would grow, because knowledge of who and what you are takes shape only in the context of who and what you aren't. And as tribal consciousness developed, so would the need for an accounting—words and sentences to tell the young who The People are and where they came from and why, so that the distinctive experience of the tribe as a whole might be remembered and passed on, and so survive.

Thus did language, like a quiver in the floor at the foundations of the sea, set in motion a ripple, a growing swell of accumulating knowledge, that built over the centuries into a tidal wave of information and change. How did The People survive that monumental Flood?

The question may sound strange to modern ears. Denizens ourselves of the much-ballyhooed Age of Information, we are familiar enough with the idea, by now a cliché, that a creature, an institution, a society needs information about the world to adjust and grow, even to survive. It is easy enough to slip over into talking as though, *thinking* as though, one can never have too much information, too much of a good thing. But that is a dangerous mistake. Too much data, taken in the raw, so to speak, can swamp a living cell, a creature, a species and destroy it as surely as too little. That is why, wherever we look in nature, we see structures that limit the amount and type of information that living things can receive. The reproductive molecule of life, DNA itself, has a particular structure—the now-famous double helix—and that shape limits what can be added to it. The double helix, so to say, protects and preserves life by preventing the accretion of too much information, of the wrong kind. And that is why there survive, in every living creature and species, biologic structures that function as "filters" of sensory data, thresholds and barriers to sensation and perception, structures that limit and direct what can be seen, felt, heard, and attended to. Without such structures, which function in effect as commands to *ignore* stimuli, data, and information, sensory creatures would be inundated by detail and difference, overwhelmed by choice, and paralyzed by change.

There are, in short, two principles that govern the relation of information to life, not one. The first is that no creature can survive with too little information about its world. And the second is that no creature can survive with too much. To these we might add the observation that it is *structures* that limit the accrual of information and that, in the biological world, increases in the capacity of creatures to receive information are always accompanied by the development of structures that reduce and limit it. In the biologic realm, what is "too little information" and "too much," what is an "adequate structure" and what is not, is determined by the configurations of the habitat in which a creature must function. Nature drives out or eliminates those with neurological structures that filter out too much difference or leave a creature distracted by too great a sensitivity to change.

We humans, of course, are biological creatures, and like others that survive, we are the inheritors through evolution of thousands of biochemical and neurological structures that limit and direct what we can sense and perceive. Without them, we would be swamped by excesses of information, drowned in static, so to say. For static is the unfiltered, the unstructured uproar of a universe everywhere and continually undergoing differentiation and recombination; it is the sound of infinitesimal and, because it lies outside the capacity of our bodies to structure it, of *disorganized* change.

But we humans are also creatures of the word. And the word is a powerful generator of new information and change. Names permit us not merely to record and recall the "wholes" of our creaturely experience, but to subdivide it, to continually differentiate one thing from another. And because words differentiate, they also permit us continually to create by combining things in new ways, in the world of thought and in the material world. The laws of nature, of course, limit what things can be separated and combined, and how, in the material world. Thus while words may allow us to construct, in imagination, a creature with the body of a lion, the wings of an eagle, and the head of a man, we cannot assemble such a creature in the material world and bring it to life... at least, not yet. But there are, in principle, no such limits in the world of words. We can, in theory, infinitely subdivide the world in language, or any set of symbols (like numbers), and reassemble the different "things" or "units" we name in any variety of novel ways. If we did so, of course, we should soon drown in the sheer volume of names we would need for all the distinctions we made, and for their new combinations. They would swamp the capacity of our memories to recall them, and therefore serve no useful function. And language is, in its origins at least, functional. That is why wherever there are humans, it has everywhere survived.

The fact is that, though words make it possible, we do *not* give a name to everything in our experience, or make all the distinctions we might. As the vocabularies of different cultures suggest, we subdivide the world of experience linguistically only so far as it is necessary or useful to do so. That is, we differentiate by naming, not *all* things, but only those things that make a difference for our behavior and are important, therefore, to call to mind. The language of the Navajo peoples of the American Southwest, for example, does not have separate words for the three distinctions we remark in our words "ice," "cold," and "snow"—not because they cannot perceive the difference, but because it is so rare that it is not worth remembering. American English does not have vocabulary items for the twenty or so different kinds of cold precipitation that the language of the Inuit tribes of the Arctic Circle names. To us, they are all one or another kind of "snow"—a generalization of so little behavioral use in the far north that the Inuit language has no single word for it. To put it somewhat differently, we remark "snow" in our language because it differs from another form precipitation may take in our clime—namely, rain—and the difference has important consequences for our behavior: how we prepare to go out, how we walk or drive, and so on. In the Arctic, there *is* no other form of precipitation to which "snow," generically, is a contrast, so "snow" would be a useless word—a distinction that *makes* no distinction. It is not "snow" generally that requires a difference in behavior in the Arctic, but the *kind* of frozen precipitate it is: soft and shifting, or hard-packed and stable, weight-bearing or not. Attending to such differences and adjusting behavior accordingly are matters of life and death to peoples of the far north. It is these distinctions, therefore, that are coded in the words of their languages and, through the use of the different words, called to the attention of the young. Thus the young learn, in learning their elders' vocabulary, the differences among things to which it is important, in their culture, to attend.

And the young also learn, by means of their elders' use of names, what differences among things may be ignored. For words both "split" or differentiate things and "lump" or liken them at the same time. In English, for example, the different words "chair" and "desk" call attention to a distinction to which, for many reasons, it is important in our culture to attend. But each of these words may itself be used for countless numbers of quite different objects in our experience. I call the thing I am sitting on now "a chair," and I call the thing I sit on in my living room the same, even though one is hard and white and made of wicker and the other is soft and rounded and made mostly of fabric, some squooshy stuff, and air. I can see the differences and feel them, and a microscope would reveal even greater differences—even between two such objects my senses would call identical. In fact, no two are in every respect the same. But language allows me to overlook that fact—in effect, to forget it and remember, by calling such different things "chairs," that for many important purposes I may treat them the same. If I discover that for other purposes, like maintaining an upright posture versus a relaxed one while sitting, I need to differentiate chairs of different kinds, language allows me to do so by adding other words, like "straight-backed" or "upholstered," in what are called *structures of modification*. These words too, in their turn, both make some distinctions and ignore others, like the variety of differences among chairs with straight backs.

The point is that language, like biology, both generates diversity and reduces it to manageable proportions at the same time. Words increase information because they allow us to split up and differentiate, in mind and thought, what our senses cannot, thus making more of less. But they also reduce information because they allow us to lump, by likening and thus ignoring differences among things which even our senses may tell us are in no wise the same. In this sense, as many have observed, all language is *metaphoric*, meaning that every word encodes a *comparison*. (The source of the Latin word for "word," *parole*, in fact, is the word *parabole*: "to compare.") To call a thing "a desk" is to indicate that it is different from some other things (called "chairs" or "cups") by comparison. But it is also to indicate that this thing is, by comparison, enough like many others to bear the same name. In fact, it is only through the metaphoric process, particularly the process of likening, that language can remain efficient as a means for coding and retrieving experience from memory. Without it, we would need a different name for every instance of something in experience—a burden on memory that would soon overwhelm it. Through the process of comparing new experience to old and remarking likeness by naming things the same, we keep the growth of vocabulary within manageable bounds. Thus metaphor is an essential process in regulating word-generated information and change.

But language is not merely experience coded in words, whether they be few or many. It is a system of words organized in particular patterns to indicate the relations among things and people named. It is, after all, the complex events and processes of our experience we heed to represent to ourselves and others, not merely their "components" in an any-which-way jumble. Grammar, of course, is the system of rules for arranging words and sounds in a language to indicate how various named things "go together," or did, or might, or will. Like names themselves, grammatical rules permit us to report or "invent" an infinite variety of experiences. The rules of English permit me to say, for example, "The pen and the cup lay on the rock while the October moon rose and the fish swam placidly in the stream." So far as I know, no one has ever said or written that before. The same is true of most of the specific sentences in this book, and of most of the utterances you produce each day. They are novel, unique, new.

But for all its capacity to produce infinite variety, to generate virtually infinite amounts of information, grammar also limits and constrains both speech and thought. The grammars of some languages, for example, require speakers to indicate, in the form of their words or the order in which they are spoken, if the speaker is masculine or feminine. Others, whether the relationship between speakers is formal or informal. Others require choices among different sounds and forms to indicate what the source of the "content" of the sentence is: the speaker's personal experience, a specific other's experience, or some anonymous others' experience, passed on over generations by the tribe. The language in which I am writing requires me to distinguish between "subjects" and "their actions," between "actions" and "objects acted upon," and to locate every event somewhere in time: past, present, or future. I must also indicate, if I speak or write in English, whether the "subject" of my sentence is "one" or "many," although my verbs do not have to specify, as they do in some languages, precisely *how* many "are" involved in some action.

The point is that no grammar allows us to codify *all* the conceivable relations among persons and things and conditions in constructing our sentences— only some of them. The grammar of each language provides its speakers, in short, with a limited set of patterns and rules for representing how things "go together."

Children learn these, along with their culture's ways of naming things, as they learn to speak. And just as names direct their attention to what is important to distinguish and what may be treated the same, so the rules for putting names together direct their attention to those relations their culture requires them to express. Through language those relationships are used not only in communicating their experience to others, but in articulating it to themselves in the silent "conversation" we call thought. Thus grammar functions, at the level of the utterance or sentence, the level of the single "event," as a set of shapes or patterns that limit the kinds of relations we attend to and remember.

If the number and variety of experiences our ancestors needed to communicate to one another and recall had remained stable, perhaps a few dozens of words and a handful of patterns for combining them into utterances would have provided structures adequate to regulate the ecology of information and life that language itself had so dramatically altered. But if that had been the case, we would be different creatures today, and I would not be writing, nor you reading, this tale. We are engaged in this strange enterprise together because the fragility of our ancestors, and the unsettled environments of their time, and the advent of the word worked together to set in motion an accelerating spiral of change. And part of that spiral was the continuous growth of knowledge—of distinctions codified in words and reassembled in patterns of relations according to the rules of grammar, as sentences, utterances, "facts": facts about plants and herbs and their uses, about tools and their making, about animals and their hunting, about kin and their relations, about thousands of encounters among people and between people and their continually enlarging and changing material world.

Now, the human memory is a wonderful thing, but we are distinctly limited in our capacity to recall miscellaneous—that is, unconnected—facts. To remember more than a handful of things, we must associate them, connect them, weave them into patterned wholes, so that the pattern of the whole can trigger memory of the parts. If I have made a shopping list, in the morning, of items I need to make lasagna and cheesecake that night, but find that I have lost the list by the time I stop at the market after work, I can jog my memory of the things I need simply by recalling what I plan to make. A lasagna is a patterned whole, and keeping that pattern in mind limits the burden on memory by limiting the possible items I need to recall. But suppose I had read off the list to my husband and asked him to do the shopping, without telling him what I planned to make. Faced by a supermarket full of choices, and no limiting pattern to jog his memory of what I wanted, he is likely to come home with little of what I asked for, and probably bags full of more. Unless, of course, he had written my list down. But our forebears would have no writing for thousands of years. How would they have remembered all that they needed to know and pass on to the next generation, without drowning in the tidal wave of their own accumulating knowledge? They could only have done so as we still do today in managing our memory of all we do not write down: by connecting it, weaving it, linking experience to experience to experience, utterance to utterance, thought to thought, consciously or unconsciously, in complex patterns. And the name we may give to those patterns when we articulate them, when we *tell* our experience to others and ourselves and by telling fix and order it in memory, is tales, or narratives.

A narrative is a structure for connecting events and articulating their relationships in thought and speech. It is a patterned way of "bringing back" experience by *relating* it (from the Latin "to bring back"), in the delightfully double sense of *telling* and *connecting* it. To put it somewhat differently, a narrative is a structure of knowledge, a way of integrating experience abstracted, differentiated, codified, represented, and called to mind through words. Since we are engaged here in exploring our roots, it is worth remarking that "narrative" itself has its roots in the Latin *gnarus*—"knowledge"—which suggests how inextricably, to the ancient mind at least, knowledge and narrative are intertwined. And it is the same root, *gnarus*, linking narrative and knowledge, that also underlies our word "ignore," suggesting by implication that what is not narrated is not known or not acknowledged; not attended to; ignored. That is very much central, of course, to the point I have been making here. Just as names, by their uses, and sentences, by their rules, direct and limit our attention to certain things and kinds of relations, so narratives by their patterns structure our memory of events. By structuring memory, narratives help us not only to remember what is important to our survival but, equally essential, to *forget* what is not. A narrative functions, in short, as a kind of information sieve, retaining only those chunks of information that fit its pattern and allowing the rest to fall away unheeded. By ignoring, in effect destroying some information, a narrative makes past experience—memory—manageable.

That is not all. By linking events in patterns, narratives also direct our attention in the present and guide our future behavior. They structure not only how we look at things, but what we will look for. Just as a familiar arrangement of silverware on a table or jewelry in a drawer may tell us at a glance what is missing and what we need to find, so do the more complex patterns of our narratives suggest "missing links" that govern our quests for new information. And they tell us, too, where new information, new experience "goes"—how and where it "fits in" with what we already know. Narratives are the means, in short, through which our thinking, speaking species constructs predictable continuities in life and, by so doing, not only manages information and change, but gives experience coherence, direction, and meaning.

At the risk of laboring what may already be obvious, I am not using the word "narratives" here to refer merely to those kinds of stories we read in novels or tell one another about the doings of our days or the events of our lives. I mean by the word *all* of the various ways in which we recount and account for our experience—of ourselves and our personal lives, but also of the world we can see and the world we cannot. We are ceaseless tale-spinners—*Homo narratans*—and our narratives are of many and diverse kinds: personal tales, tribal tales, and world tales; mythologies and histories and scientific accounts. Our different kinds of narratives attempt to account for different things, and they follow different patterns and rules. But they are all human constructions, and arise out of the human need for order, coherence, and predictability in a ceaselessly changing world. Beyond that, our tales arise through similar processes of thinking and speaking, and they are related to our social experiences and tools of knowing and doing in similar kinds of ways. What those processes and ways are, and how our explanations of ourselves, and of the material and social world, and of the world we cannot see, have changed over time are questions that are explored in the following pages of *this* tale.

CHAPTER SIX

Metaphor, Explanation, and Tales of the Self

And the Lord God called unto Adam and said unto him, "Where art thou?"

And he said, "I heard thy voice in the garden, and I was afraid, because I was naked; and I hid myself."

And He said, "Who told thee that thou wast naked? Hast thou eaten of the tree, whereof I commanded thee that thou should'st not eat?"

And the man said, "The woman whom thou gavest to be with me, she gave me of the tree, and I did eat."

And the Lord God said unto the woman, "What is this that thou hast done?" And the woman said, "The serpent beguiled me, and I did eat."

Genesis 3:9–12

We shall never know precisely when and where some primal ancestor of ours first recounted some urgent experience to another who did not share it and constructed, with sounds and reenactment, the first human tale. The event must have been nearly as ancient as speech itself—indeed, so closely woven with it that we might say, along with Genesis, that if language began in the morning, and consciousness at noon, narrative would have arisen in the cool of that same day. In fact, there is much insight to be gleaned from Genesis and its imaginative reconstruction of the world's first narrative, its account of Adam's tale. It is a remarkably short one—only three sentences long. But in those sentences Adam and Eve begin what humans have been doing ever since: recounting their experience as a sequence of events over time and accounting for it—explaining the world to themselves, and themselves to themselves, and themselves to their God—by connecting different realms of experience in relations of "cause."

In effect, Adam and Eve give us, in three utterances, the world's first history. The chronology of their tale is "backwards," to be sure—a telling from the present moment to "before that" and "before that"—but it is a chronology nonetheless, as most of our narratives are. Temporal ordering—the representation of experience as a sequence of events over time—is in fact one of the major patterns in which we relate things, simply because relating, in the sense of *telling in words*, requires us to say one thing at a time. Our eyes, our ears, all our senses working together, allow us to experience the world with simultaneity, as everything-happening-at-once. But we cannot tell it that way. The human vocal apparatus does not permit us to speak in chords. We must string speech out, one sound, one word, one utterance at a time. Thus there is always a temporal dimension to our recounting, whether we are telling another about some experience he did not share, or entertaining our children with family tales, or recounting to ourselves in silence the events of our own lives.

There is also a temporal dimension to our *accounting*—our explanations—for the language-engendered notion that every event has antecedents to which it is connected is also our earliest and most profoundly held notion of cause. To put it more simply, telling events in sequence is not merely a way of describing how they go together, or did, but also of explaining *why*. That is, if two things go together in sequence, or we tell it that way, we usually think that the first was the cause of the second—as you would think if I said to you, "The boy threw the rock and the window broke." Thousands of years after the beginnings of speech and thought and narrative, when the development of writing allowed us to "freeze" thought and study it, logicians would point out that *post hoc ergo propter hoc* is an error in reasoning, a fallacy. They meant, and mean, that what comes before something is not necessarily its cause, even though the two things may invariably go together in sequence. This is easy enough to grasp by parodying, "post hoc" reasoning: every morning the cock crows, and shortly after, the sun begins to rise. Does, the crow of the cock cause the sun to rise? Of course not. And yet... and yet when two things go together in the same space and before our very eyes, when they go together in sequence in our tales, we cannot seem to help "seeing" causal connections between them. That is because *conjunction* is the very basis of sensory learning, of all "conditioned response," and *priority plus conjunction* is the way we codify how things go together in our sensory experience and relate it in our tales. If I say, "My sister bumped my arm and I dropped my cup of coffee," you will read cause into the conjunction "and," and feel that I have not merely described what happened, but explained *why* I dropped my cup. And all the fervent lectures of semanticists and scientists and teachers of logic and critical thinking make scarcely a dent in these recalcitrant habits of mind. As soon as we leave the classroom, we will slip back into talking as though, *thinking* as though priority plus conjunction equals cause. Millions of years of evolution and thousands more of narrative condition us to think so; in the struggle for survival it is, so to say, our best bet. And it reflects, besides, our own pre-linguistic experience, and therefore our deepest intuition, that the world is a complex whole. Something in us knows, though we cannot say it, that "My sister bumped my arm and I dropped my cup" is *one* complex event, not two different ones put together; that sister and bump and arm and cup and drop are all aspects of the same thing—a single happening—in which *everything* is required and therefore a "cause" of the whole. It is naming the parts and stringing them out in speech that creates the illusion of different "things," different "actors" and "actions," different "events." It is the complex utterance—its breaking the whole into two "independent clauses"—that is the illusion, the "error," not the impression of cause arising from the conjunction "and."

The point is that all the "ands" in Adam and Eve's tale make it the prototype, not only of the kind of narrative we call a chronology or a history, but also of the kind of account we call an explanation. In our own time, we might say that a chronology or history tells us *what* happened and *how*, while an explanation tells us *why*. But in the more ancient times from which this tale comes down to us and even before, in the very earliest of times, we may guess, that distinction was not yet made. "What?" and "How?" were indistinguishable from "Why?" In answer to God's question, first Adam then Eve names the "parts" in that piece of the whole event which each experienced: for Adam, it involved himself and Eve and eating and the fruit; for Eve, herself and the fruit and the snake. And there their account stops. (The wily serpent, earlier so limber-tongued, keeps silent.) For them, as for the early tellers and hearers of this tale, and of many others that survived through generations of oral retelling until they were written down, the relating of observable doings and their antecedents is enough. It answers adequately to what we of later times think are two different questions: What happened? and Why?

But perhaps you noticed, among all the "ands" that give Adam and Eve's tale its basic structure, a lone, anomalous "because." "I heard thy voice in the garden," says Adam, "and I was afraid, because I was naked; and I hid myself." That "because" is worth remarking, for it provides us, in this primordial tale, with the prototype of still another kind of human narrative: what might be called the world's first *theory*.

A theory differs from a descriptive explanation of events by postulating a "cause" that cannot be seen or heard or otherwise made available to our "external" senses. It makes reference to an invisible agent or agency that is somehow involved in observable events and accounts for how they unfold. The story that there is an unseen force, called "gravity," that operates at a distance on the mass of material bodies and accounts for their actions, for example, is a theory. So is the story that the world is supported on the shoulders of a giant we cannot see. I call Adam's first statements ("I heard thy voice... I was afraid, because I was naked... and I hid") the prototype of a theory because Adam invokes an invisible intervening agency accessible only to himself—his feelings—to link observable facts and actions. In particular, Adam constructs here a psychological theory: relations between oneself (*I was naked*) and others (*I heard thy voice*) give rise to internal feelings (*I was afraid*) and these feelings are the immediate antecedents (i.e., "causes") of actions. The lone "because" in Adam's tale answers, in short, to a different meaning of "Why?" from the What/How/Why of the rest of the account: a "Why?" that asks about *motive*. The distinction is an important one, because the idea that there is an invisible world, a hidden world somewhere below or behind the world as we see and touch and hear it, and that there is an "internal" world in people that somehow generates their actions, is a monumental turning point in the development of human language and cognition.

In one way or another, all our science, our myth, our religion, all our psychology, our literature, even our art centers around expressing and explaining the relation between the visible and the invisible, the material and the nonmaterial, the objective and the subjective, the "inner" and the "outer" worlds. Indeed, it is not too much to say that all our history and civilization, all that makes us distinctively human, goes back to the second great awakening reflected in Adam's lone "because," which answers to a second, unutterably profound meaning of "Why?" For this is the "Why?" that asks, not about observable events and their sequences, but about invisible forces that lie behind; not about actions, but about motives; not about antecedents, but about ends. It is the "Why?" that imagines or recognizes in human life and the universe not just pattern, but purpose, without which pattern by itself gives us predictability but no direction, order but no significance, sequence but no sense.

"Why?" and "Because" are so central to our own experience of significance that it is easy to think, if we think about it at all, that surely humans come into the world with that question, if not on their lips, at least in their minds. But this seems not to be the case. Children come quite late, in their understanding and use of language, to statements about their motives and feelings, their "inner lives." They are able to give and understand accounts of events in terms of their observable antecedents long before they can either ask or answer the "motive" question, "Why?" One of our notable comics, Bill Cosby, has built a very funny routine around what he calls "universal brain damage" in children, the chief symptom of which is the "I dunno" the very young produce in answer to "Why?"—as in this familiar dialogue:

"What did Daddy tell you about the soda?"
"Daddy said not to drink the soda."
"Well, what happened to the soda?"
"I drank it."
"But what did Daddy say?"
"Said not to drink it."
"So why did you drink it? *Why?*"
"I dunno."

Cosby's routine makes us laugh because it highlights what everyone who lives or works with young children knows to be true: that the simple question, "Why did you do that?" seems to leave them speechless. Not because they are brain-damaged, of course, or even recalcitrant or evasive. They say "I dunno" because they *don't know* what the question wants from them or how to answer it. They have not yet learned to introspect—to reflect on their inner feelings and see these as causes of their actions. Even the youngest of children *have* feelings, of course—inner sensations of hunger, thirst, fear, distress, as well as pleasure, relief from pain, satisfaction. And they "know," in the behavioral sense, that changes in these feelings are somehow correlated with things and events in the "outer" world. But in the very young, "inner" and "outer" are not clearly separated. "Feeling good" comes with drinking soda, for example, but is just as much bound up with *it* as with *me*. In fact, as our temporal sense develops, the "goodness" attaches more firmly to *the soda*, since the drinking of it comes before the sensation it produces "registers." Thus it seems that the "goodness" must somehow be "in" the soda, and the act of drinking gets it into me. Certainly, this is the way we most commonly narratize the event, and not only when we are very small. "That soda," we say, "was good." Or, "I drank the soda, and it was good." Far more rarely do we say, "I drank the soda and it made me feel good." And even when we put it that way, we make it seem that the soda is the "active agent" or cause, and our feelings the result.

The point is that we do not separate our feelings, early in childhood, from the objects and actions to which they are connected. And even when we do (long after speech begins), we understand our feelings as *results* of actions first, and only much later as causes. Children up to the age of five or so are, so to say, the original behaviorists, busy learning how the observable world of things and people and actions go together in terms of antecedents and consequences. They are conscious of their own actions on the world and of the reactions of people and objects to them. But they have not yet learned to see themselves as independent agents who consider options, weigh consequences, make choices and decisions from some internal center of feeling, willing, wishing, wanting. The world to them is a given; it does not require, for the purposes of the young, invisible forces to make it work. "Mad" is a way Daddy looks and sounds when certain things happen—a look and a sound that has unpleasant consequences for me. "Happy" is a different way he looks and sounds, with nicer consequences. And children learn quite well how to convert "mad" to "happy" by altering their behavior. The notion that "mad" and "happy" correspond to some internal state of affairs inside Daddy is quite unnecessary. In the adult controlled world of early childhood, any "Why?" that cannot be answered by pointing to antecedents and consequences comes down to "Because I said so...and what I say goes." So far as the experience of young children is concerned, that is not merely a way to end discussion. It is an entirely accurate fact.

The early narratives of children, then, do not make reference to their hopes, wishes, longings, angers, fears, or to their thinking, because they are not as yet able to reflect on that inner world and the role it plays in mediating their actions. Their "mind's eye," so to speak, has not yet opened; they do not "see themselves," mentally, as tiny figures acting and interacting with others in a miniature landscape located somewhere inside their heads. In a word, young children do not, so far as anyone can tell, introspect. How and when they begin to do so is very difficult to say; the processes through which we come to that "second awakening" are long and complex. Certainly the child's increasing ability to manipulate the world of objects plays an important part, for the discovery that there are things inside of things that produce a sound even when they can't be seen, for example, provides a major model or metaphor, later on, for the conceptualization of "I" as a little person somewhere inside who generates our speech and movement and actions. The increasing conflict between biological and social "goods" is also involved. As children learn that the same actions—drinking the soda, for example—have both pleasant consequences (its taste and feel) and unpleasant consequences (Daddy's response) at the same time, they are required to make choices between actions more frequently and to regulate more and more of their impulses by "internalizing" the responses of others. So long as those others are in fact present most of the time, it "makes sense" to locate what are in fact becoming internal controls "out there," in them. But children spend more of their time outside the immediate supervision of adults as they approach school age, and they must make more and more choices without visible others to guide them or bring about anticipated consequences. Who is it then, or rather, *where* is the adult whose "voice" tells the child what to do?

For a considerable time, children solve this problem by assuming that an adult other is somehow present, watching and giving direction, but hidden from sight. Their own experience, in games like hide-and-seek, for example, provides them with a ready basis for the notion that one can see without being seen, and the parental practice of giving children direction from distant rooms ("Stop running around in there!" "Close that refrigerator door!") reinforces the assumption that adults can both see and command without being visible. Thus the childhood belief in the omniscience and omnipresence of invisible adults not only has a firm basis in experience, but maintains the sense, also based on early experience, that one's choices, actions, and decisions are governed and directed by "external" though invisible others, not an internal, independent "self."

Two factors, though, eventually lead to the downfall of this behavioral "theory." One is the fact that the "voices" that direct children's behavior when alone do not, of course, come from outside; they come from memory, and do not have the same sound as voices falling on the outer ear. They are heard within, in the mind's ear, the heart's ear. How they *get* there is not a pressing problem for children; if people can see without being seen, they can also speak without being audibly heard. The more critical factor in the discovery of the autonomous internal person, the awakening of the introspective "self," arises from something else: the fact that as children encounter and "internalize" a larger variety of important adult others—daycare providers and school teachers, for example—their voices do not always agree. At the same time, children begin to face more situations, and more complex, unfamiliar situations, in which they must make choices of action without adult supervision. A child leaves a jacket behind at school. He has been reprimanded a dozen, a hundred times for coming home without things he left with. But he has also been taught never to re-enter the school after the children have been dismissed for the day. And to come straight home, "Straight home! Do you hear me?" What is he to do? How to choose among conflicting commands and consequences?

Not once, but dozens of times, on a daily basis, the more complex world of the child of five and six and seven presents dilemmas, forced choices, where one internalized command or another must of necessity be disobeyed. Choice becomes problematic, and thus raises to consciousness the activity of choosing. Who and where is the person who stands listening to the conflicting commands falling on the inner ear? Whose little voice enters the internal argument between teacher and parent and says in the end, "O.K. Here's what to do"? It is the voice of the mediator self, the internal listener, the chooser, the little "I" inside myself who tells me, when all else fails, how to act. Thus we become aware, through conflict and the inevitability of choices that require us to disobey, and the ready metaphor of things inside of things, of the self *as a self*—as an internal instigator of our actions, a little person inside who watches and listens and worries and fears and weighs alternatives and consequences and decides. We become conscious, so to say, of our own consciousness, of the psychological "I" that goes with the grammatical "I." And we project it onto others, seeing them as likewise moved by internal selves like our own. Thus introspection—accounts of the doings of my internal "I," and hers, and his, and yours—enter our narratives as an essential part of their structures, as the means of linking actions and antecedents, as new meanings of "Why?"

I have asked you to endure all this admittedly longwinded reconstruction of how children come to account for "I" not only because it is central to understanding how our personal narratives develop, but also because it sheds light on much that is obscure about how tales have evolved in the history of our species, and are evolving still. For it is clear that the way we humans tell our stories changes, not only from person to person and culture to culture, but over the course of time. Some of those changes are striking—so striking that ancient narratives sound odd to the modern ear. More accurately, they read odd to the modern eye, for few of us are accustomed, past childhood, to the oral recitation of tales. And writing makes the strangeness of ancient stories even more visible. All those "ands" in Adam's tale, for example, or in the tale of the creation, or in Isaac and Abraham's tale. Surely they are superfluous, as your English teacher or an editor would quickly point out.

But equally as odd as what is there in too great measure is what is there too little. Something is missing in these accounts that makes them even stranger to the modern eye and ear. And that something, of course, is introspection. What was in God's mind when He made the world? What did He think He was doing? Yes, he "saw" that it was good—but how did He *feel*? And what of Abraham, when he heard God's awful command, to sacrifice his only son? Did he not grieve, deliberate, debate with himself the right and wrong of such a monstrous act? And young Isaac, as he walked up the hill with his father and that knife at his back. What went through his mind, and what did he feel as he lay bound upon the sacrificial stone and the blade flashed upwards in the sun? On such matters, it would seem, the writers of Genesis had nothing to say.

What kind of people could tell so baldly, so emptily, such a densely emotional human tale? People, perhaps, who *felt* no less strongly than we, but had not yet come to see the internal world of feeling, of thinking, deliberating, choosing, of personal motive, as a world separate from and causative of acts, and who therefore did not include that world in their recounting and accounting of events.

Several scholars have argued that the kind of introspective self-awareness so familiar to people of our own time and culture, the consciousness of our own consciousness that so thoroughly permeates our own accounts—"I thought," "I wondered," "I considered," "I realized," "I decided"—is a relatively late development in the history of the human mind. And at least one has proposed a neurophysiological explanation for it. In his daring and provocative book, *The Origin of Consciousness in the Breakdown of the Bicameral Mind*, Julian Jaynes links the way in which our oldest tales narrate events—particularly, the absence of introspective reports—to their repeated reference to "voices" of gods who direct human affairs from "outside." Jaynes proposes that people before roughly 1100 BCE literally *heard* such voices as *auditory*, not "mental" events. He does not mean that the "voices of the gods" reported in early narratives in fact came from outside people's bodies. They were the voices of memory, of past experience with others, internalized. But Jaynes argues that early people heard these as "externally" as we hear the voice of a friend across the room—because, he suggests, the neural pathways that allow us to distinguish "internal" voices, remembered voices, silent voices falling on the inner ear, from "outside" voices were incomplete, or different, or not yet laid down. When these neural pathways *were* laid down, through the process of selective evolution in response to a more complex and demanding physical and social world, the "voices" as *auditory* experiences disappeared, and consciousness of them as our own internal thoughts and feelings emerged. The poignant pleading of later people—those who speak, for example, in the Biblical Psalms—for the return of a God who has fallen silent, whose voice can no longer be heard, reflects, according to Jaynes, the confusion and despair of the transitional era in which the auditory hallucinations were breaking down.

It is a bold hypothesis, but difficult to confirm in the absence of solid information about the structure and workings of the human brain in the times Jaynes writes of. The narratives and behavior of our own children, however, and of peoples of different cultures in our own time, suggest that neither "auditory hallucinations" nor neurophysiological evolution is necessary to explain how our conceptualizations—of self, of others, of gods, and of how the world works—change and have changed. There is no evidence in children's behavior, for example, that they experience the promptings of internalized others, even in early childhood, as sounds falling on their *outer* ears. They do not turn their heads to listen, or start, or search for the source of the sound, as they will do for the audible sounds made by hidden things. Nor do the peoples of living cultures whose ways of explaining themselves and the world preserve many of the features of ancient tales, including the lack of the introspective "I" and the attribution of their own decision-making to invisible others, including various gods, show signs of "hearing voices" in the auditory sense. The "speaker" may be felt as "other," "not-me," "outside," but the voice seems clearly to be experienced as inside. The experience of peoples who move rapidly from isolated, tribal conditions to "integration" in citified, technologized cultures, moreover, argues against an explanation of narrative change rooted in neurophysiological evolution. People who undergo such rapid change may shift over the space of a single generation to ways of accounting for themselves and the world that fully incorporate all the indications of a self-conscious, introspective "I." And a single generation is too short a time for evolutionary processes to be at work.

The dynamics of narrative change, in short, seem to lie more in social and metaphoric than in neurophysiological processes. To put it as plainly as possible, our explanations of what and how and why things go together, of what and how and why things work, are shaped by the world as we experience it at a given time and by the particular problems we encounter in trying to manage that world successfully— that is, to avert disastrous consequences and accomplish our ends. Our ends, of course, change as the material and social world we experience grows larger and more complex, so we are always encountering new problems, and consequences for which our prior experience has not fully prepared us. But we need some basis for guiding our behavior in new situations, some way of predicting the likely outcomes of our actions and using those predicted consequences to govern what we do. And that basis is provided through the processes summed up in the word *metaphor*.

A metaphor is a way of dealing with the unfamiliar, the novel, the unknown by likening it to something known—that is, to something we have already learned to predict and control with relative success. It is a means through which we bring our past experience to bear, consciously or unconsciously, on new situations, anticipate how they are likely to work, and adjust our behavior on the basis of those anticipations. When I meet a new student, for example, I assume she is like other students I have known, and likely to respond in similar ways, therefore, to things I have said and done with other students in the past. The more like the new student is to particular others I have known—in age, speech, dress, movements, appearance, etc.—the more specific my predictions of what will "work" with her are likely to be, and I will use those predictions quite without thinking to tailor my behavior accordingly, at least initially. I may discover, of course, that my metaphor—my unconscious assumption of her likeness to others I have known, based on a few behavioral cues—is wrong: that my predictions and therefore my behavior aren't "working." If that is the case, and the problems that result are too pressing to ignore, I will find some other metaphor for this student—different others in my past experience she is like—and base my predictions and behavior on that. All the while, of course, my experience with this particular student is increasing, and providing its own basis for predicting how she is likely to respond to different actions of mine. If we work together long enough, and successfully enough, she will herself provide me, eventually, with a new model or metaphor for what some future student may be like.

Our behavior in new situations is also governed by metaphors—by conscious or unconscious assumptions about something in our past experience they are *like*. We would have no idea what clothes to dress ourselves in for the first day in some new job, or how to walk, sit, stand, carry ourselves, what to say and what not, unless we assume that this situation is like other jobs we have had—or at least like enough that the dress, speech, and behavior that served us successfully in the past will work in this case too. If someone has no direct experience of the world of work, then learning from secondary sources, like television, will provide the metaphors. In our own culture, of course, it is school that provides most young people with the initial metaphor they need to guide their behavior on their first job; that is the reason why business leaders in this country take an active and critical interest in the conduct of public education.

Our attempts to make the material world, the world of nature, predictable and so bring our relations with it under control are also governed by metaphors. The history of natural science, we might almost say, is the history of different answers to the question, What are the invisible things inside of things *like*? Particle physics is the working out of the metaphor that inside things are things *like* little balls in continuous motion, colliding and bouncing off each other in different directions and at different speeds, just as visible balls do in a game of marbles or billiards, for example. Since we know quite a lot about the behavior of visible balls in motion, the metaphor provides a basis for predicting how things will work out at the "atomic" level. So long as those predictions work, the metaphor and the narrative we construct around it will endure. But sooner or later, we will try to do something on the basis of our metaphoric predictions and they *won't* work. If this happens often enough so that we can no longer accomplish our ends, we shall need to find some new metaphor for what the invisible world is like. Waves, perhaps. But sooner or later, that metaphor too will fail to work for some situations and purposes—because "atoms" or "electrons" are *not* in fact little balls or waves; they are only like them in some respects. And not like them in others.

For no two things are precisely the same in every respect—that is, identical: not visible balls and electrons, nor beams of light and waves in the sea, nor, for that matter, any two students, any two jobs, even any two electrons. Each is unique in some way, different from every other. Happily for us, most of their differences don't make a difference for most of our purposes. We can get along in the social world and even the material world quite well, generally speaking, with only a "lumpish" level of predictability and control. I like my drinks in the summer, for example, to be cold, and I know from past experience that I can achieve that end by adding a couple of ice cubes. I do not stand at the refrigerator door and ponder which two from the tray I want. For my purposes, they are all identical, and so long as my expectations are met—they all chill my drink—I will continue to treat all ice cubes, even think of them, as the same. At least until I run into some problem with ice cubes—like the fact that I have to get up too often for more, since they melt too fast. That problem may add another purpose to my ice-cube agenda, so to speak: not just to cool my drink, but with slower-melting cubes. And that new purpose may direct my attention to differences among ice cubes I never attended to before, like differences in shape and their consequences for rate of melting. Thus I may discover that my original metaphor—ice cube 5 is like ice cubes 1, 2, 3, and 4 in all respects—is not adequate, and come to revise it.

The continuous enlargement and complication of our experience of the world, and of others, gives rise to new needs, new purposes, new problems. These require different predictions and therefore different assumptions about what things are alike and how *much* alike—that is, different metaphors. These metaphors are themselves suggested, of course, by our prior experience—experience not just in the material world, but in the social domain, since from earliest infancy we must learn to negotiate both realms to survive. In fact, in the socially dependent world of the human infant, and of the human species, object learning and social learning are not separated but closely interwoven. We cannot even suckle without another person; from the beginning, our social and physical experience is integrated. And throughout childhood, even after we distinguish people from things, the world of objects and the world of others remain experientially tied. Not only do we interact with others around and through material "things," like food and bottles and toys, but our encounters with things are mediated by others as well. Thus social and physical experience are interdependent in the child's world, and both are drawn on in predicting what new experiences are like. When prior experience with material objects is inadequate to suggest a metaphor for some new thing, social experience may provide the basis for predicting what it is like. And the converse is also true: when social experience is inadequate to suggest what a new situation or psychosocial event is like, we may draw on our experience of the physical world to provide the metaphor. Nor is this process confined to the very young. Adults and children alike use metaphors drawn from social experience to account for the behavior of non-human things—as when we attribute "stubbornness" or "disobedience" or "tiredness" to our machines, and "anthropomorphize" our cars., ships, and planes with the pronoun "she." We also use metaphors from our experience of inanimate objects to account for human psychological and social processes—as when we talk about our feelings in terms of "pressures" and "stress," worry about nervous "breakdowns" and the need to "let off steam," or think of our minds as complex data-processing machines, or of social history as a process of "Darwinian" evolution determined by the principle, "survival of the fittest."

I mean to suggest, by all of this, that the conception of self as an internal person (or persons) who directs our actions arose in the history of our species, and came to be reflected in our narratives, through much the same social and metaphoric processes as it develops in children. Reason and the evidence of ancient narratives suggests, moreover, that this notion of self develops in two stages. Early in our personal lives, and in human history, we seem to account for the inner "voice" that tells one what to do by attributing that voice to an "other" who has somehow "gotten into" one. That idea, based on the metaphor of sound-making things inside of things in the material world, is neither so farfetched nor so alien to us moderns as it may at first sound. We preserve it in our own ways of speaking, as when we ask, "What's gotten into you?" or "What put that idea into your head?" Our language also provides some clues about the extension of that metaphor to the process by which the "other" *gets* into one—namely, as most things do in our earliest experience: by our ingesting them. It is scarcely possible to speak about ideas and how we get them without using metaphors of food and eating. A new idea is "food for thought," "something to chew on," something to "get your teeth into"; but it shouldn't be "swallowed whole." We "devour" the contents of books and magazines, but take our time "digesting" them, perhaps because we fear being "fed a line." In these and countless other expressions, language preserves what is perhaps our earliest sense of the source of our own thinking: someone or something outside ourselves who has gotten in, not through our ears but through our mouths, by eating. It may well be, in fact, that the ritual cannibalism apparently practiced by many of our cavedwelling ancestors and later tribal peoples reflects the rounding out of this metaphor: if one's behavior is guided by others who speak within oneself, and they get in as most things do, by our swallowing them, then one may add to one's own store of wisdom by literally incorporating—taking into one's body—those others whose living voices and actions have been most powerful or courageous or wise. You are, so to say, not only what but *who* you eat. And cannibalism, not imitation, is the sincerest form of flattery.

Traces of this early conception of self—as an other who inhabits us, lives and speaks from somewhere inside—and the associated idea that "it" gets into us by ingestion, are found everywhere in the history of thought, and throughout our narratives even today. It underlies not only religious practice, as in the symbolic eating of one's God in the Christian mass, but also themes of "possession" wherever they appear: in the "psychology" of the Middle Ages, in our fairy tales, even in such popular films as *Invasion of the Body Snatchers, The Exorcist, Aliens,* and others that play upon our fascination with, and terrified awe of, the transforming power of things that control us by getting in. The pervasiveness and persistence of this theme suggests that it has old and powerful roots, not only in the development of our species, but in the social and metaphoric experiences of our own early childhood.

Such experiences, and the narratives to which they give rise, never quite go away. They are not expunged by later learning or entirely replaced by newer narratives, but are subordinated, transformed, reinterpreted in the light of new problems we encounter as our social and material experience expands. New experience, we might say, provides a new context for older narratives, and by recontextualizing them, modifies and gives them different meaning. Thus we are always re-reading our older stories, our past, from the point of view of our present state of knowledge and culture. Contemporary Protestants, for example, "re-read" the Eucharistic feast as a symbolic act of *remembering*, not magically restoring the moment of the original Last Supper, and the bread and wine as *symbols* of the spirit of God, not his literal flesh and blood. But underneath lies a far more ancient story, based on very different experience in a world far removed from us in space and time: the world as our ancestors knew it at the dawn of time, and as we once did at the dawn of our personal time, in earliest childhood. And it is those more ancient stories, living transformed within the new, that connect us to our past and invest our present acts and tales with compelling significance and power.

The changing patterns of narratives passed down from earliest times suggest that just such a process of overlay occurred in the conceptualization of the self in history. Among some peoples, at least, the early notion of the self as externally motivated, "inhabited," "other"-directed seems gradually to have been subsumed by a different notion: the idea of the self as an independent, autonomous thinker and decisionmaker who reflects on the various internalized "voices" of past experience, weighs alternative promptings and predictions, chooses among them, and moves us to act. There is no question that such a conception did arise in history, for it is our own, and it has been given expression in our narratives for at least 2500 years. There is no question that it also develops in our children—or at least in most—and begins to be given expression in their narratives by about the age of five years, though there is little indication of it before.

The dynamics of the process through which the conception of self was transformed in history are much the same, I would argue, as the dynamics of the process through which it is transformed in childhood. That is, the metaphor of the self as an outside other who speaks in one and directs one's behavior breaks down because it proves inadequate when novel situations are repeatedly faced and the internalized "other" no longer "speaks" in a coherent "voice." Instead, the authoritative voices of past and present social experience give conflicting directions, make competing demands, project alternative and conflicting consequences. Such situations require, over and again, the invocation of another "self"—that "mediator" self or "meta"-self—to choose. And because such situations are problematic, filled with tension and stress, we become more aware of our own choosing, and thus of the lonely, autonomous, independent "I" who must decide.

In our personal lives, these situations arise when we move physically and socially outside the relatively controlled and coherent realm of the home and family, and into the larger, more diverse social world, where different others and institutions impose competing rules and demands. In the history of our species, one may find such circumstances writ large in the great movements of tribal peoples in the lands we now call "the Middle East," beginning some 9000 years ago, or in the emergence of the first "cities," following the development of agriculture, in roughly the same fertile area at about the same time. Both sets of events thrust into more or less sustained contact peoples of different languages, different ways of doing things, different learnings and expectations, different rules for behaving and interpreting the behavior of others. Both, but especially the demands of civilized life, confronted people with novel situations, filled with stress and competing obligations, conflicting commands. Both required individuals, often cut off from the coherent predictability and direction of kin and tribe, to choose among competing "voices"—not once, but a score, a hundred, a thousand times—and in choosing to become aware of the chooser: the lonely, autonomous, independent "I." Thus, as in the development of language itself, encounters with new problems in an expanded social and material world fostered, and foster still, change in how we experience our own experience, how we recount "the self" to the self.

But what difference does it make, in the end, how we tell that particular tale? If Jaynes is right, and other historians of consciousness, and I, then people got along quite well for thousands of years, and many get along quite well still, without continuous reference to the troublesome, introspective, independent, wishing, wanting, *will*-ing "I." True enough. People get on as well (or as badly) with or without it. But they get on very differently, and with important differences for the world. For the way we narratize ourselves to ourselves is related to the way we narratize the world to ourselves, and that in turn plays a critical role in how we see it, and identify our problems in it, and act upon it. As we shall see.

CHAPTER SEVEN

Connections: Tribal Tales

One of the world's most ancient and pervasive ideas, and the very wellspring of all our tales, is our sense that above and behind and all around the world as we experience it there lies something more: a "reality" more real and more complete than our senses can give us, a truth more true than any of our sentences about it can say. All our philosophies, all our sciences, all our religions—indeed, all our attempts to account for our experience; all our tales—are attempts to explain that other, invisible world and how it is reflected or made visible in the here and now of our daily lives.

Whence arises the universal intuition of such an invisible world, and the need to incorporate it in our narratives? The intuition, I believe, arises from the interactions of our senses and the "discovery," which dogs and kittens and other sensory creatures make no less than we, that there is more to things than meets the eye—or the nose, hand, ear. Thus even the rudest puppy "knows" that where a sound is, or a scent, there is something more that goes with it, though it may not yet be visible, and a dog, having followed a scent to where it stops on the surface of the earth, will dig. Creatures closer to us on the evolutionary "tree" have an even livelier sense of the world hidden beneath the appearances of things, perhaps because the vagaries of their diets and the use of their hands to manipulate things fostered a wider range of discoveries about what lies under and inside. In our own children, the curiosity to discover—to remove the outer wraps of things with teeth or hands and bring to eye or mouth what lies inside—is so insatiable (and so hazardous to health in a world filled with electrical and chemical products) that adults around the newly-mobile crawler or toddler maintain constant vigilance, and whole industries have developed to prevent prying little fingers and teeth from opening things to find what lies hidden inside.

There is another source of our intuition that behind the world as we know it lies another, greater world, and that is our almost daily experience of frustration, puzzlement, surprise. All of these reflect, in one way or another, the shock of the unexpected, which is to say, the incompleteness of our knowledge, the failure of our predictions. Every surprise, every frustration, is a little lesson, so to say, that things don't work quite the way we think they do; that there is more to things than we have noticed or thought. Some surprises—most, one would hope—are delightful: they bring new pleasures and thus spur our curiosity and optimism about the world unknown. Others, alas, are rude or downright nasty: they give us unexpected pain or frustrate beyond tolerance some purpose it is vital for us to accomplish. These, too, perhaps more than the pleasant surprises and forgettable frustrations, heighten our sense of the world unseen. More important, they intensify our need to give that world and its interactions with our behavior an accounting: to find or construct the patterns in it and in our experiences with it so that we may better predict and control the results of our actions and more successfully accomplish our ends. Thus the great invisible world, the world not present to our senses, enters into our tales, our narratives—our attempts to order the data of our experience and. relate it to what is unknown so that we may achieve, if not a perfect predictability in life, at least enough predictability to govern our own behavior by anticipating certain results.

Even a puppy, I have said, knows from the interaction of its senses and its experience that there is more to things than its nose or eyes may tell; that where there is a part, there is usually a greater whole. But there is something the puppy does not know that humans, through the agency of language, do know, and that something gives our intuition of a non-sensory world, and our accounts of it, a totally different dimension. For language allows us to preserve and, through speech, articulate and pass on *memory*. Through the device of words, we can keep in mind experiences of a world unfolding, not here and now, within the range of our senses, but elsewhere and elsewhen: in the kitchen, for example, where I stood a moment ago. In the coffee shop across the street, which I can neither see nor hear from where I sit, but I remember. In Amsterdam, which is far away and long ago, but lives on in my mind. Through speech and other symbols, moreover, we humans have access to the experiences and memories of others, and thus glimpses of other realities, of a world we have never known directly, but is somehow connected to our own. And that world stretches out in two dimensions: not only beyond the boundaries of our own spatial and kinesthetic senses—beyond our sight and hearing, smell and taste and touch—but beyond our personal memory or even living, tribal memory of it. It reaches beyond our knowledge of it not only in space, but also in time.

Of course, that is a culturally specific way of putting it—a habit of talking and thinking directed by the structure of the great family of languages, including English, that separate space and time into two different dimensions.

There are other languages, other cultures, where time and space are not two separate things, but one; where every "elsewhere" is also "elsewhen." It is very hard for speakers of English and other Indo-European languages to hold onto this idea—the interdependence of time and space—although we remind ourselves of it every time we say, usually in irritation, "I can't be in two places at the same time." Just so. At the level of our personal experience of them, different "places" are also different "times." In going from kitchen to bedroom, for example, I move not only through space but through time. The bedroom is where I "am," here and now. The kitchen is where I "was"—not only *there* but *then*: earlier, before. We also preserve this sense of the connectedness of space-time in the double meaning of our word "present," which we use to refer both to things "here" in a spatial sense (as in "My brother is present as I speak") and "now" in a temporal sense ("in the present"). Thus in at least some rudimentary ways, even speakers of English preserve a conception of space-time that at first mention seems so odd as to be unthinkable: namely, that things not present to the spatial senses are also not "present" in time; that they are both "otherwhere" and "other*when*."

The significance of this point is that it helps us to understand why our ways of accounting for how things and people behave almost inevitably involve actors and agencies and events not only imperceptible to us (as "forces" like gravity, or human "motives," or our remote tribal ancestors are imperceptible), but also occurring elsewhere in time. In the West, we identify that "elsewhere" with the past, which we imagine as a line running backward from this moment to before that and before *that*, all the way "back" to some point out of personal memory, tribal memory, even human memory, when everything began. Thus if our attempts to explain the invisible forces that keep the stars in their places and bind atoms together, or families, or our individual personalities, we trek back and forth along the line of the past, to "when you were born," or "when great-great-grandmother's family first came from Russia," or "when the universe began." Cultures of radically different languages, and non-linear conceptions of time, locate "elsewhen" otherwise: not so much "back" in historical time, but in a changeless present that lies imperceptible all around us—above and behind the secular time of daily experience. For them, *that* is the otherwhere and otherwhen, the "dreamtime," the realm of hidden causes and the time of origins that was and is and ever shall be.

Different as our cultural conceptions may be, we have this in common: that all our explanations, ultimately, rest on some notion, some construction, of what happened and is happening elsewhere and elsewhen: in a realm not "present" to the senses and in a time before memory. In the beginning. To put it in loftier terms, every physics and every psychology, no less than every mythology, invokes both an ontology—a theory of the true nature of things, of existence, and of reality—and a cosmogony—a theory of how things came to be, of how things were with the world and with ourselves, "in the beginning."

In saying this, I have no wish to minimize the differences between the cosmogonies of 20th-century science and those reflected in the world-tales that have come down to us from earlier times. The origin stories constructed by contemporary particle physicists and astrophysicists to account for the present world of appearances are as radically different from the world-tales of earlier times as modern accounts of the self are different from those of the ancient past. In fact, the two kinds of tales, of world and of self, change together, not only because they are dynamically connected to one another but because both are linked to the changing experiences of human talespinners—*homo narratans*—in the same way. Human accounts of the world, the self, and yes, even of the devil, change over time because the world encountered by people changes. And this means that people of different times have different things to account for in their tales—and different experiences to provide the metaphors that lie at the heart of all accounting.

On the first point, there is little, I should think, that needs to be said. Just as your personal life-narrative is different from mine and everyone else's because it must account for experiences uniquely your own, so the world narratives of different peoples are different because people who live in different environmental situations, and within different social and economic structures, will encounter quite different kinds of problems in dealing with the world and one another and thus must explain quite different things. People of different times, moreover, live in different knowledge environments, different noospheres, as they have been called, because knowledge grows and changes over the long course of the human experience.

As knowledge grows and changes, new questions and new problems arise, demanding new and different ways of accounting for the invisible world that generates our changing experience of it. Our tools and technologies of doing and knowing—our striking flints and hoes and sails, our telescopes and microscopes and television sets, our mathematics and logics and computers—are deeply implicated in such changes. They make more of the world accessible to us and allow us to operate on it symbolically in new and different ways. So they change the state of our knowing, and also the world to be known and explained in our tales.

The different worlds encountered by different peoples not only give them different things to account for, but also provide the key to *how* they will account for them. Our experiences do this because our only way to explain the unknown, the invisible, the hidden world we intuit is by likening it, consciously or unconsciously, to what is familiar. Our world tales, in short, always rest on some metaphor—some implicit assumption about what the unknown is *like*—and these metaphors are drawn from what is most familiar to the people of a given place and time. To put it somewhat differently, we *project* what is best known to us directly—the natural environment we encounter, our social experience, our experience of ourselves, the workings of our symbol systems and technologies—upon the world we cannot know directly, and because we are largely unconscious of this process, we come to believe that that is how the world *is*.

But these matters are even more complex than that. For having come to believe that we have explained, through our metaphors, how the *world* is, we then use those accounts to explain to ourselves what is mysterious about ourselves, our social encounters and arrangements, and the working of our symbol systems and technologies. Thus our personal and social and technical and symbolic lives are not merely *projected*, metaphorically, in our explanations of the invisible world that lies outside our skins. They are also *introjected*, in a disguised form, as ways of accounting for what is invisible and mysterious about ourselves. If we humans lived only in the worlds of our own accounts, explanations, theories, narratives, this "loop" of projection and introjection would be a perfect circle, and our tales would never change. However, we are also creatures of biology, and for all we may sometimes wish it, our experience is not totally the product of our thoughts and beliefs about it. Those are abstractions, codifications of the world and our experience. No matter how comprehensive we think our accounts to be, something is always left out that will arise to frustrate our expectations and require us to revise our tales. So it has been throughout the human experience, and so it will always be.

For now, however, let us keep our eyes on the past. How might the experiences and the processes of metaphoric projection and introjection have shaped the world and self stories of earliest times, and yoked them together?

To say that the tribal and nomadic peoples of the distant past lived "close to nature" is something of an anachronism—a projection of our own way of thinking, with its division of the world into "nature" and "us," "human" and "non-human," backward into a time when no such schism was possible. Reflections on our "human-ness" and "culture," and their difference from everything else in the world, are products of both a highly developed consciousness of self and a world of walled settlements that keep "nature" at bay, and neither had yet arisen when our ancestors first began to recount and explain their experience to themselves.

Thus they lived and thought themselves not "close to" nature, but part of it, not different from the other creatures with whom their lives were interdependent. I do not mean, of course, that the people of the time before agriculture and permanent dwellings could not distinguish one of their own kind from a horse or a bear. Of course they could—just as they could distinguish the horse from the bear and those from the plants of the field. They would have seen that people were different from other animals—but only in the ways that horses and bears, foxes and rabbits and coyotes are different from each other: in appearance and skills, hunting patterns and dwelling places, the noises they make.

Living in circumstances far removed from those that would lead eventually to our own oppressive preoccupation with our internal lives, our own minds and thinking and how they work, and living in a time long before systems of inscribing the spoken word would make human language a visible object for the curious to wonder about and study, the cave dwellers and plains dwellers and tundra dwellers of the late Pleistocene would have no reason to believe they were unique among the other creatures on whom they were dependent. And no reason to feel set apart from them in any distinctive way. Like other creatures, they hunted and were hunted; like them they dug for roots and searched for nuts and berries; like them they sought shelter against rain and the winter cold; like them they mated and gave birth, and made dens to protect and raise their young; like them they lived in groups, and made noises to one another to call each other, greet each other, give warnings, communicate their wants and needs. If their noises were different, and their ways of finding or making shelter, and their hunting patterns and weapons of attack and defense, well so were the those of the fox different from those of the cave lion—but such differences did not set them apart from other creatures in any unique way.

To the tribal and nomadic peoples of the ancient past, the creatures with whom they shared their lives were, like them, animated and motivated in the same way: they spoke among themselves in different tongues; had memories like their own, and wishes and wants; experienced fear and malice, grief and rage. And just as members of the same tribe were different from each other—some quicker of foot, some stealthier, some more timid and easily frightened—so it would seem that the creatures of other kinds were different: the rabbit, timid; the hawk, sharp of eye; the lion, stealthy; the fox, cunning. Thus the earliest narratives of the human experience would have been peopled with such animal creatures and their doings—as are the oldest world tales, preserved through centuries of retelling, of those tribal and nomadic peoples who still live among us today.

Such accounts would serve a double function in the lives of our ancestors: the vital function of preserving critically important information about the natural world by organizing it around vibrant repeated figures, familiar and easily called to mind, and the equally vital function of providing the basis for an *explanation* of the world and how it works. That is: the world works as it does because it is animated just as we ourselves are, not only by creaturely feelings of hunger and thirst and the need to mate, but also by the socially elaborated human feelings of sorrow and delight, affection and jealousy, fear and rage.

The close interdependence of early peoples with the other creatures that shared their environments would also have provided them with ways of accounting for their own behavior, because the process of metaphor—of grasping likeness— cuts in two directions at once. That is, every perception or assertion, conscious or unconscious, that A is like B implies its corollary: that B is like A. Thus our tribal ancestors, in assuming that other species were like themselves, would also assume that they were like them: that they had in themselves something of the wolf or the coyote, the deer or the bear. And indeed they did, in far more than some poetic or fanciful sense. For to be a successful hunter requires that one has so internalized the habits and movements and responses of one's prey that one can anticipate them and have the countermove ready when the prey's own movement has barely begun. This is particularly the case when the hunter is less strong, less fleet of foot, less able to jump and bound than his quarry. He must know the mind and habits of his quarry, so to speak, better than it knows itself, and be able to call up those habits and responses in himself with all the speed of reflex. So it is, too, if one is to survive as the prey of larger and stronger species: one must know in advance the moves of the lion or boar to avoid or dodge it and so escape. In this sense the successful deer hunter is successful because he can call up the deer in himself; the survivor of repeated encounters with bear or boar or lion survives because he can call up in himself the part that is lion or boar or bear. Thus the early conception that people have in themselves a part that is some animal—a spirit shared with that animal— was not merely based on the observation of superficial likeness (this one is easily startled—thus like the hare; this one is fierce and strong in battle—thus like the lion). It was also deeply grounded in the *internal* experiences of early humans—in how they experienced themselves.

Such experiences and conceptions, of a world animated at least in part by human-like characteristics, wants, and feelings, would have been given expression and thus reinforced not only in the narratives of earliest times, but in the met- aphoric nature of language itself. It is important to remember that language is useful as a code only because it compresses and organizes experience into a smaller number of categories, indexed in memory by words to represent and recall it. In so compressing experience, we focus on likeness in naming things, so that the same words are used for things that are in some respects quite different. But there is a kind of mental loop in this process, for the more we name different things the same, and talk of them in the same words, the less we attend to their differences and the more we think of them as the same. If the naming practices of the tribal peoples who still live today serve as any guide, we may guess that our nomadic ancestors often named the people of their tribe for the animals with whom they were most closely associated. But far more important than that, they used the same verbs and adjectives to refer to the actions and characteristics of humans and animals, or so we may guess from such patterns as they still appear in living languages today. In English, for example, wolves and men both "snap" and "growl" at one another; children and dogs "whimper" and "whine"; the hungry coyote "steals" eggs and the starving man "steals" bread. Such codifications of the likeness between human and non-human, passed down through language itself from one generation to the next, both reflect and reinforce the early conception that human and animal share a kindred spirit.

Names and verbs and narratives would not have been the only form in which the tribal peoples of the distant past expressed this early conception and encountered it. Mimed enactments of encounters with animals, originally necessary to supply the missing visual context of signalic speech, developed into more complex forms of dramatic enactment, supplemented by the use of animal skins and heads or claws and antlers as costume, and these in turn hardened into ritual. They too would have provided the people seeing them by the flickering and distorting light of fire with ready visual memories of moments when men turned into beasts and beasts into men. The impact of such enactments, seen largely in darkness, on children in particular, would be especially vivid.

So, too, would be the impact on the uninitiated and on those of other tribes who might come upon them unaware of seeing, again in the profound shadows of flickering flames, such half-human, half-beast figures leaping at the from the walls and ceilings in the deepest recesses of caves. For we know that the cave drawings of the late Pleistocene include such composite human-animal figures among those more recognizable as early bison and elk and deer. There is no reason to assume that the only people to see such images were those who had put them there. Indeed, there is no reason to assume that the impulse and skills to create such drawings were evenly distributed among all the small bands that successively inhabited the caves over a period of some ten centuries. More likely, on many occasions those drawings were encountered by people who had no experience themselves of producing such art. And to them it must have seemed that the stones themselves had taken on the shapes and colors and movements of the elk and bison and deer—and of the other fantastic creatures that seemed to move in the flickering shadows there. For the capacity of symbols to survive beyond the original context that produced them—language, drama, and ritual by repetition down through time, images by being limned or incised on durable stone—generates different ideas, different meanings. To a tribe whose rituals include the dancing by firelight of men garbed as deer, and whose members include one gifted at drawing, the image on the wall serves as a mnemonic—an externalized reminder—of that ritual and its entire context. But a different tribe, at a different time, may not have shared that context. So it must supply the decontextualized symbol with some context drawn from experiences of its own and the clues provided by the surrounding images. And this process, this recontextualizing of the decontextualized symbol, gives it different significance, different meaning. Thus the half-human, half-animal figure amid the bison and deer might be assumed by the newcomers to be, like the deer and bison, some awesome creature of nature not yet encountered by the tribe, and the drawings themselves a further demonstration of the ability of stones to take on the character of living things.

This would not have been a new idea to the people of the late Pleistocene, who for centuries before the great flowering of cave art had been finding bits of stone and bone molded to the shape of animal or human form. These they would keep and carry about with them as objects of special significance and power, which they treated with signs of great reverence and awe. But in the depths of the caves, the illusion of movement among the creatures of stone created by their placement and the flickering of shadow and light, and the further impression of their dreadful sounds created by the winds moaning and howling through the narrow passages, would have raised to new heights the terror of the power of the inanimate to take on living form—to come to life. It would have been a mystery as awesome as the more familiar but no less fearsome mystery of its counterpart, in which the animate creature turns as cold and hard and still as stone in the rigor of death.

Taken together, the circumstances and experiences of early tribal and nomadic life—the close interdependence of people and animals; the experience of the animal's "thinking" as one's own; the evolution of dramatic enactments of encounters with animals into ritualized performances with men in animal heads and skins enacting the animal's part, the development of the capacity for seeing the likeness in form between animate and inanimate things and for highlighting, in colors, suggestive shapes on cavern walls, where they seemed to move and groan in the noisy shadows; the metaphoric projection in language of human qualities and characteristics onto animals and other phenomena of the non-human world and the introjection, in the same process, of their characteristics into the self; the recurring mystery of death—all these combined and interacted to give rise to a set of ideas, unconscious at first but becoming more conscious and coherent as they were articulated and elaborated in tales and dramatically enacted around the fire.

What links these ideas together is the great central metaphor of animism, the idea that all things that move and change are moved and changed in the same way: by an invisible something inside them, like the wind—which moves and changes things and can be felt and heard, but cannot be seen. This wind or breath or spirit gets into things through their openings or cracks or crevices and animates them, each in its own way: the wolf to be wolfly, the lion to be lionly, the boar to be boarly, the man to be manly, the woman to be womanly. But the spirit that animates each creature is not permanently confined to that body. It may get out as it got in—through the natural openings of the creature's body or through rents made in it by accidents or battles with other creatures. When the wound makes an opening large enough, or is not closed quickly enough, the spirit may pass out of the creature entirely; then the creature becomes still and silent, as cold and hard as stone. But the spirit set free seeks another home—another form close by to enter through any crack or opening, and when it does, it imbues that form with the character of whatever creature it last animated. When the spirit does not immediately find another home, it wanders, searching, and the voices of such disembodied spirits may be heard in the whispering and whining and howling and animal cries borne on the wind. These spirits are a source of danger to the tribe, for one cannot know from which creatures they may have come. Thus it is doubly important to guard the openings of one's body and to quickly close or cover any wounds—both to prevent an unknown and unwanted spirit from entering and to keep one's own spirit from running out. It is equally important to stop up the openings and cover the inanimate bodies of those whose own spirits have fled, lest the wandering spirit of some other creature enter it and the people wake to find a jackal or bear in their midst.

Since what most visibly and invariably runs out of the bodies of animate creatures when they are wounded is their blood, and there is a perceptible loss of mobility, speech, animation with the progressive loss of blood, it would seem inevitable that the animating spirits of creatures should be closely identified with their blood, and that blood would come to be seen as the major "medium," so to speak, through which the spirits of creatures migrated, in whole or in part, from one creature to another. Thus in consuming the flesh and blood of the deer, for example, one would acquire the spirit and knowledge and skills of the deer—and even, in some circumstances, its outer form. And the wolf, by biting and drinking the blood of a man, might take on something of the human character—and again, in some circumstances, human form. Even stones and the earth itself might be so transformed—reshaped, animated, brought to life by the blood of creatures seeping into the cracks and crevices of rocks and sinking into the ground.

The great world-tale of animism, as I have sketched it in a few sentences here, is probably the oldest and most universal of human ways of accounting for the world experienced. Like the scientific theories of our own time, it arose from observations of the world. It arose from the perceptions of early humans of likenesses among diverse things, and the codification and extension of those likenesses to other things via language. And it arose from the need to make familiar, orderly, and predictable those things that were dangerous, frightening, and mysterious, so that rules for how to behave with such things could be formulated and passed on as guides for conduct that would enhance the survival of the tribe. Like the best of modern theories, the world-tale of animism had enormous explanatory power. It could account for almost every aspect of "subjective" and "objective" experience: how it was that a man could feel in himself the thoughts of the lion or deer; why men should roar and snarl and thrash with the strength of the bear after being mauled; how men took on, after the most successful of hunts and the greatest of tribal feasts, the form of the beast on whose flesh and blood they had fed; how it was that all could remember seeing wolves or jackals or deer that stood on two legs and danced in the moonlight at the dimmest edges of the fire, and spoke with the voices of men; how stones took on the shapes of living things, and living things turned again to stone; why children took on the features of those from whom they suckled the whitened blood, and spoke in their high voices until they were blooded by men; why the earth itself might be heard to groan and bellow and felt to tremble with animate life, and things that drank of the earth, like trees, be seen to move and sigh and groan with the voices of animals and men. These and countless other sensations, perceptions, observations, experiences and vital problems of tribal and nomadic life could be accounted for by the great world-narrative of animism, and this accounts, in part, for its endurance, universality, and power.

But more important even than that was its pragmatic and predictive power. Like the great scientific theories of later times, animism flourished and spread and endured because it *worked*. And it worked as most theories do: by reinforcing, perpetuating, and also generating practices and attitudes and rules of conduct that in fact enhanced the survival of the tribe. It *is* important to cover and close wounds, and to staunch in injured people the flow of escaping blood. For a host of reasons, including the dangers of putrefaction and contagion, as well as of attracting predators, it is a good idea to remove the dead from places of human habitation and to cover with earth both humans and animals that have been killed. Because creatures that feed indiscriminately on a wide variety of others, including many not freshly killed but already long dead, incorporate in their own flesh and blood a host of bacteria and parasites harmful to humans, it *is* best to shun the flesh of carrion-eaters and of scavengers like swine, which feed on the leavings of many others and include in their diets substantial amounts of human and an-imal waste. The discoveries of much later times that the flesh and blood of such creatures is dangerous to humans because it contains parasites and pathogens that are transferred from one host to another by eating, and not because it contains a babble of competing spirits that would madden the eater, make little difference in the outcome—or in the pragmatic utility of proscriptions against consuming the carrion- and offal-eaters' flesh. And it was the pragmatic utility of animism that gave this oldest and most universal of world-accounts its extraordinary power to survive.

It survived, of course, not in some mysterious "race memory" of ancient times, but in the only way that the fleeting, substanceless, no-thing we call an idea can survive: by being codified in the very fiber of language itself, and expressed in a thousand tribal tales, and reiterated in countless enactments of ritual, and perpetuated and reinforced in hundreds of rules of conduct passed down from one generation to the next until their origins had long disappeared in the mists of a hazy "otherwhen." Different tribes and different generations would, of course, tell the tale somewhat differently, each as its own circumstances and experiences dictated. When circumstances changed radically—as they did with the develop-ment of agriculture, settled life, and writing, and again with the explosion of in-vention, technology, and printing at the dawn of modern times—people would so re-write the older tale and reexplain their old, inherited practices that animism might seem to disappear.

But an idea of such explanatory and predictive power, so embedded in lan-guage and tales and rituals and practices, so preserved in writing and images, and so consonant with the early perceptions, experiences, and "theories" of every generation's children—such an idea cannot be made to disappear. It survived with only minor transformations as the underlying "text" of the agrarian earth-mother religions; in the rituals of human and animal slaughter, of the blood sacrifice so that the earth might be watered and the gods fed with the animate spirits that give them the power, in turn, to bring forth new life; in the dietary and blood-atonement laws, and the burial practices, and the prohibitions of contact with women when they bleed, and the purification rituals of early Judaism; in the trans-migration of souls of Hinduism and the reincarnation doctrines of Christians and Moslems. Animism survived in a more disguised form in the early "science" of Aristotle, in the vitalism of the 19th century, in the notions of "possession" that have served as an explanation of human evil and madness in every era and culture, including our own. And it survives today in dozens of children's tales, in our habits of talk—"Whatever got into you? Whatever possessed you?"—in images incised in the cornices of buildings, in countless legends, books, plays, and movies that keep alive the fearful images of shape-changers like werewolves and vampires and the terror of the spiritual and physical transformations wrought by exchanges of blood. Thus with respect to its endurance alone, it may well be said that animism is the world's most powerful theory.

But in several important respects the world-account or world-view I have sketched in a few paragraphs above and summed up in the word "animism" is not a theory at all—or was not in the early tribal times that gave it birth. It certainly was not a scientific theory, in the sense that most educated people would use those words today. To begin with, the ideas I set out in twelve or so general statements or propositions would not have been formulated in that abstracted way in the earliest of tales. The narratives of peoples living in a time long before the development of writing, like those of peoples who have never been exposed to writing today, were occasioned by and tied to specific events and happenings in the life of the tribe. It would not have occurred to anyone to enact all of the tribe's repertoire of stories at one sitting—or rather, at one dancing, for there is little doubt that the earliest of tales were embedded in the communal celebrations, feasts, and preparations from which they come. So it is with our own festal accounts and our retellings of them even today: we do not recite and enact the tale of the first Pilgrim harvest around the Yuletide fire or decorate pine boughs and sing of a wondrous birth under a miraculous star at Easter. There is more than "custom" at work here. In our own time, the sense of the sacred and of the awesome power of the spoken word and ritualized enactment to call forth what is named and enacted are so diminished that only children and the most deeply religious tremble at the recitation of even our most sacred litanies. Even those raised in the church, the mosque, the synagogue might be hard-pressed to explain, if they admit it at all, why the recitation of the litany of Communion or the Mass for the Dead in some casual setting—a classroom, say, or a restaurant—is felt to be not merely inappropriate, but much more profoundly *wrong*. For the rest of us, I would guess, the recitation of the Christmas story at the beach in midsummer, or of the Passover tale at the winter solstice, would occasion only a vague sense of disorder. We have, after all, been accustomed by 5000 years of writing, painting, and engraving, and 500 years of books, to words and tales and images taken out of their contexts of space and time and communal activity. We can, if we wish, read an entire corpus of sacred liturgy, as collected for example in the Book of Common Prayer, whenever and wherever we wish. So too all of the creation stories, covenant accounts, festal narratives, prophetic and holy sayings, and miracle tales of the Jews, Christians, and Moslems, as collected and reproduced for our solitary and distanced contemplation in the Torah, the Bible, the Koran. We can, if we want, read at one sitting the story of the pilgrims and of the virgin birth, or the various creation stories of different peoples around the world—and we can do so without participating in the least in the feasting and singing and dancing, the vital preparations and dreadful transformations, the wild joy and terror, the trembling in the presence of awesome mystery that provided the original context of those tales. So distanced and detached, we may even, as scholars do, compare and contrast and analyze without emotion the common threads, themes, patterns that weave through the stories collected and set out for our quiet study; move back and forth from one to another without so much as stirring, except to turn a page, from our own fixed and solitary context of time and space.

It is writing that allows us to do this, if we choose—writing and printing and the dozens of more recent ways we have invented, like the phonograph and audiotape, movies and videotape, to represent and record our words and actions and carry them out of the full contexts of their origins. It is writing, too, and the habits of thought engendered by centuries of literacy, that so attenuate the connection between word and action that we no longer sense the magical power of speech and ritual to bring about the things spoken of and enacted.

Early humans had no writing, no books, no audio and videotapes—no way to separate their narratives from the full and specific contexts of tribal life that occasioned them; no way to divest their tales and rituals of the profound sense of mystery and awe that accompanied them; no way to collect and study and compare at leisure their own accounts of how and why different things happened; and therefore no way to identify the common themes and articulate them as a set of conscious, abstract, general propositions. In the sense that such conscious, abstract, and general propositions are what we mean by a "theory," then the animism at the center of the oldest human tales was not a theory.

Far less was it a "scientific" way of accounting for the world of appearances, despite the fact that, like scientific theories, it was firmly based in empirical observations of the natural world and had enormous explanatory, predictive, and pragmatic power. For what distinguishes "science," in the contemporary use of that term, is not its empiricism or its insistence on prediction and proof. It is the search, not for evidence that *confirms* one's theories and assumptions, but for instances that might *refute* them. To put it in more familiar terms, the "scientific" theory is only tentatively held, and subjected to intense critical scrutiny. Its propositions and predictions must be scrupulously tested in carefully controlled conditions, and such tests must be exactly replicated not once but dozens of times by independent observers, with exhaustive cross-checking and comparison of the results. If those results vary even occasionally from what is predicted, one is obligated (at least in principle) to admit that the theory is wrong or inadequate, and to revise it or give it up. In practice, of course, scientists do not always work that way. They are as human as the rest of us, and as prone to both error and passion. Thus the scientist is as wont as anyone to fall in love with some theory—because it is socially useful, or particularly exciting, or a favorite of those who are in positions to grant tenure and fund research, or simply because it is beautiful—and having fallen in love, is prone to overlook the theory's shortcomings and failures. But modern science is a vast social enterprise, and most of its rules and procedures are intended to act as checks on such human foibles and thus reduce (though they cannot prevent) the persistence and accumulation of error.

The rules and procedures of modern science, like its abstract theories, are thoroughly dependent on writing, printing, and other means of recording and disseminating observations, measurements, and reports of procedures. The unaided human memory is simply not adequate to the tasks of precise and detailed recall that are required to report the exact conditions of some observation or to permit a listener to remember those conditions and replicate them. Nor is the spoken word, which vanishes on the breath, an adequate means of preserving and disseminating detailed reports across space and time, so that different accounts may be compared and the results checked and cross-checked.

Our distant ancestors had only speech and memory, carving and drawing, en-actment and ritual to codify and preserve and communicate their experience and accounts of it. They had neither the means nor the detachment from their experi-ence and accounts to develop the attitudes and procedures we identify with modern science. And they were too busy, we may guess, with the pressing problems of day-to-day survival to attend much to what we think of today as the abstract pursuit of "truth." Their theories of the world were pragmatic theories, not scientific theories; theories embedded in their world tales, not abstracted from them; theories codified in practices and rules for conduct, not in general principles. For the most part, in the environmental and social and symbolic contexts of early tribal and nomadic life, those theories worked. Thus they endured, and endure in disguised ways still, as perhaps the world's oldest ontology: the metaphor of the visible world as the house of the invisible, animating, transmorgrifying spirit.

So too is the great world-tale of animism intimately connected to what we may be the world's oldest cosmogony—that is, to the earliest human notions of space, time, and origins. To understand those notions, so radically different from our own, we shall have to accomplish an all-but-impossible feat: to imagine what it would be like to live in a world without calendars and clocks; without hours, minutes, days, months, years; without birthdays to count the ages of children; without Mondays, Tuesdays, and weekends; without schedules and appointments and the segregation of time into fixed units for schooling and dancing lessons, work and vacations; without even breakfast, lunch, and dinner—just eating when you are hungry and there is food. And we shall also have to imagine a world without maps and recorded locations, without feet and inches and miles, without drawings and measurements to show us where we are in location. It is hard even to imagine that such a world could exist. But it did—and for a short time in our own infancy, each of us lived in a world something like it, in the sense that though clocks and maps and schedules existed, we knew nothing of them. In the life of a modern child, that period is very brief indeed, for everyone and everything else around children goes by the calendar and the clock and the schedule, and long before they can count or tell time, they will be living on a schedule too. Still, the world of infancy and early childhood gives us our best clue to how time and space might have been conceived before systems of marking and charting them began. So let us begin our feat of imagination there.

To the newborn, everything that exists exists by means of sensation; *only* those things exist that register as sensation; and things exist only *so long as* they register as sensation. Something not seen, felt, heard, smelled, tasted is simply not part of the newborn's world, for the newborn has not yet learned that objects persist when they are not seen, heard, or otherwise registering on the baby's senses. We may say that at birth, then, the baby's universe has only one dimension, one "where" and "when," and they are the same: the universe is the *present-to-the-senses*.

From birth onwards the neonate is correlating dozens of patterns of sensory wholes and storing them in that mysterious process we call "memory." Within the first few weeks of life, the infant can already distinguish a familiar from a novel pattern, in what we call "recognition," and somewhere between six and twelve months or so shows signs of active looking for or wanting a *specific* something that is not present. I am not talking here about the fretful distress of a two-month-old when, for example, its pacifier falls from its mouth. True enough, the infant feels that loss—but it may be consoled by any number of similar objects that produce roughly the same sensations. I am talking about the later stage at which a baby searches for a specific something that is gone, and is not satisfied until someone proffers the right thing. This suggests that the baby has in mind a memory of the object that persists even when the object is not present. And now the baby's universe is considerably more complicated, because things exist, we may say, in two different states or ways: they are present-to-the-senses or present-but-*not*-to-the-senses or, as we adults would put it, present in mind. To us that may seem a clear-cut distinction, but to the baby and the young child it is not—not only because the baby has no conception of "memory" and "mind," but also because things are always moving from one state to the other. The pacifier is not-present-to-the-senses, let us say, but is present otherwise, as a pattern in mind. So the baby enacts its pacifier-sucking behavior, with signs of distress, and Lo! the pacifier appears. The two-year-old's blanket is not present-to-the-senses, but is present otherwise, as the blanket-in-mind. She moves the teddy bear, and—Ah!—the blanket appears.

These experiences are wonderfully amplified and intensified by words, when the child begins to understand them and then to speak. For words both bring things into memory and hold them there, and at the same time cause them to happen or appear. Or so it seems in the world of early childhood. Mama says, "Eva—want a cookie? Cookie?" and the cookie experience comes to life in little Eva's mind. A moment later, the cookie materializes in the world of the senses. When she learns to shape the right sounds herself, moreover, Eva discovers her own power to bring things from their not-present-to-the-senses state into their present-to-the-senses state: to call forth the cookie from the hazy otherwhere it resides when it is not here to the sensory world where it can be seen, felt, touched—and eaten.

In this and countless other ways, the daily experiences of young children with objects lost and found, here and gone and here again, present in the vague otherworld of memory but not in the sensory world, then in the sensory world, then again only in the nonmaterial "elsewhere" of memory; with objects called forth from "otherwhere" to "here" by words—such repeated experiences suggest and daily confirm an early construction of the universe as two different worlds or states of things, not one: a state or place and time where/when things are present-to-the-senses and a state or place and time when/where they persist forever but cannot be seen, touched, or heard—until they materialize in the sensory world of themselves, or by being searched for and discovered, or by being called forth by the proper enactment or the saying of the proper words.

Such a world-construction may seem to us bizarre, but it is in fact a quite sensible way of accounting for the way things have of disappearing and reappearing; yet always, somehow, somewhere, somewhen persisting; for the world experienced by the senses and by "the mind." And it is a particularly sensible world-view if one has as yet neither the introspective self-awareness nor the symbolic tools for inventing the ideas we call "memory" and "mind."

Some of the world's oldest languages, in fact, codify experience in just this way: in two great grammatical categories that indicate whether objects and events are present-to-the-senses or not-present-to-the-senses; in their perceptible or not-now/not-yet perceptible state. Such languages are radically different from our own, of course, in their treatment of space and time. Things present to the senses are also, as we would say, "present" in space and time. Things not present to the senses—including all of what we would call "subjective" experiences like thoughts, memories, dreams, wishes, ideas, and all of the not-here/not-now, the "past" and the "future"—are simply elsewhere, elsewhen.

These notions—that space and time are not separate, that every "elsewhere" is also "elsewhen," and that things not here-and-now cannot be precisely located in time—are entirely consonant with the conditions of both early childhood and of nomadic life, for both children and nomads are always on the move, and neither have maps or clocks or calendars to "fix" things in space and time. To the child at home, the park is not only a different place but a different time, for it takes time to get there, and the park isn't "here" or "now" until one has arrived. To the nomad, different times—different risings of the sun, different "moments" in its movement through the sky—are also different places because in their experience they do not stay in one place while the sun moves. Our own notion—that space remains the same while time "passes"—is very much a function of permanent dwellings and sedentary life. And, of course, of ways like clocks for representing changes in time.

To people without clocks and maps, without calendars, without fixed times for eating and working, schooling and playing, without marks on wood, stone, paper to record where they are in relation to where they have been and might return again, or when which things happened in time, "where" and "when" are not only integrated, but also much more diffuse notions than our own. Just *how* diffuse you may remember from your own childhood. My sister likes to remind me of the long nights we once spent, when we were very young, sitting wide-eyed with fear at our bedroom window, watching and listening for the tanks and soldiers with flame-throwers and guns whom we expected at any moment to appear. We had heard our parents and the radio talk of them "in Korea," which we assumed was, like everything else in our experience, somewhere vaguely down the block and around a couple of corners. And I remember an even earlier time when we would pass the long, dark hours before falling asleep (they were probably only minutes) in eager discussions of where exactly Christmas *was* and how we might go there before it came, instead of waiting for it here. The idea was no more strange to us than the idea that we could go down the hall and see our brother asleep; the only difference was that in the case of Christmas, we didn't know the *way*. You may wish to say that in this belief and dozens of others like it, my sister and I and other children were and are merely victims of a kind of confused over-generalization or metaphoric projection: that since *most* things that we experience, talk of, and remember, like absent brothers and misplaced teddy bears and lost tennis balls, both persist when we don't see them and are located somewhere in time and space, so do other recurring things that we name and remember, like Christmas, persist when we don't experience them—and so are they located somewhere in time and space, though exactly *where* is hard to say. That is precisely the point. Through just such a process children even of our own time may construct a short-lived cosmogony or conception of the universe quite different from that of adults: a notion of two different worlds or dimensions where things exist in two different ways—a sensory world where things are perceptible but come and go, appear and disappear, are present and absent, here and gone and here again; and another world where they persist forever, out of hearing and sight, unchanging and unchanged. Like the world of sensation, that world exists somewhere in time and space, but not here and now. It is elsewhere and elsewhen, has no precise or fixed location, but is there somewhere nonetheless, everywhere and everywhen that is *not* right here and now. And that world is the *source* from which things come, from which they emerge and into which they disappear when they are not here-and-now.

In the lives of our children, in our own lives when we were children, that world-view is very short-lived—done away with by pictures and maps and televisions, by clocks and calendars and counting, and by the thousand, thousand adult explanations that things are *things* and thoughts are *thoughts* and the two are not "really" connected; that "Christmas" is not a "place" but a *time*, and that these are separate, and one cannot "go" to a time but must wait for it to "come"; that a story is only a *story*, made up of *words*, and that *words* cannot hurt you; that "Santa Claus" is only an idea, not a real thing or person, and that "ideas" don't exist in the world; that the sensations and feelings of terror that wake the child screaming in the night are "only a dream" and not "real"; that the things the child *knows* are under the bed and behind the closet door and running up the stairs from the dark cellar behind her frantic feet are not "there"—just products of her "imagination." "Look. Here: I'm opening the closet and putting on the light. See? There's nothing there. Just your imagination." (No wonder children think adults are fools. Of *course* there's nothing there when you're *looking*, idiot! It's only there when the light's off and you *can't* see it!)

But even in the clocked and mapped, scheduled and explained world of modern times, this early construction of the world persists. Why else does Stephen King sell millions of books, set adult hearts to pounding again with primal terror, move fortyyear-olds to turn on all the lights, check the windows, and bolt the basement door? We buy the books, go to the movies, feel the terror, bolt the doors, not because the books and movies *invent* a world we have never known, but *resurrect* it—or resurrect the powerful echoes of something we once believed, before language allowed us to express it and the adult world taught us to forget it.

If this is the case in our own time—that the power of our childhood experiences and conceptions can survive all our later learnings about space and time, clocks and maps, the teachings of science about language and memory and mind, we should not be surprised that in the much longer "childhood" of our species, when language was new and strange and there were no clocks, no maps, no calendars, no "adults" and no science to teach us about "memory" and "imagination" and "mind," the same construction arose and endured for centuries, codified in language and given expression in dozens of different tribal tales, as perhaps the world's oldest cosmogony.

In that cosmogony, the universe is divided into two different dimensions or domains. One is the world of daily, mundane experience as given to the senses: the world of appearances—fickle, fleeting, here and gone and here again. The other is the world hidden from the senses, secret, sacred (in its old meaning of "set apart")—permanent, enduring, eternal, unchanging. The sensory, mundane (or as the scholar Mircea Eliade terms it, "profane") world is here-and-now; the sacred world is otherwhere and otherwhen—not fixed in space and time but everywhere and everywhen that is out of sight, touch, hearing. It lies at the boundaries of perception: below the ground, at the horizon where the sun and the earth vanish from sight, above the black blanket of the nighttime sky, beneath the surfaces of deep waters, inside the impenetrable walls of mountains, within and behind and beyond the things and events that appear out of it and disappear into it. That hidden world is the important world, the real world, the enduring world out of which the world of perceptible things and events emerges, to which they return, and from which they come again in a continuing process of appearance and reappearance, creation and re-creation. It is the world in which the present world of experience, the world of here-and-now, has its origins, its source. To participate in that world and thus ensure their own perpetuation and renewal, their continuing survival in the here-and-now, people must maintain their connection to it, by finding or creating the openings, doorways, passages, physical links between the two worlds: finding them by discovering the deep fissures in the earth, the places where streams gush out of the ground, the mountaintops that spew forth smoke and flame, the groves where bolts of lightning flare between the sky and the trees, connecting them to the sacred; creating them by driving poles deep into the earth and opening smoke holes to the sky.

Such spaces and places and physical connections were not the only doorways between the sacred and the profane, in the cosmogony or early peoples. So were such altered states of consciousness and sensory experience as dreams and near-dreams—the trance-like fugues that might be induced by the elevated emotions, the smoke and fatigue, the rhythmic chanting and repetitive movement, the continuous flickering of firelight against darkness that were the conditions accompanying the communal enactments of tribal tales and rituals. We know well enough from our own dreams and nightmares, fugue states, experiences with hypnosis, and even the repeated chanting of mantras their power to create alternate realities in a place-less otherwhen where time is distorted, suspended, stands still. We have our own cosmogony, of course, to account for such experiences, and a vocabulary of dozens of words to taxonomize them. In the cosmogony of ancient tribal times, dreams and trance-like states were gateways—en-trances, transitions—into the otherworld: points at which the here-and-now of mundane sensory experience met and dissolved into the timeless everywhen of the sacred; at which the eternal, unchanging present at the source of things was not only revealed but was experienced, reentered, *restored*.

The repeated incantation and enactment in ritual of the tribe's own past experiences, its codified memory, its practices passed down from generation to generation until their origins were long lost in the mists of time, had several complex functions. The sensory and temporal distortions induced by the conditions of such enactments led early peoples to "locate" the origins of what they experienced during ritual, not in themselves, but elsewhere—just as we may experience our dreams, while we are in them, as originating not in ourselves but elsewhere. Since the elsewhere and elsewhen where the tribe's rituals and practices were experienced seemed to them to be the timeless world, the world-that-endures, the permanent world behind the unstable and fleeting world of appearances, the world that perpetually generates and regenerates the here-and-now of life, those rituals and practices were taken to be manifestations of the sacred and all its awesome power. Thus the practices and traditions of the tribe, as codified in its chanted and enacted tales and rituals, were not pale "customs" or "memories" or "stories," but were *sanctified*, imbued with all the power of their source in the timeless world-of-origin. It was this source and power, their connection to the sacred, that gave the tales and rituals and practices of the tribe their authority; through their enactment and en-chantment, the tribe maintained its own connectedness to the world-that-endures, to the generating and perpetually regenerating source of all that is momentary and transient, the source of enduring life.

The cosmogony of the sacred and the profane served vital social functions. The rooting of tribal customs and practices in the otherworld of the sacred, rather than merely in human memory and tradition, gave them an awesome significance, for it meant that deviance from custom carried with it not merely loss of standing in the tribe, but the infinitely more dreadful loss of one's connection to the sacred and therefore of all that was enduring in life. Thus the sacralization of tribal customs served as a powerful instrument for the social control of deviance and the regulation of potentially threatening impulses. It also strengthened the unity of the tribe by adding to the existing bonds of blood relations, co-dependence, and reciprocal obligation a new kind of bond: the bond of a shared sacred "history." In effect, the cosmogony of the sacred and the profane provided the different peoples of ancient times with the beginnings of their tribal and cultural identities. For a "culture " is not merely a group of people who share the same territory, the same ways of hunting and eating and tool-making, the same customs, even the same language. More than that, a culture is a group of people who share the same *meanings*: the same ways of accounting for and interpreting themselves and their customs.

Different tribal groups told the story of their sacred origins in different ways, populated it with different animal and human-like figures, identified different sites as their major sacred "center"—the feature of their landscape most awesome and enduring yet least knowable, and therefore the most likely passageway between the sacred and the profane, the font of creation and re-creation. In some tribal accounts, the senseable world is laid, like an egg by some creature in the world of the sacred; in others it is spewed forth, as by a volcano; in still others it is given birth, or spoken or sung or breathed into being. In some accounts, The People are instructed in the proper ways to do things by animal figures; in others by First Woman and First Man; in others by different talking gods. In almost all, they are given songs, words, dances, dreams, drawings, incantations to keep open their connection to the sacred world, in which the moment of creation is always and perpetually going on, to be re-experienced, re-entered, restored by those who have kept the way.

In the specifics of their details, then, the sacred origin tales of different tribal groups were different, as the environments and experiences of the peoples were different. And these differences gave each group a unique tribal "history" and identity—an identity reinforced and perpetuated and elaborated with each reenactment and reenchantment of that group's specific origin tales. Thus they served to unify and maintain the group, to cement ties of place and necessity with ties of shared meaning, shared culture. And thus the cosmogony of the sacred and the profane underlying all those tales—codified and perpetuated in them and in the customs they reinforced, passed on from generation to generation in ritual and dance; image and song, even in the grammatical structures of speech—endured.

Like the great ontology of animism, the cosmogony of the sacred and the profane long outlived the environmental and social and symbolic conditions that gave it birth. It survived at the foundations of the Pyramids and in the great temples of the Jews; in the sacred groves of the Greeks and in the eternal cycles of the Hindu faith. It is the idea that raised the great stones of Stonehenge and the soaring vaults and spires of Chartres. It echoes in the allegory of Plato's cave and in the Christian refrain repeated everywhere to this day: "As it was in the beginning, is now, and ever shall be... world without end." It fueled the passions that launched the Crusades and lit the fires of the Inquisition, perpetuates the struggles over Jerusalem and other holy places even today, is given voice in the anguished cries of modern peoples whose sacred spaces have been violated by the violent intrusions of the profane. It shows its face, disguised, degraded, and ashamed, in contemporary advertising, where images of the sacred—the awesome heights of mountains, geysers erupting from the earth and towering to the sky, the ever-changing, ever-enduring surfaces of the sea—are used to sell cigarettes, chewing gum, and other paltry things. We see its dark side in our monster books and movies, where evil always lurks beyond the boundaries of the visible: beneath the surface of deep waters, in the bowels of the earth, at the frozen edges of the world, beyond the planets and stars. And we see its bright side, too, in books and movies and images of endless regeneration and return, like *Ghost* and *Starman* and *E.T.*. Even our physicists invoke it, when they have pondered too long on the beginnings of the universe, gazed too long on galaxies without end.

Successive generations have so heavily written over the ancient cosmogony of the sacred and the profane that it is barely recognizable in its original outlines today. But it has never quite been erased—perhaps because for each generation's children there is, however brief, a time like that earliest of human times: a time without clocks and hours, calendars and years, maps and miles; without consciousness of one's unique self and words to map the inner world of memory and mind; without writing and photographs to record where one has been and is going or what happened when; without the tools of communication and mind to invent history and science; and so a time when experience presents itself, not as a tidy "objective" and "subjective" nor as "past, present, and future," but simply as here-and-now, elsewhere-and-elsewhen. In the conditions of early childhood, that cosmogony is good enough: it accounts for the ways things change and the ways they endure, and given what children know and what they need to do, it works.

In the parallel conditions of early tribal and nomadic life, the great world tales of animism and of the sacred and profane were also good enough: they accounted for what early people experienced, served as vital ways to organize, codify, preserve, and communicate acquired information to the young, generated and perpetuated practices that enhanced the survival of the tribe, kept social deviance and group-threatening expressions of impulse within safe bounds, reinforced the unity and cultural identity of the tribe. In the environmental, social, and symbolic ecology of tribal and nomadic times, they worked—and so endured through centuries of tribal wanderings.

But then conditions changed.

CHAPTER EIGHT

Transitions and Transformations: The City, the Self, and the Sacred

Spring came. Not our local and transient spring, but a global spring, a lasting spring. It came, not in a period of weeks or months or even years, but over the slow course of centuries, as the earth warmed and the dense glaciers of the last Ice Age melted and shrank back toward the poles of the planet. Behind them they left deep hollows and channels in the earth, where trapped ice melted into inland lakes and the waters given up by the retreating glaciers rushed in rivers and streams. The seas rose, some to flood the land, some to refresh with their minerals and salts the inland seas created eons earlier by the drifting and colliding and rending of the earth's crust. And still the planet warmed, until the northern lands grew temperate once again and the lands to the south turned hot.

In the great and gradual spring that marked the ending of the last Ice Age, the ecologies of place changed and changed and changed again, and with those changes came change, as well, in the lives of the hardy bands that had survived and toughened and elaborated their tools and skills, languages and world-tales in the long centuries of the passing winter. Game and grains grew more plentiful in the warmer, wetter springtime of the earth, and as they did, the hardships of the hunt moderated, diets improved, and populations grew. Time and again it must have happened that some nomadic band wandered into an area particularly favored by just those stable conditions of sun and soil, temperature and rain that promoted, perpetuated, and continually renewed an abundance of plant and animal life. And there the tribe would settle, to wander no more. But they would not long be alone in such a favored clime, for others would come and settle too. And still their numbers grew, until even the most bountiful terrain could support no more. Nor would the terrain be always uniformly and perpetually bountiful, for the earth continued to warm, and as spring turned to high, hot summer in the plains of the lands we now call Egypt and Israel, Iraq and Turkey, for example, their lakes and streams began to dry and the land to bake, until once-lush ecologies of life turned barren and bare and their peoples were set to wandering again, to those more fertile lands in the valleys watered by the great rivers of the Nile, the Tigris, the Euphrates, the Jordan that ran down out of the Galilean mountains and lake to the trapped salt waters of the now-Dead Sea.

It was some 10,000 years ago, the climatologists tell us, that the earth reached the peak of its last interglacial warming, drying the Saharan plains to desert sand and driving its tribal peoples north and east to the water-rich valleys of the great rivers of the Middle East. There the newcomers struggled and contested, we may guess, with those already settled on the now too-populous land. And in those struggles, the losers would be driven out of the lush valleys where the waters flowed and the game abounded and the fruits of the earth lay ripe for the taking—driven to the outskirts, to the hillsides above the valley floors or farther out on the plains, where eking out a living proved more challenging. There some scattered bands developed sickles and pounders to reap and crush the wild grains; others domesticated the wildfowl, the lamb, the swine drawn to the leavings of human habitation. And there a primitive form of trade arose among the thinly spread bands: the simple exchange of what one group had in abundance for what they needed or cherished and another could supply. And with the barter of goods came an even more vital form of exchange: the exchange of ideas, knowledge, information. For one does not visit another's habitation to trade with blinders on. One sees how others live, what they have done: scratched shallow channels in the earth, perhaps, to direct the precious water from infrequent rains or a distant stream to where the grasses grow; shaped mud into rounded bricks to harden in the sun and made of these round shelters in which to dwell; woven reeds into baskets hardened with clay to carry and store grains and eggs; covered meat with salt to dry and preserve it. With even primitive forms of barter, people come away with more than eggs or grains or tools. They also take home and leave behind ideas and techniques that, applied to the different materials in their own environs, may produce somewhat different and sometimes better results—giving them something new to trade.

But trade is, beyond a medium for securing needed goods and exchanging and enriching ideas, something more. It is in itself an idea, or a practice that requires, institutionalizes, and promotes an idea, an attitude, a set of dispositions. At its most abstract, this is the idea that peaceable exchange among strangers provides a viable—indeed, less costly and therefore preferable—alternative to the taking of things by force. Of course, peaceable exchange, cooperative interdependence, and the suppression of the impulse to take were in themselves nothing new; families could not have knit into clans or clans into tribes without them. But the early forms of trade that emerged with the beginnings of settled life extended cooperation beyond the boundaries of family and tribe, beyond the circle of people connected by common experience, common practice, common blood. They required and promoted cooperation among, and therefore the suppression of aggressive impulses toward, strangers—or at least toward those who came to trade, not to take.

In the earliest of settled times there would have been many, of course, who came to take, for the drier, hotter climate would produce periods of drought in even the most productive terrains, driving their peoples out, and among them would be many who had neither the habits of settled life nor anything to trade. We may imagine that, as the population pressures on the lands of the Middle East grew, small and scattered agrarian villages linked by barter were time and again overrun, their peoples decimated, their domesticated flocks and fowl carried off and dispersed by wandering tribes who kept to the older ways and moved on. But some must have survived, their scattered people returning to the land and the landmarks that now marked for them not just a village center, but the center, as well, of their sacred space. Perhaps, too, the numbers of those who returned would be increased by those the wanderers left behind: women with child, or with children too young to keep up with the tribe; the wounded, the aging, the ill, the temporarily disabled who could no longer sustain the rigors of the hunting and gathering, nomadic way of life. Others may have been drawn to such lightly settled centers by the geological features that signified connections to the sacred—a bubbling spring in the desert, a towering pillar of salt, a still-smoking mountaintop—and there gave up their wandering to reap the wild grains and swell the numbers of those who scratched out a living from the land and met warily in the peaceable exchanges of trade.

However it may have been, the numbers of tribal peoples settled here and there on the lands of the Middle East grew, and so—at least in one harsh and stony place—did cooperation among them. We know this must be so, because some 10,000 years ago, long before they had learned to fire clay pottery or mix mortar for bricks, the peoples around the oasis at Jericho came together to dig a great circular trench, raise a tower, and build a wall. What drove them to do so we cannot know. Perhaps the need to defend their fragile settlements from the depredations of wandering tribes brought them together in this first great communal labor. Perhaps it was to protect their flocks and grains from the beasts of the wild. Or perhaps the great tower, with its interior stairway descending from the heights to a point where it vanishes beneath the ground, was constructed as a passageway to the world of the sacred, and wall and the ditch were built around it to protect that vital gateway to enduring life.

Whatever may be the case, the peoples at Jericho some 10,000 years ago built a wall. It was a massive project—raw stone placed carefully on stone, with mud between, to a height three times and more that of a person, and circumscribing an area some ten acres in measure. And the ditch around it must have been an even more grueling labor, cut by hand 9 feet deep, 27 feet wide, into the solid rock of the stony hillside, and in Jericho's blistering heat. We do not know the peoples who undertook such a project, but the silent stones they left behind tell us much about them. They must have produced food and channeled water efficiently enough to support large numbers who could expend their strength, not in hunting or bearing water or reaping the wild grains, but in digging and hauling and smoothing the stones to build the tower and wall. They must have divided among themselves the tasks necessary for daily living and for the great construction project, special-ized their labors, differentiated their roles. They must have developed structures for making decisions, organizing and coordinating the work, and adjudicating disputes that arose in its course. They must have found ways of communicating that bridged differences in tribal speech and meaning, perhaps by developing, over the years of common effort, a common tongue. And they must have learned to tolerate, to accept, to accommodate themselves to strangers—to the other-ness of peoples of different clans, different customs, different blood.

They are 10,000 years gone now, the nameless peoples who came together to raise that ancient tower, dig that vast trench in living rock, and build what is our planet's oldest known wall. But the trench, the tower, and the wall survive, and they mark a great dividing line in the history of our species: a dividing line between the nomadic and the settled ways of life; between forms of social organization based on common blood—the family, the clan, the tribe—and forms of social organization based on the common needs, interests, and labors of strangers; between economies of scarcity or sufficiency and economies of surplus and exchange; between "nature" and "civilization," in its old meaning of *citification*, with all that implies: permanent dwellings, the gathering in one place of peoples of diverse origins, cooperative public projects, the diversification and specialization of skills and roles, increasing complexity of social organization, an intensification of trade and exchanges of in-formation, the flourishing of crafts, arts, and the building trades—and with these, the steady growth of knowledge about the patterns and processes of the natural world and of techniques for altering nature to serve human needs.

Perhaps in the end that is the greatest significance of the tower, the wall, and the trench at ancient Jericho: they are works that mark, by the grandness of their scale, a great watershed in the relationship between humans and nature, a dividing line between ways of life in which our species, like all its predecessors, accommodated itself to the givens of the natural environment and ways of life in which the natural environment was altered to accommodate human needs. For in gouging their trench in the living rock and piling stone on stone, the builders at Jericho transformed the face of the land to their own ends. And while it goes too far to say they harnessed the forces of nature to serve their needs, at the least they channeled them—for the silt-filled grooves at the top of their wall indicate that water ran there, if not as part of a larger project of irrigation, then perhaps as a means of collecting and directing waters produced by condensation and the infrequent desert rains. And the tower suggests a shift, as well, in the relationship of humankind to the sacred, for its stout walls hide a passageway between the worlds not found by happenstance or revealed in nature, but created by human design. Perhaps this is the very site that gave rise in later years to the ancient tale of Babel, where human efforts to penetrate the world of the sacred by means of such a tower brought down the confounding wrath of God for their hubris. It is a remarkable story, that—one of the earliest to link the arts of building in stone with an enormous increase in human knowledge, pride, and power, and to warn of the dire consequences that might befall any who extended their newfound control over nature too recklessly and too far.

It is doubtful that the cautionary tale of Babel was told at the Jericho of 8000 BCE, but if it was, it was given little heed. For men continued to build and rebuild, not only at Jericho but at other sites in the lands we call the Middle East. And as they built and delved and channeled, and learned to plant and store as well as to harvest the evolving hybrid grains, they vastly extended their knowledge of the workings of the natural world—particularly, of the transformations wrought in things by interweaving them, combining them, mixing them with water, subjecting them to fire. By 7000 BCE the city dwellers of the Middle East had invented mortar and plaster, fired clay pottery, and woven mats. By 6000 BCE, they had spindles, looms, and textiles, and these supplemented an already extensive intercity trade in such locally-occurring natural products as salt, flint, seashells, the razor-sharp but durable and easily worked volcanic byproduct, obsidian, and the various pigments derived from the oxides of iron, copper, and manganese. With every new discovery, the power of men and women to transform the natural world increased. The trade in shells, obsidian, and pigments, and other archaeological evidence from the early cities of the Neolithic Age, tell us that the transformations they wrought served more than utilitarian ends.

The earliest of pots and clay-strengthened baskets, of woven mats and worked leather pouches, of hearths and floors and plastered walls, of flaxen fabrics and blades of polished obsidian and bone were no doubt prized primarily for their functions. But as the techniques and leisure for producing them grew more familiar within early city walls, attention shifted from function to surface form. At first the designs on pots mimicked the interwoven reeds and rushes that had formed the baskets that preceded them; fabric patterns and colors reflected the subtle variations in the natural fibers of which they were woven; thumb indentations and cross-hatching on bricks served the functions of marking them for placement and providing a better surface for the adhesive mortar. But later, as artisans produced goods in a wider variety of media—leather, plaster, obsidian, bone, fabric, wood, clay—and exchanged their products more widely, they began to transfer the simple designs from one medium to another. Thus liberated from the contexts of their origins, patterns, colors, and shapes were also divorced from the functions of the pots, fabrics, and tools from which they derived, and achieved both a new visibility and a new value in their own right—an aesthetic value as pure decoration. With the separation of surface form from function, moreover, came a spurt of innovation and inventiveness, a new playfulness in the arts of decoration and design that transformed fabrics from simple woven garments to possessions prized for their beauty and plain plastered walls into complex colored murals combining representation—of houses, landscape features, animals, and humans—with a profusion of geometric patterns and abstract designs.

At Catal Hüyük, a city of some 32 acres and perhaps 6000 people on the Anatolian Plain in South Central Turkey, which carbon-dating of its artifacts places at around 6500 BCE, such elaborate wall murals abound, most of them in buildings associated with religious rites. There the abstraction of design from any specific context reached such a peak that artisans cut the patterns they wished to reproduce into the flat surfaces of small pieces of clay, baked them, and used the hardened seals to stamp the patterns onto fabrics, wall coverings, and perhaps even human skin. These seals are a find of great significance, not only for what they tell us about the capacity of early city dwellers for abstractive seeing, but also for the link they suggest between religion, art, and the evolution of writing, in which such incised seals play a critical role. And if indeed, as some archaeologists suggest, the seals were used to pattern not only fabrics and walls but also human skin, they confirm what other artifacts found in the earliest of cities suggest: that the men and women of 8000 years ago were not only occupied in transforming the natural world by their labors, and their functional creations by their arts, but were also deeply engaged in transforming themselves.

In one sense, the practice of transforming the human body through costuming, scarification, the application of colored pigments, and even tattoo was nothing new. Such practices no doubt date back to the earliest of tribal times, where they are connected to the evolution of dramatic enactments of events such as the hunt, to sacred ritual, and to such other integrative activities as rites of passage and of to-temic identification. But the artifacts found in the early cities of 7000 to 5000 BCE suggest a subtle shift in the functions of face and body coloring, of costume, and of ornamentation: a shift away from their earlier use in connection to the sacred and to rites of tribal integration and towards their secular use as enhancements and distinctions of the individual person. The finds of makeup pots, colored pigments and various implements for applying them to face and skin, necklaces and other objects of ornamentation, and highly polished ovals and rounds of gleaming ob-sidian among the household and grave goods of women indicate a heightened attention to the arts of personal ornamentation, and their separation from the contexts of sacred ritual. Of particular importance are the hand-sized, smooth-surfaced, highly polished bits of obsidian, for their shape, their placement among other cherished possessions, and their admirable ability to reflect light suggest that they were used as mirrors.

The personal use of mirrors reveals something more significant about the men and women of early cities than their attention to outward decoration. It suggests an important step in their *inner* transformation: a subtle shift in consciousness, a changing conception of self. For a mirror allows one to see oneself from a van-tage point outside oneself; to see oneself as an object of interest; to see oneself as others do, and to note one's similarity to or difference from them. A mirror may lead one to like or dislike what one sees—to be critical of oneself or, like Narcissus, enchanted—but in either case, it heightens selfawareness and the sense of one's personal uniqueness. It provides a vantage point, in short, from which the eye may see the "I"—or at least its outward manifestation. For a mirror does not, of course, provide a reflection of one's inner life, of the psychological "I" that corresponds to the unique figure in the glass and moves it, as we think, to speak and act, ponder and decide. The full awakening of that inner "I," and of the habits of scrutinizing and reflecting on it in the processes we call introspection, would have to await the evolution of a different kind of mirror—the mirror of the mind that is created by the imprisonment of thought in writing. That great revolution in thought, culture, and communication still lay some 3500 years in the future from when the earliest of city dwellers first began to look into their obsidian mirrors.

Nonetheless, the mirror, along with the heightened attention to personal adornment and decoration, both reflected and intensified a set of psychological and conceptual transformations that arose with the beginnings of cities. For cities, with their intensification and diversification of the arts and crafts, their varieties of goods and products, their complexity of social structures and roles, their diversity of peoples, customs, and gods, offer people far more choices and opportunities for self expression than do the more fixed and limited contexts of tribal life. But at the same time, cities require greater restraints on the self: both a more stringent control over biological impulse and the subordination of tribal ways to the requirements of living, building, trading with quite different others in an emerging "public."

The mastery of the more aggressive aspects of human nature apparently did not come easy, and the evidence of skeletal remains from early cities indicates that the control of impulse and of intertribal conflict was shaky at best. According to one source, "no single group of persons until the bellicose days of the Roman Empire suffered so many head wounds" as the inhabitants of the burgeoning Neolithic city at Çatal Hüyük. Nonetheless, their capacity for self restraint was good enough to foster cooperation on a grand scale, for Çatal Hüyük's extensive building projects could not have gone forward without it.

The opposing pulls of city life towards a heightened expression of self on the one hand and an increasing suppression of self on the other are important be-cause the conditions they create—more choices, more decisions, less predictability, greater internal tension between the biological and social self—lay the groundwork for the awakening to consciousness of the internal, individual, decision-making "I." It is unlikely that this conception of the self as internally and individually directed had as yet arisen among the peoples of 8000 to 5000 BCE, for despite the diversity and complexity of city life, the dominant structures that controlled and directed activity and behavior, thought and belief, were still the family, clan, and tribe, and people lived outside those fixed and predictable structures too briefly and intermit-tently to see themselves as autonomous, self-directed individuals. But the ground was being prepared.

If the people of early cities did not yet fully see themselves as individuals, they did see themselves in a new way as a group: that is, as people, as *human.* With permanent dwellings, walls between themselves and "the wild," the diminu-tion of hunting and increased reliance on domesticated flocks and grains, came a weakening of the close bonds of interdependence between people and the beasts that had for some fifteen million years shared their wandering way of life. Gathered in increasing numbers behind their sheltering walls and interacting more with one another than with the aurochs and deer, lions and jackals that had earlier been their sustenance and competition, hunters and prey, city dwellers became more aware of their differences from them than of their similarities. There is nothing like a wall for creating distinctions between "us" who are within and "them" who are without. The domestication of animals, moreover, heightened the awareness of difference between herders and their beasts, for it provided ample opportunities to observe the divergence of their ways. Goats and lambs and chickens do not build, as men had come to do, or cook and weave and clothe themselves. Nor do men come running, or turn and wheel, to the sheep's command or the dog's bark. It is man who commands, and they who obey. The arts, and mirrors, too, intensified the differences between beasts and humans, by directing heightened attention to the significance of surface form. Humans simply did not look like any of the other beasts, and in that, too, they were set apart, of a special kind: different.

It would be another 3500 years before the first use of the word "humanity" was recorded. But the artwork of the citydwellers of 6000 BCE reveals a growing awareness of the significance and special estate of humans. Human forms begin to appear more frequently and in greater detail in the wallpaintings of city dwellers, along with depictions of their buildings and habitations. But nowhere is the new attention to human-ness more apparent than in representations of the sacred. For as people became aware of themselves as humans, so did their previously faceless or animist conceptions of the great invisible forces of nature begin to take on human form. They began, in a word, to be personified.

The humanization of the sacred was a long and gradual process, not an abrupt transformation. Indeed, it is hard to determine from the wall paintings and carvings in the shrines of early cities, where animal and human figures are almost invariably linked, together, whether the animal or the human is the god. It would be many centuries before the gods lost completely their animal qualities and came to be concretized in exclusively human form. But the beginnings of that transformation lie here, in the cities that date to 7000 and 6000 BCE. And the increasing dominance of the human form over the animal with which it is associated in ancient city shrines reflects the projection into the sacred world of both a dawning human consciousness and a growing sense of control over the physical world and the human's "animal" nature.

The heightened attention in sacred art to the human form also intensified the distinction between gods and goddesses by role and gender. The female form, especially swollen with child, had been associated from the earliest of tribal times with the mysteries of creation, fertility, and the capacity of the earth to bring forth grains and creatures in an endless process of regeneration. Perhaps because of the litheness of maidens and their fleetness of foot, and the role of women, children, and the hearth in the domestication of dogs, the female also came to be associated with such coursing creatures of the hunt as leopards and wolves. The figures associated with the human hunting of large and powerful game like the aurochs, bison, and bull, on the other hand, were almost exclusively male. Over time, the female form came to represent all that was most mysterious and transformational—in a word, *biological,* for human understanding of biological processes has always lagged far behind our understanding of the mechanical, even to this day. The male form, on the other hand, came to represent the physical forces of nature, overwhelming strength, and mechanical power.

As the forces of nature took on more human form in the early cities, the evolving gods and goddesses apparently lived together in harmony, for there are shrines devoted to both, and some archaeological evidence suggests that their interactions were metaphorically modeled on that most central of human institutions, the family. As hunting declined in significance for city dwellers, however, and dependence on agriculture and domesticated flocks increased, the evolving female deities seem to have become more central in importance, and the conception of the increasingly humanized sacred world took on that hierarchical structure we call a matriarchy, with the male figures, even in the sacred family, in subordinate positions. It is not unlikely that in this, too, the sacred world re-flected the social structure of early cities. For the cities depended on trade, and there is good reason to suppose that the earliest of spinners and weavers, jewelers and mirror makers, basket-weavers and potters, sculptors and even painters were predominantly women, not men. Even agriculture and the tending of domesti-cated wildfowl and flocks, associated as they are with gathering, child-rearing, and the hearth, may have been more the work of women and children than of men, while men undertook the heavier and riskier tasks of mining the local ores, cut-ting and hauling blocks of stone and salt, erecting the walls and houses of the city, organizing and coordinating its building projects and defense. If this were indeed the case, then women would have held roles of central importance in city life, and the preponderance of female deities in the shrines and sacred objects of the early cities would make much sense. All the more if women were the earliest of the city's weavers, sculptors, and painters, for we do incline to shape our gods to our own ways and image.

In retrospect it is easy to see that the gender identification of the forces of na-ture, their personification as gods and goddesses of human character and form, the identification of the female with the more potent and awesome mysteries of the biological world, and the subordination of the male in relations of sacred, if not secular power would lead eventually to disaster for the relations between the sexes, and especially for women. For the mysterious and unpredictable forces of nature and the goddesses who came to represent them were objects of awesome fear, and while one may serve, one more often hates than loves what is most powerful in inspiring dread, particularly if one is relegated to the state of servant.

As the cities evolved through history, men both learned the female arts and crafts in their extended childhood at their mothers' knees and expanded their own mastery of the skills of mining and building, organizing and acting in units and groups. And in the end it was organization and physical engineering that made the later cities of the Bronze Age centers of power and might, channeled the rivers, tamed the land, brought nature more and more under man's control. As shrines expanded to temples, moreover, becoming centers of precious goods, repositories of surplus, hubs of human congress and trade, the men who began as servants of the goddesses became the keepers and disposers of their wealth and the intermediaries of their frowns and favors. And when the marking and recording of goods and transactions evolved into writing, the servants of the goddesses became the keepers of their secrets and the writers—and re-writers—of the sacred tales. Then there would be revolution and war between the sexes in the sacred, if not the secular world, and powerful sons and consorts of the goddesses would rise up to trick and depose, banish and slay their awesome mothers, subordinate them to the male will, drive them out to the deepest recesses of the world and imprison them there in the darkness at the margins, forever controlled and limited in their power by the superior knowledge and force of the gods and of god-sprung men. Such was the fate of the goddesses in their great reversal of fortune, and it would echo forever in the written tales of the sacred and in the relations between the sexes in the secular world of citified men.

All that was as yet far off at the beginnings of cities, but the seeds were planted then. Among those seeds was the evolution of shrines from their probable origins as simple markers of holy places where the sacred was revealed, into houses, homes, dwelling places for the increasingly human-like gods. At first these were, like the houses of the people on which they were modeled, simple affairs, distinguished only by the richness of the carvings, wall paintings, and fabric hangings that represented their sacred occupants. But as the gods grew more attached to specific places, in the minds of the men and women who elaborated them, larger numbers of people from the outlying fields and villages would travel to their shrines for the communal enactment of sacred rituals, bringing gifts for their gods and produce to trade for the crafted goods of the city's artisans. As the size of the gatherings at shrines and their stores of sacred objects and offerings increased, so did the buildings that housed them and the attention required for their maintenance and care.

At first, it seems, these were communal responsibilities. But as the size and functions of shrines increased, the custom grew of housing caretakers there. Perhaps these were, in their origins, the surplus people of the city: maidens not yet married, and a burden on their too-populous households; men rich in tribal wisdom but too elderly, infirm, or disabled by accident to hunt, reap, build, or practice their trades. To these would fall the special role of tending the growing shrines, guarding and maintaining the ritual objects, lighting the sacred fires to burn the offerings of grain and sweet-smelling grasses and, when these exceeded what even the hungriest of gods could smell and eat, storing them or trading them for more durable and precious gifts. Thus grew up, we may imagine, that special role among the diverse occupations of city life that consisted of serving the gods and goddesses in their shrines: the role that would evolve, as shrines grew into larger and wealthier and more complex temples, into the increasingly complex and powerful role of priests.

But the centralization of communal activity—particularly, the enactment of sacred ritual—around the Shrines that served as the local dwellings of increasingly personified gods and goddesses did more than concentrate the leadership of ritual and the enchantment of sacred tales in the hands of an emerging class of priests. It also contributed to the growing complexity of social uses of space, and there-fore to subtle changes in *conceptions* of both sacred and secular space. In particular, it intensified the differentiation of spaces according to the kinds of activities and engagements of others that occurred in them, and simultaneously differentiated activities and engagements of others by the spaces in which they took place. As *communal* activity and engagements with strangers centered more around shrines, the home became more differentiated as a space where those most closely linked by ties of blood were separated from others, set apart. In effect, we may say, by intensifying the idea of a *public* space, the shrine gave rise to its opposite: the idea of *private* space, centered in the home.

The development of the shrine as the central location for the communal cel-ebration of sacred ritual also intensified both the separation of the world of the sacred from the world of the profane and the localization of the sacred in a partic-ular place. In saying this, I do not mean that the city dwellers of 7000–5000 BCE would have thought of their gods as bound to the shrines that came to be seen as their local homes. Far from it. The gods were more inclined, in fact, to wander than to settle, changing both their abodes and shapes at will—for their human character was as yet but a shallow overlay on their old animist and nomadic nature.

Keeping the gods with the people and maintaining their favor required their continuous wooing with gifts, enticement with ever larger and more splendid homes, and propitiation with thank offerings from those things the gods (if they are happy and well-fed) perpetually regenerate and provide: the grains and other produce of the land, the wild and domesticated beasts on which humans de-pend to survive. For as the unpredictable forces of nature came to be modeled metaphorically on the human form, they also became the repositories—the out-ward projections—of human feelings and needs: took pleasure in the delights of the senses, in objects of beauty, in the comforts of home; were inclined to wrath when hungry or thirsty or disobeyed; were mollified by flattery and gifts, by sweet perfumes and song; felt anger and envy, jealousy and pride, lust and pity. And they made these feelings known, grumbling and roaring their displeasure in the voices of violent winds and thunder, shaking the ground and spewing forth fire in their wrath, bringing forth new life in abundance when well-fed and pleased.

But it was not only in nature that the gods expressed their rage and delight, their lust and envy, pleasure and greed. They also spoke and moved in the bodies of women and men, making them tremble with desire or shake with rage, moving them to strike out in anger or dance in ecstasy. Or so it seemed to the people of that time, judging from the patterns of the tales that long outlived them and left their traces when they came to be written down in the later cities of 3000 BCE. In those earliest of written tales, transcribed from the oral accounts repeated in chant and dance across decades of centuries, it is the gods who speak and move in the passions of women and men—not the men and women themselves. And thus it must have seemed to be. For having projected the most visible and vital aspects of themselves and their experience onto the mysteries of nature to give the outer world an accounting, the people of early cities introjected their own metaphor to explain themselves to themselves, to give the inner world an accounting.

This is not to say that the new conception of the human self as god-inhabited, god-driven replaced the older, animist account. Rather, it was overlaid on and integrated with the older metaphor, just as human figures were overlaid on and integrated with the animal figures that had dominated the cave art of the Pleistocene, in early city wall paintings and carvings, and as these composite figures would be overlaid in turn by images of god as father, as sculptor, as architect and engineer, lawgiver and judge, as clockmaker, as mathematical equation, as chemist, and, in our own time, perhaps as computer programmer and systems engineer. With each such projection of our own changing experience onto nature and the invisible forces behind it, we internalize a corresponding metaphor of ourselves that guides the way we explain ourselves to ourselves—what "drives" and "moves" us, "struggles" within us, "shapes" our thoughts and "governs" our feelings, "programs" our responses and "directs" our learning, makes us "tick" or makes us "explode."

Each age gives rise to new metaphors of the world and of the self, and the new may eclipse the old for a time, giving rise to new ways of treating ourselves and each other and the world: new ways of defining our problems and new social practices and programs for remediating them, new institutions and designs for improving ourselves, our relations with other, and the natural world. But the older metaphors do not disappear. They are codified in our languages and techniques, preserved and reiterated in drawings, carvings, and paintings, resurrected in dance and song and drumbeats, passed on in old and modern tales. And they are also born each generation anew, in the ages and stages of our personal encounters with the world and with others, with symbols and machines, with animals and earthquakes, with joy and terror, with death and newborn life.

And so our accounts of the self are not a simple story but a palimpsest—a tale sung or written over time and time and time again, in layers too dense with age and fused by experience to peel off and string out tidily in a single, simple line. Beneath the modern conception of the cool computing self, there still lie the clockworks and steam-driven psyches of the mechanical age, and the animal snarls and hungers and howls of rage that go back to far earlier times. And overlaid and intermixed with them we may still hear the thunderous voices and tremble with the awe and pity that are the marks in us even today of the earliest personified gods. If the conception of self of early city dwellers seems less densely layered, more simple than our own, that is because they had as yet no machines, few encounters with others, and only a handful of media—speech and enactment, carving and painting—to preserve and complicate their tales.

But they had media enough to set in motion another conceptual change that would, in its Bronze Age flowering, alter forever the telling of human tales. For with settlement and building in stone, and the carving, stamping, *marking* of surfaces of every kind that accompanied the flourishing of early crafts and art, there gradually evolved a new conception of time. And while that conception did not yet correspond to what we mean by "history," it was a necessary forerunner to it.

Human settlement—the long-term attachment to a single place—is of itself an important step in the evolution of the conceptual separation of space from time, for it provides a fixed vantage point from which to observe changes in the world around. Such a stable vantage point is critically important in helping us separate changes in ourselves from changes in *it*—in the world that moves while we stand still, changes while we remain the same. Our own stillness, moreover, heightens our attentiveness to the changes around us, and the longer we are still, the more likely we are to become attuned to the patterns and rhythms of change in our surroundings. To the occasional visitor of a hospitalized friend, for example, the comings and goings of doctors, nurses, and staff, the rattle of meal trays and medicine carts, and the frequency of interruptions may seem chaotic and unpredictable. But to the patient who has been confined there long enough, they have a familiar rhythm that, if he is well enough, may by itself tell him the hour and day in the absence of a calendar or clock to mark the time. To observe the longer cycles and periodicities of the natural world—the tides and seasons, the slow circling of the stars—would require, though, a much longer place-bound time.

The early cities of the Neolithic Age were not, of course, the first experience humans had of being confined to a single place for a significant time. The caves that had sheltered earlier tribes during the preceding age of ice must have been home at least to some for times as long as a season—long enough, at any rate, for those who kept watch at the mouths of caves in the enforced stillness of the perilous nights to note the continuous changing of the inconstant moon while they remained in the same place. Or so it seems, for here and there among the carved bones and stones of those earlier times have been some with mysterious marks that archaeologists have read as early representations of the phases of the moon. They well may be—for the moon dominates the night sky, even when seen only in part from the overhang of a cave. It appears when men and women themselves are still, and it changes in cycles short enough to repeat several times during a period of relatively short permanent habitation. Perhaps it is these factors that account for the fact that the earliest of calendars everywhere are tied to the phases and cycles of the moon.

But it is a long way from observing cycles in nature to the idea of ordering human events around them, and then counting by them, and then counting back along a line of repeated events to distinguish one moment from another in the retelling of one's sacred—and secular—history. It is easiest, perhaps, to see how the first of these developments emerged and was intensified by the gathering of increasing numbers of people around the earliest of cities and their shrines. While the bringing of offerings to the personified goddesses and gods and the communal enactment of their rituals would not, at first, have been "scheduled" (in our modern sense), it would seem natural enough that the largest numbers would gather at those phases of the moon that are most visually striking and most awe- and fear-inspiring: its fullness, in which the goddess is at the height of her power and potency, rich in fecundity and smiling with favor; its darkness, at which the goddess withdraws from sight and her people, perhaps never to return; and its first reappearance, at which the goddess both returns and demonstrates her awesome power by mysteriously regenerating herself out of nothing. At such moments, we may guess, the crowds that gathered and the communal rituals of thanksgiving or propitiation would be at their peak of intensity. Thus the most elaborate and significant of sacred activities might begin to be tied to a "calendar" of lunar events. Since such celebrations would also be filled with emotional fervor and intensity, and thus stand out in memory, they might also come to serve as the markers, in speech, of other significant events coinciding with them: this child was born at the last coming of the full moon; this dove is set aside to thank the goddess at her next return. While such habits of thought and language are still far from what we call "dating," they lay the groundwork for it by organizing memory and forethought around events tied to a rudimentary "calendar" marked by periodic, and *visible*, changes in the natural world.

In one important respect, however, the periodicities and cycles of natural change are not what we mean by a "calendar" at all. For our ideas of calendars and of time—and especially our ideas of *history*—are not based only on the idea of cycles and periodicity. They are also based on the idea that time *passes*—and passes permanently, not in a cycle of eternal renewal and return, but in a stream, a progression that permits no "going back" or "coming again." Our notion of history, in short, is a notion of events strung out in succession, each one occurring (as we would say) at a different moment in forward-moving time, like beads on a string or stones in a wall to which we may point and say, "There. That is where we were *then*. And this is where we are *now*."

The people of the earliest cities did, of course, link beads on string. More important for their conceptions of time, they built not one, but many walls. And a wall may serve, over the time of its construction, as a new kind of calendar: not a natural and sacred calendar, like the cycles of the moon, but a human and secular calendar showing the forward movement of events over time. Its stone and levels are permanent and visible indicators, to the people who are raising them, of the difference between "today" and "yesterday" and the days that came before, which stretch back over space in the visible structure of the completed parts of the wall. It is likely, too, that some of the sections and levels of their walls served the people who raised them as markers of significant occurrences during their construction: Here is where the earth shook and the stones rained down and many died; there is where my arm was crushed; here is where you were born and your mother died. Here was a time of plenty; there a time of famine. Thus a wall might come to function not only as an extensional mnemonic device—a physical structure for storing and retrieving memory outside the human skin—but also as a rudimentary timetable for the unfolding story of its builders' secular life. In both respects, walls and the processes of building played an important role in the changing architecture of human conceptions of time, adding to the perpetual circles and cycles of nature the beginnings of a quite different idea: the idea of human events as a sequence, a movement forward and upward, like the sections and levels of a wall or a tower, in a progression over time. And that, we may say, is the beginning of the idea of history.

But we must be careful not to think, in our own attempts to construct the human past, that "history" is a smooth, unbroken line, a single path that all peoples trod to some inevitable destiny of their own progressive making. We are not so uniform, or so powerful, as that. The peoples of the past, like ourselves, were shaped differently by the different ecosystems into which they wandered—by the vagaries of climate and geological formation that gave rise to different kinds of shelters and sustenance, different natural resources for building and trading, different needs for protection, association with others, cooperation, defense. Some settled and some did not. Some built in rushes and mud, some in snow, some in wood, some in stone; some had no need to build at all. Some made boats, not walls. Thus different peoples in different places developed different ways of doing and thinking, different paths to travel for a while, with unforeseen twists and bends. And so the cultures and conceptions and consciousnesses of ancient times differed and diverged.

And sometimes, for some peoples, the paths they followed came to abrupt and disastrous ends. The ruins of the earliest cities do not tell a tale of continuous habitation by the same people, evolving steadily toward the great civilizations of the Nile and the Indus Valley, of the Mediterranean and Mesopotamian Bronze Age. They tell, instead, of successive abandonments and rehabitations by peoples of different ways. What befell the original inhabitants, or those who followed them and were replaced by others in their turn, we cannot say. Perhaps their walls and their gods failed them and they were overrun by others, or famine and drought, deluge and disease came upon them and those who survived were driven out, or carried off, or simply wandered away. But they would not have left as they came, for just as the centuries of settlement and building, agriculture and trade left their marks on the land, so did they leave the settlers and builders and traders changed. And they would have carried those changes with them when they left their cities to enter again the restless stream of people in perpetual movement across the still-changing, lifting and settling, warming and drying land.

For all the haunting imagery and profound point of Shelley's "Ozymandias," the traveler who narrates the tale has it wrong when he says, of the vast ruin in the desert, "Nothing beside remains." Sand, wind, and water may destroy what humans build, but they do not easily erase the memory of building or the habits of thought and social behavior that result from building, trade, and generations of city life. The survivors who fled or were driven from the earliest of cities would have carried with them something of their skills and learning, if not their artifacts—and every artifact is in itself an embodiment of a possibility and how to achieve it, a material repository of a skill and an idea. More important, they would have carried with them, in their speech and graphic symbols, their rituals and chanted tales, the evolving conceptions of human-ness and personhood, of self and the sacred, of time and space that arose out of the complex material, social, and symbolic ecology of early city life. What others the outcasts met, and whether they settled to build again, and where other cities of a century or a thousand years may lie beneath the rocky mounds or modern metropolises or shifting desert sands today, we do not know. But the idea of the city and all its nascent conceptions spread and survived. The great and powerful city-states of the Bronze Age did not spring up in a century or a millennium out of delta soil or desert sand. They were built, like Bronze Age Jericho, on ground prepared thousands of years before by people drawn together by weakness, not strength, to gouge a trench, erect a tower, and raise a wall.

CHAPTER NINE

Sounds of Silence: The Evolution of Writing

As I write, the scientific community is astir with excitement and perplexity at the news of an unexpected discovery about the movement of the galaxies at the farthest reaches of the universe—a discovery that, if it stands, may require astronomers and astrophysicists to revise, once again, the way we tell the tale of cosmological origins and endings. It is too early to say what far-reaching consequences the Postman-Lauer findings may have for our accounts of the cosmos, the world, and ultimately ourselves. But it is a safe bet that whatever those consequences may be, they cannot approach in scope or significance the world—and tale—altering impact of a little heralded change in the more mundane affairs of men and women some 5500 years ago, in the bustling Bronze Age cities of 4000–3000 BCE. The change I am speaking of was neither a discovery nor an invention, in the sense we usually use those words. It was an innovation in the practices of those who stored and supervised the exchange of surplus grains and oils and fruits for livestock, and who crafted goods and labor in the lively and complex trade that fueled city-centered life where the Tigris and Euphrates rivers met, in the Mesopotamia of the Fourth to the Third Millennium BCE. The innovation consisted of adding to the clay tablets on which items were identified a set of marks that were neither pictorial representations of the objects nor images associated with their owners, but symbols indicating the sounds of the owner's spoken name.

Thus began the process of inscribing the spoken word that would culminate, around 1500 BCE, in alphabetic writing—and an entirely new way of encountering, constructing, and accounting for the world.

The evolution of writing is itself a rich and complex tale involving many of the world's people and places, and many a mystery that we are unlikely ever to understand. Indeed, even to choose a particular event as the "beginning" of the story of writing is in some measure arbitrary, for while it is accurate to say that the development of true writing hinged on the use of inscribed signs to represent speech sounds, it also depended on a host of earlier practices and of circumstances that fostered and modified them. Thus it might be argued, for example, that writing originated when people first began to draw, paint, or carve on their shields, knife handles, and pots the image of that god or animal whose power, favor, or skill was particularly important to the user of the article. Over time, such images on objects, originally employed for their religious/magical powers, would also come to serve as ways of identifying articles with the particular persons whose distinctive designs they bore. This was indeed a critical condition for the evolution of writing, for writing is connected to trade, and such identifying marks are essential to the idea of *property* on which complex trade depends.

I do not mean, in saying this, that prior to the use of identifying marks on objects people had no sense of possession, no feelings that correspond to our words, "This is *mine*." Of course they did. The impulse to hold onto what one has and to defend it against the encroachments of others plays a major role in the survival of most animal species, and is easily observed in the behavior of children who do not yet speak, let alone draw or write. But in the absence of identifying markers or signs, "ownership" is entirely a matter of immediate physical possession: what is "mine" is what I have in my hands or on my person and can hold against takers; what is "yours" is what is in your possession, so long as it remains with you. But the idea of *property* goes beyond those things that are in one's physical possession. It is an extension of one's person to objects not in one's grasp, by marking them with one's personal sign.

In its origins, this practice is not very different from the animal's marking of its territorial "property" by leaving its distinctive scent on the trees and stones that establish its boundaries. And there is little doubt that the early human "property signs" were equally potent in their effects on others. It is important to remember that in the early uses of images and inscribed signs, as in the early uses of speech sounds, people did not fully grasp the signal/sign distinction. Images of things were experienced not as mere arbitrary representations of the objects they depicted but as deeply connected to them—*part* of them, as the scent of an animal is part of the animal. Thus the image of a god or of an animal sacred to the god, drawn on one's shield or carved on one's blade haft, was no mere decoration; it imbued the object with the spirit and power of the god so "captured." It also imbued the object with the spirit and power of the person who drew or carved the image. For in the thought-world of the early Bronze Age, the animist "theory" of life and nature still dominated human ways of accounting for the world seen and unseen, and a central conception in that worldtale is the belief that part of the animating spirit in persons passes into those things they create or have long and close contact with.

It is well to remember, if we are inclined to deride such beliefs and doubt their potency some five or six thousand years ago, that they linger in many a rational mind even today. Though I am embarrassed to confess it, I am among those whose desk drawers overflow with letters from loved ones long out of date, because I feel a strange reluctance to destroy what seems so imbued with the spirit of those who inscribed them. I have file drawers full of the finger paintings and childish drawings of my long grown niece and nephew, and something more than fond recollection slows my hand when I am moved to trash them in favor of my tax records. Others handle with the special reverence of communion the useless objects that were once the intimate possessions of the cherished dead. Or find more than nostalgic comfort in preserving unchanged the room where a lost loved one dreamed in the bed, sat at the desk, handled daily the objects on the dresser, and so imbued them with her lingering spirit. Even collectors of original works of art, and fans who bid thousands of dollars for, say, a headscarf worn by Marilyn Monroe—or some doodle scribbled on a napkin by Picasso—are often moved by more than the intrinsic appeal and social cachet of the article and its investment potential; they feel, as well, that secret stirring of the untutored heart that tells them what they hold in their hands is more than a fine drawing or a lovely piece of silk: it is also a fragment of the spirit of Monroe, a piece of the soul of Picasso. If such whispers of archaic belief are loud enough to echo in the mind's ear even today, after 500 years of science and of habituation to endlessly-reproduced images and words, how much more awesome and compelling must have been the magic of the inscribed word and image when they were new. And that magic was the underlying power that made possible the idea of *property*—of articles invested with the spirit of their owners and the protection of the gods because they bore upon them the god's own image and the absent owner's distinctive sign.

As techniques of irrigation and agriculture improved in the villages surrounding the nascent cities of ancient Sumer (in modern Iraq), some 6000 years ago, and techniques of building and producing crafted goods improved in the growing cities, surplus goods increased. So did the means for storing and transporting them across distances for trade: stoppered jars and pots of fired clay protected grains and oils from spoilage and pests, and by 3500 BCE, the wheeled cart had been invented to transport them. And as the use of containers grew and the traffic in trade goods increased, new needs arose for identifying both owners with their property and containers with their contents.

An early solution to the problem of efficient property identification, at least among those with many goods to trade, was the cylinder seal—a small stone shaped into a smooth cylinder and carved around its surface with the drawing, usually some set of sacred images, that served as the owner's distinctive sign. Rolled across wet clay, the cylinder seal would reproduce, quickly and without variation, the pattern identified with its owner. The shape of the seal suggests that it was originally used to roll a continuous pattern around curved surfaces, such as the rims of pots and jars before they were fired, thus marking both the containers and their contents as the property of the person or family whose sign they displayed. But such seals could also be used to impress the image on small, flat tablets of clay which, holed and fired, might be attached as "tags" to goods of any kind—including those not suited by their shape for storage in jars. It is likely that a similar solution was found to the problem of identifying, at a glance, the contents of the opaque pots and jars in which seeds, grains, and oils of different kinds were stored and delivered for exchange. Initially, we may guess, the pots were marked while wet with a design whose pattern pictured the objects to be stored in them: wheat sheaves for the grains, palm fronds for the dates, and so on. Indeed, some of the early pot designs that we admire for their aesthetic value are like to have served not primarily as decorations but as identifying signs of their contents. In time, these signs too came to be transferred to small, perforated tablets that could easily be attached to plainer, cheaper pots to indicate their contents.

The shift from inscribing or impressing pictorial signs directly on the objects they identified to inscribing them on detachable "tags" was a critical step in the development of writing. It parallels the separation of sounds from the immediate contexts of their use that was necessary for the evolution of full symbolic speech, and had much the same consequences. For when the direct physical connection between objects and their picture-signs was broken, and the signs stood alone on tablets, they became available for a different "connection": not to their objects, but to the *words* that represented them. And that is the beginning of logographic writing: a system of visible marks that stand, not directly for objects and events, but for the words of spoken language.

To say that marking picture-signs of things on clay "tags" and detaching them from objects made those signs "available" for the connection to words, however, is not to say that the new connection was made immediately, or that the signs were quickly used for "writing" as we understand it. Several steps intervened between the use of picture-signs on trade-good tags and the early logographic or word-sign writing system the Sumerians developed around 3500 BCE. To understand its evolution, we need a clearer picture of social and economic life in Sumer's burgeoning cities, principally Uruk (Biblical "Erech") and Lagash, as archaeologists have drawn it.

As in the earlier cities that predated them by 4000 years, life in Uruk and Lagash centered around their numerous temples. Unlike the simple one-room shrines that preceded them, the temples of Sumer were large and lavish structures that climbed, step-like, toward the heavens, as layer upon layer of new bricks and buttressed walls were laid upon older foundations. The largest of the temples were dedicated to the four nature gods and goddesses of heaven, earth, air, and water. But they also housed the extended "families" of deities to which these had given rise, some of whom had in addition separate temples of their own.

According to some estimates, the Sumerians honored some 3000–4000 deities by the Third Millennium—evidence of the diversity of tribes and clans who mingled and enriched knowledge and culture in the cities and surrounding villages on the soil-rich plains. Their rites and the continuous expansion and elaboration of their temples required the services and skills of many—not only priests and priestesses, but stonemasons and carvers, potters and jewelers, sculptors and weavers. And the working of the communal lands set aside for the needs of the gods and their temples required still more laborers, all of whom must be housed and clothed and provided with the tools and household goods needed for daily life.

Thus the temples of Sumer not only served as centers of religious activity and public gathering, and as ideal storehouses and redistribution centers for the surplus fruits and grains that preserved well in the cool darkness within their layered walls; they also served as major employers of both city-dwelling artisans and agricultural workers in the surrounding countryside. One set of temple accounts recorded after the development of writing, around 3100 BCE, shows that it provided 1200 men and women with daily rations of bread and beer, and employed 205 women and their children as spinners, weavers, and dyers in a cloth-making shop, in addition to cooks and bakers, herders and fishermen, guards and scribes. Moreover, since the lands in the plains surrounding the cities of Sumer were rich in soil but devoid of the stone, alabaster, marble, and steatite needed for building and sculpture, the temple also engaged in extensive trade for such materials with caravans that traveled from the distant mountains of the north and east, and even from such far off lands as those we now call India, Afghanistan, and Iran.

All of these activities required careful inventories of the temple's goods and resources, ways to track what came in and went out, the development of standard units of both time (for assessing the exchange value of labor) and measure, the establishment of uniform rates of exchange, and the development of methods of counting. Above all, they required ways of storing all this information outside the limited capacities of human memory. For while the ability of people in oral cultures—i.e., cultures that have never known writing—to commit experience to memory and retrieve it intact, is astounding in comparison to our own limited ability, the demands of trade posed an unprecedented problem of information storage and retrieval that human memory alone was, and is, incapable of handling. That problem had to do only in part with the exponential increase in the *amount* of information that trade generated and required. Much more important, *trade introduced into human affairs a new kind of information—information of a type that rendered inadequate all the strategies and devices of oral mnemonics.*

To understand why trade overwhelmed the strategies of oral memory, it is necessary to reflect briefly on the ways in which people managed the preservation of information in the long eons that intervened between the evolution of spoken language and the development of writing. Many fine books have been written on this subject, and the reader curious about oral mnemonics will want to consult them. But for the sake of economy here, let me reduce what has been said to a handful of points.

The most central of these is that the unaided memory works by weaving events and experiences into patterned wholes, so that the whole triggers recollection of the parts. In Chapter 5, I used the homey example of a dinner plan—for lasagna and cheesecake—to illustrate how a "whole" (like lasagna) helps us to remember individual items needed in the absence of a written list—assuming, of course, that one has made lasagna many times and thus knows what goes into it. This is in fact a critical requirement, for if one had no experience of making lasagna, or if the ingredients were totally different each time, the "whole" would be quite useless for generating recall of the individual parts. Thus patterned wholes work as means for remembering only repeated experiences that do not much vary in their "contents" over time.

Of course, we frequently need to remember things much more extensive or complicated than the few ingredients of cheesecake and lasagna. In such cases, we may weave them into quite different patterns. I have a friend, a frequent traveler, who packs for his extended journeys not by making a written list (as I do), but by standing before his open suitcase and telling himself the story of his day. "I awaken late..." (in goes the alarm clock) "after a sleepless night..." (sleeping pills; pajamas; boring book; cigarettes) "and head for the shower..." (soap; shampoo) "to clear my head..." (aspirin; Alka-Seltzer) "and scrape the night's growth off my teeth and jaw..." (toothbrush and paste; mouthwash; shaving cream and razor)... and so on, through dressing, reviewing his notes (glasses; speech, yellow pads; felt pens), meeting his hosts (appointment book; phone numbers), dining and traveling about the city (cash and credit cards; coat and umbrella), and returning at last to his room for relaxation (comfortable clothes), calls to home (phone card) and sleep. In effect, my friend constructs a narrative of his life on the road, and the structure of the tale reminds him of the things he will need. He does not always tell the story in the same way, of course. Over the years of his travels, he has made various insertions and amendments—like "It is hot," or "But the weather has turned"— that reflect somewhat different experiences and give him slightly different tales (and reminders of different things to pack). Nor does he repeat the whole story on every occasion. I first learned of it in a drugstore where we happened to stop a few days before an upcoming trip and he decided to resupply his toiletries—to the cadences of the part that might be titled (if it were written) "Morning." I have since heard other segments on different shopping expeditions. Each unit has a structure of its own, marked by personal doings in temporal sequence, and can be pulled out for some particular purpose, or skipped, or moved around in the whole (if some part of the packing is already done). And it doesn't much matter which part comes first, since the days will cycle round in much the same way whether he begins with morning, afternoon, or evening. The pattern as a whole remains largely the same, because that is in fact how his days away largely go, or so it seems to him when he reflects on his oft-repeated experiences.

My friend's "packing narrative" has many of the characteristics of the oral narratives in which people before writing recounted and communicated the experiences most important to the family, clan, and tribe: their sacred histories and accounts of the origins of things and practices; their genealogies and ties of kinship; their observations of the ways of animals and of growing things; their beliefs about the awesome gods and how they might be pacified. Like his, their stories were patterned wholes whose over-all structure helped them to remember the parts. As in his, the parts were units with structures of their own, "episodes that could be skipped" or moved around for different occasions and purposes, or might stand alone. Like his, their narratives were not precisely uniform, but incorporated variations and amendments as experience changed over time. And like his, their narratives preserved the memory of what they recounted and triggered recall of countless other events and practices it was vitally important not to forget.

But the narratives of oral peoples in the time before writing were also different from my friend's in important respects. His is memorable to him because it is tied to a figure of central importance: himself. It is a *personal* account. Those of tribal peoples were communal accounts; to be memorable, they had to be tied to figures familiar enough for ready identification yet powerful enough to capture the imagination and passions of all. And they were. Through the processes of person-ification and the linking of animals and tribal ancestors to the world of the sacred there emerged in oral tales central characters that were both recognizably human in their traits and vastly larger than life in their powers and exploits. In his work on the narratives of oral peoples, Walter Ong calls these central figures "heavy" characters, drawn to greatly exaggerated proportions yet oddly "flat" or stereotypical in their outlines: this creature always cunning; that hero always wily; this god soft of speech; that one always vengeful. Such characters strike the modern reader as strangely one-dimensional in relation to the subtle complexity of, say, an Anna Karenina or a Holden Caulfield. But in the context of an oral environment, their exaggerated features, like the vastly amplified intensity of their struggles, clashes, and passions, make them and their doings far more memorable.

Of course, personification and exaggeration did not *arise* out of the intent to make characters, and therefore tales, memorable—any more than narratives arose for the conscious purpose of remembering things. To argue so would be to make the fundamental error of confusing the origins of things with the functions they may come to serve—akin to arguing, for example, that speech evolved for the purpose of giving directions, or flowers so that people might have gardens. The roots of narrative, of personification, and of the superhuman scale that characterizes oral tales lie in complex social and symbolic processes stretching back to the origins of speech and even beyond, as I have tried to show in preceding chapters. But the storytelling practices and features to which they gave rise also functioned superbly well as means of storing and retrieving vast amounts of vital information from memory, and passing it on.

Like the narrative structure and the "heavy" character, the internal rhythms and rhymes of oral tales, and their incantation to the sounds of accompanying music and the regular movements of dance, also date back to their roots in ritual enactments. And these features, too, played a central role in the mnemonics of oral peoples. As anyone knows who has tried to commit a list of any kind to memory, assigning it a rhythmic beat and reciting it in a sing-song cadence of pitches and pauses is an enormous help. Indeed, most of us would find it difficult to recognize, let alone recite, even our own phone numbers without the rhythmic 3–4 beat and patterns of stresses we give them, or our social security numbers without their 3-2-4 beat and distinctive modulations of pitch. You will also know, if you have ever tried to recall a poem you have memorized, how important rhyme is for filling in the blanks where memory has temporarily failed. And as for music—well, you might be surprised how quickly the words of songs you would swear you know by heart disappear from memory if you are required to *say* them without singing. You might try, for example, "The Star-Spangled Banner"—no chanting or singing permitted. (Most people can't get beyond "light" without a quick hum through.)

Modern advertisers are, of course, well aware of the power of music, rhyme, rhythm, and repetition to carve into our memories even things we will ourselves *not* to remember. Thousands of New Yorkers of my generation are walking around today with the mysterious number, Melrose 5–5300, engraved indelibly on their brains—and no idea what it *means*—because it was sung *ad infinitum* on the radio (before there was TV), to a catchy tune and the accompaniment of a little bell. Even long lists of unfamiliar names can be committed to memory by otherwise normal people, if the lists are subdivided into units, rhythmatized, set to song, and performed communally. I know this because my entire third-grade Sunday School class was set to memorizing, for the greater glory of God (or our teacher), the names, in order, of the 66 books of the Old and New Testaments—many of which we could not even pronounce. These were divided into uneven groups (the books of Law, History, Poetry, etc.), each group given a little melody of its own, while the whole was linked by a repeated refrain whose mindless repetition gave us time to recall which set/song came next. Forty years later, I know them still, as do my siblings, who were set the same task in their turn. And this on no motivation stronger than, as I remember, the pleasure of the task, the singing, the company, and the performance before our properly astonished parents. But perhaps that should not surprise. The ease and apparent joy with which children of all ages learn the lyrics of countless popular songs confirm that there is something deeply pleasurable in it that makes the feats of memory of oral peoples, not the less prodigious, but somewhat less astounding.

To sum up, then: people without systems of writing committed enormous amounts of information to memory, and preserved and passed it on, by weaving it into narratives composed of episodic sub-structures with patterns of their own, linked by means of over-all continuities of theme, metaphor, occasion, and character. These narratives dealt with the repeated experiences of the group and with matters of the utmost concern: the nature, origins, and history of things and people and the relations among them; accounts of the worlds seen and unseen and how they worked; the origins and proper conduct of practices of all kinds, from the sacred to the mundane. In addition to preserving tribal memory of what was recounted, the tales of oral people served as reminders of other associated experiences and practices. The tales themselves were made memorable by such internal devices as rhythm, rhyme, repeated phrases and epithets, familiar but "heavy" and stereotypical characters, bold sensory images, action stressing conflict and strongly aroused passion. The mnemonic power of these features, moreover, was reinforced and amplified by such "external" devices and conditions as their accompaniment by music, dance, and enactment in communal settings deeply associated with ritual and the awesome world of the sacred. Finally the tales were themselves repeated in whole or in part many times, and the experience of participating in their enchantment was both exciting and pleasurable—particularly, we may guess, to the young, whose minds were (and are) particularly susceptible to mnemonic learning.

But if oral peoples were able to preserve information so well through such devices, why should memory suddenly falter in the cities of 3500 BCE? What was there about trade that rendered useless the oral mnemonics that had served effectively for some 50,000 years?

The answers to those questions lie in the nature of the transactions that trade involved. Each was, to begin with, a different event, involving different participants and different goods exchanged in different quantities at different times—and it was the particulars of such exchanges, not their general patterns, that needed to be remembered. To be sure, there were some features of trade that came to be standardized over time—in particular, rates of exchange for those things most regularly traded: how many loaves of bread for how many days of labor, how many jars of oil for how many sheaves of grain. But these generalizations alone would not have been sufficient to track who contributed what to the temple's store of goods and was entitled to how much on presentation of a claim. While such details may well have been memorable to the individuals and families who brought their surplus for storage and trade, or spent their days in labor to receive bread and beer in exchange, they would scarcely be of equal import to the priests and assistants who oversaw hundreds of such exchanges daily, and of goods not their own.

Moreover, on the whole, those transactions involved people not linked to the priests by ties of family, clan, or tribe, but strangers. And as strangers they fell outside the mnemonic structures the served to remind people of their genealogies and the blood bonds among their own families and clans. Indeed, it is unlikely that those who conducted the temple trade would have thought to narratize the individual transactions at all. The narratives of oral peoples, after all, were not about the doings of strangers, but about their own-experiences and the ways of others, like animals and the gods, who were intimately connected to them.

But what most rendered the mnemonic techniques of oral people useless for the transactions of trade was the fact that the exchanges to be remembered changed daily. Even supposing there had been singers enough to compose a chanted hymn to remember each transaction by, what would have been the point? By week's end, the hundreds of transactions so committed to song would be out of date, and hundreds of new songs would be required.

Beyond all this there is one more point, speculative to be sure, but that must be considered. Among the most important details of the exchanges involved in the processes of trade were data about the *quantities* of what came into the common coffers and went out. And while there is no way to document it for certain, there is good reason to believe that, in early systems of counting, there were no spoken words that corresponded to our "twenty" or "nine" or "twelve." Though we may find it well-nigh impossible to grasp how people could have functioned at all without words for numbers, in the time before writing, it is quite likely that they did, and that number *names* evolved after, not before, visual means of counting.

By visual means of counting I mean the substitution of some token—say, a pebble or pot shard or notch carved in a stick—for each item in a set of things one might need, or need to keep track of, so that each token stands for one of them and the set of tokens as a group answers our question, "How many?" If one is building a wall, for example, and needs additional bricks to complete a section, so one might substitute a pebble for each missing brick, give the pebbles to an assistant, and send him to fetch a brick for each pebble he has. Such systems of "counting" by matching tokens to items work quite well so long as the items to be "counted" do not run into numbers so large as to make the tokens themselves difficult to carry around. In many early cultures, this problem was solved by substituting for pebbles and potsherds such more convenient "tokens" as knots tied in a rope or string and, later, by the convention of using a larger knot to stand for five or ten (or whatever) of the little ones—as we might use, for example, a closed fist to mean all five of the fingers. The point is that these means of "counting" by direct substitution of tokens for items do not require the use of number words. And in fact these seem not to have been in use before the development of writing. This gives us still another reason why oral mnemonics were useless for the transactions of trade: it is hardly possible to weave such transactions into narratives if one has no words to use for the quantities involved.

And judging from the oldest of inscribed ledger tablets found at Uruk, it was the quantities of goods and their kind, rather than the names of donors, that were most important to the temples to track. This makes sense if we assume that in the earliest days of trade, exchanges were made on the spot—i.e., so much oil handed over for so much grain brought in, with a measure for the temple gods set aside. In such transactions, the donor's name would not be necessary to recall, since his or her interest in the matter would terminate with the trade. But not so the temple's, for it would be vitally necessary to know, at the end of the day, how much of what goods had come in, how much of what had gone out, and what remained in store for the next day's trades—and for the temple's transactions with its own (or the gods' own) property. To provide such accounts, the temple elders set their young assistants the task, probably towards the end of the day, of tallying the identifying "tags" detached from goods as they were exchanged. These tallies were recorded on larger clay tablets by means of sorting the tags according to the items pictured on them, sketching that picture-sign on the wet tablet with a sharpened reed, and entering a mark for each tag that bore that sign.

But how did the picture-signs come to be understood as standing, not for the objects directly, but for the spoken words for those objects? The answer most probably lies in remembering that the tablets so created would have been useless unless they could be *read*—and by others than the recorder who inscribed them. And to be easily read, the drawing had to be uniform—stripped of the individual flourishes that characterized different recorder's drawings, and conventionalized. To this end, schools were established to teach the young inscribers how to make their marks the same. We may imagine that, for the purposes of drill, their teachers initially both pointed to the object to be rendered in a picture-sign and named it. As the number of objects and picture-signs for them increased, however, it would be less and less feasible to have the objects themselves available for pointing. (As any teacher can imagine, it would be difficult enough to maintain an orderly classroom of bored and restless young people without introducing into it, for instructional purposes, a flapping and squawking chicken or a lunging and bellowing bull.) Thus the young scribes would quickly come to drilled in their picture-signs by dictation of the spoken words alone—and through such repeated association, the signs would come to mean, for them, those *words*. Thus we may say that written signs changed from pictograms (object signs) to logograms (word-signs) through that process of de-contextualization (the separation of the pictures from the context of their object) and recontextualization (their use in the context of speech) that invariably underlies changes in meaning.

The intimate connection between the "writing" and the reading of ledger tablets also helps to explain how names for numbers evolved. If the young were trained by dictation and taught to "read back" their practice tablets aloud, they would soon have needed sounds for the quantities represented by their different number-marks. Different scribal cultures solved this problem differently—some inventing new sounds for numbers and some pressing existing sounds into double duty. But whatever the spoken words for numbers, they made it possible for scribes to record transactions, not from tallies of tags at day's end, but from dictation on the spot.

This change in practice, along with the increase in the speed of "writing" that came with standardized signs and repeated drill, may have played an important role in the evolution, around 3100 BCE, of the Sumerian cuneiform, or "wedge-shaped" script. The original pictorial signs used to represent objects, then words, in the earlier "writing" of 3500 BCE had been rounded, as were the shapes of the objects they initially depicted. But as fluency and familiarity with the signs increased, and scribes began to record transactions on the spot, the need arose for faster means of inscription. Because it is quicker and easier to impress straight marks on clay with a pointed stick than to draw curves, the logographs lost, over time, their roundness and were reduced to more abstracted shapes composed of a few straight marks. Since the impress of the point was heavier when the stylus was set on the wet clay and lighter as it was withdrawn, these marks left a characteristic wedge-shape, from which the newer style of writing, "cuneiform," takes its name. Cuneiform may have originated in the scribal schools of Sumer. But it is likely that its widespread use for trade was given impetus by the demands for speed in inscription that came with the practice of recording exchanges as they occurred.

By 3100 BCE, in fact, many changes had developed in the patterns of Sumerian trade. Among these was the separation in time between the donation of goods and labor and the payment (in other goods or services, not money) taken in exchange. This change—i.e., the notion of a deferred claim against goods and services rendered—made it important to record, along with the goods received and paid out, the identities of their donors and recipients. And that posed a new set of problems for the scribes of Sumer, because not everyone who came to trade had a cylinder seal or even a readily identifiable pictorial sign to distinguish himself or herself from others who may have chosen a similar design. Such devices work well enough to serve as identifiers of property and persons among smaller groups of people already known to one another, as in villages or tribes or when the person associated with a particular design occupies a position of such status and power that his or her mark is recognized even by strangers. But the identifying pictorial sign is not adequate for distinguishing the different people involved in hundreds of exchanges, particularly if many of them have no such recorded signs.

But everyone has a spoken name, and in the cities of ancient Sumer, the names of people contained enough information to distinguish one from another. The same complexity of names that allowed them to serve as distinctive identifiers, however, made them difficult to record by simple logographs and combinations (e.g., as one might record a simpler tribal name like "Flying Deer" by the picture of a bird flying and the picture of a deer). That principle—that complex words and names might be represented by combining signs for other things that the more complex word *sounded* like (e.g., "season" by combining for the *sound* "sea" and for the *sound* "sun") had been discovered much earlier, probably by bored young scribes in the back rows of their writing schoolrooms. (I say this only partly in jest. With apologies to Jane Austen and to dedicated teachers everywhere, it is a principle universally to be observed that healthy young people set to repetitive tasks in schoolrooms get bored, and in their boredom resort to playing with whatever limited materials they have at hand. I think it more than likely that the phonetic principle in writing originated in the doodles and whispers of the young in droning scribal schools, who entertained themselves by discovering combinations of logograms that generated the similar sounds of insults, vile names, and dirty words. Since true writing and all its world-changing consequences could not have evolved without the discovery of that phonetic principle, there is an important moral for frantic teachers here: we should not strive too desperately to control the wandering attentions of the young. Greater things may emerge out of their boredom than out of what we think important for them to learn.)

However the early principle of partial phonetic transfer evolved—that is, the use of word signs not for their original referents but for other words with similar sounds—this alone was not sufficient for the writing of complex names. Many of these contained sound-variations that could not be rendered by association with the 3500 or so logographic signs in use by around 3500 BCE. These sounds came to be represented by a new set of signs: signs not for whole words but for such smaller units of speech sound as syllables, such as the sign *li*, which stood interchangeably for the syllables with the sounds *li* and *le*.

The incorporation of syllabic signs in the Sumerian cuneiform of 3100 BCE, and the mixed "word-syllabic" system that resulted, were significant advances toward full phonetic writing—that is, the use of written signs to represent *only* the sounds that make up the words of human speech. But it also made reading and writing much more complex tasks, requiring long periods of training for the growing class of scribes. To grasp just *how* difficult cuneiform was to master, consider: in any purely logographic writing system, where each sign represents a different spoken word, one would need to commit to memory as many different signs as there are words in one's language. Since most of the world's languages have a vocabulary of 40,000 to 60,000 words, this would be a task that overwhelms even the imagination of it. The task was simplified greatly in the Mesopotamian writing systems by combining a much smaller number of written signs to produce more complex words, and by using the same sign to represent several different words that either sounded alike (e.g., "son" and "sun") or had related meanings (e.g., sun, day, light). While this made the process of writing somewhat less difficult, however, it intensified the difficulty of reading, since the same written sign might mean "sun" or "day" or "light," or "son," or the sound-element "son" (as in "season"), depending on the context. In addition to these complexities, moreover, the Sumerian system also required the learning of independent signs for syllables, numbers, number names, and the mathematical relations (like "plus" and "minus") that developed as methods of calculating evolved along with trade and writing. In the earliest stages of writing, the pictorial character of the inscribed signs had been of great help in remembering them and what they stood for. But as the pictures were reduced to more abstract shapes, then turned (for some mysterious reason) on their sides, then further reduced to a set of disconnected wedgelike marks, the signs lost any resemblance to what they stood for. They became conventionalized and arbitrary symbols whose meanings could be learned only through memorization and endlessly repeated drill.

The complexity that characterized Sumerian writing also marked the writing systems that had originated independently in other trading centers of the early Bronze Age and developed in similar stages, like the hieroglyphics of early Egyptian civilization. Indeed, the Egyptian hieroglyphic system was, if anything, even more complex than the cuneiform that had some influence on its later stages, as trade increased contact between the two civilizations. Like the Sumerian system, hieroglyphics originated in property marks and signs to identify goods, developed into a pictographic system, became logographic through the principle of phonetic transfer, and then incorporated a very large number of syllabic and consonantal signs as well as others to indicate different "readings" of the "base" signs. By 3000 BCE, hieroglyphics was an intensely complex system of rebus-like writing, in which some signs stood for objects, some for words, some for consonant sounds, some for homophones, and some for "instructions" that told the reader which signs stood for which. These elements were combined in various ways to generate the sounds of human speech—as children of my generation used to invent combinations like the rebus "♥ ⋒ 4 U" to be read as "My heart pants for you."

The difficulty of mastering the reading and writing of such "mixed" word-syllabic writing systems had several important consequences. One was to restrict literacy to those who could devote a significant part of their lives almost exclusively to the long years of training required to master the written signs, their uses, and their meanings. Those who did were almost invariably drawn from the ranks of the young who served the temples, and it was the temple schools that provided their training. Thus literacy came to be almost exclusively the province of the temple, the priesthood, and the priestly subalterns who constituted the rapidly expanding class of scribes.

The priesthood already held a dominant position in the emerging hierarchical structure of Mesopotamian and Egyptian life by virtue of its role in mediating between the people and the sacred. And that position had been vastly strengthened by the temple's central role in trade and its steadily increasing wealth. With the identification between the priesthood and literacy, the temple now also achieved a dominant position in an emerging hierarchy of information, for reading and writing were quickly becoming indispensable tools for preserving and retrieving information of all kinds, sacred as well as profane. And the means of using those tools—of encoding and decoding information in little inscribed marks—were, to all but the priests and scribes, secret. Though the word "hieroglyphics" is used in contemporary parlance almost exclusively for the Egyptian writing system of 3000 BCE (as "cuneiform" is used primarily for the Sumerian system), the root "hiero" might be applied to all of the word-syllabic systems of the time, for it has the double meaning of "sacred" and "secret." And the writing systems of the Third Millennium were both.

Writing would not begin to lose its sacred and secret character until the development of the alphabet, some 1500 years later, and of widespread schooling in reading and writing, centuries after that. But by then, the sacred and secret scripts of 3000–1500 BCE had already transformed the human social, psychological, and symbolic world in ways that would shape the contexts of the future, and thus give such later developments a particular bent. As we shall see.

CHAPTER TEN

Kings, Consciousness, and Intimations of Immortality

Ironically enough, the early systems of writing that so increased the power of the temple in the trading centers of 3000 BCE also fostered the institution that would in later centuries come to be its major adversary in a continuous struggle for wealth, power, authority, and the allegiance of human souls. I am speaking here of the rise of kings and all the complex machinery of laws and treaties, titles and deeds, rights and obligations, taxes and armies that constitute "the state."

The structures of authority and decision-making that would evolve, in Mesopotamia and Egypt, into the institution of kingship and the hierarchical order of the city-state had their roots, of course, in the tribal times that long predated writing and complex trade. In every human group, even the family, conflicts arise between members that must be resolved if the group is to survive. Structures of leadership—even if ad hoc and temporary—must evolve to organize the group's response to crises. Families linked together into clans, and clans into tribes to gain the advantages of cooperation and protection and the need to resolve inter-tribal disputes gave rise to decision-making councils—probably composed of tribal elders known for their wisdom, their ability to command large numbers of followers, and their prowess in hunting and battle. Such councils of elders, now also including the chief priests of the temples and gods on which so much depended, probably served much the same functions in the early days of city life.

But as trade evolved and the idea of "property" came to be extended to the lands that different tribal groups had occupied and successfully defended over long periods, a new criterion for membership and status in the councils of elders began to emerge. For some whose tribes had long held lands began to exchange those lands, in bits and pieces, for other goods and services. And those who held the richest lands and traded with cunning soon began to amass disproportionate amounts of wealth—not in money, but in the material resources needed to engage the services of builders and artisans, architects and engineers, laborers and guards. Indeed, in some cases such newly prosperous tribal leaders had sufficient resources in their own storerooms and documented claims enough in the temple coffers, to hire, provision, and maintain professional soldiers who could, in times of crisis, swell the ranks of the clan members whom bonds of blood and tradition obliged to answer the summons to fight.

Such summonses came more frequently as the number of cities on the Mesopotamian plain grew from two to eight, and the competition among them for the outlying lands between them increased. As sporadic skirmishes intensified to pitched battles between cities in the years between 3000 and 2800 BCE, larger and better organized, directed, and provisioned armies were required to defend the cities and their outlying lands. When crises arose, the councils of elders would elect from their members a "lugal" (originally, "big man") or temporary ruler to marshal the city's forces and direct its defense. As the personal prowess in battle of tribal leaders became less important than their ability to command, provision, and direct large numbers of soldiers, the choice for leadership fell more often on those who could provide the best trained and equipped fighters and who could manage problems of organization and supply most effectively. These were usually the more economically powerful leaders accustomed to directing the largest estates.

Those who commanded successfully in battle were quick to consolidate their power and maintain the allegiance of their troops through the ample and even-handed distribution of the riches that fell to the victors in war—among them, both lands and people captured. The latter may have been taken initially as hostages against counterattacks, or for the ransom they might bring. But soon enough, those who were not redeemed were exploited for their labor, which might be leased to others without their consent. Before long the captives of war would come to be counted among the "property" of their "owners," to be traded like other goods at their holders' will.

The extension of the idea of property to humans captured in war was a major impetus to the widespread extension of slavery throughout the lands of the Middle East, for it attached to captives an "exchange value" that made them far more desirable than did the simple exploitation of their labor by their original "owners." The institution of slavery also served an important military function, for the prospect of capture and enslavement by others vastly intensified the ferocity and desperation with which soldiers would fight. Beyond this, the enslavement of conquered peoples effectively removed them as a future threat, while at the same time providing a cheap supply of labor for the vast building projects that victorious rulers undertook to fortify their cities, enhance civic life, and perpetuate their own fame among their people and favor among the gods. Thus it was that most shameful of human institutions, the enslavement of others, came to be entrenched among the city-states of the Bronze Age, and so woven into the fabric of economic, political, and social life that it would spread from there through almost all the centers of the "civilized" world.

The struggles between city-states for the control of trade routes and lands became so frequent as to require the perpetual maintenance of armies and of readiness for attack and defense. As such, the rule of the "lugal" who had at first been only a temporary "crisis" leader was extended over longer and longer periods of time, until it became a more or less permanent condition. The more sagacious rulers used their positions and talents not only to consolidate their military power and increase their personal wealth, but to maintain the favor of the gods through lavish gifts and the erection of new temples. They enhanced civic life by commissioning public works, and by adjudicating with wisdom and skill the disputes brought before them and the councils of elders they now led. And like modern leaders, they used every means available to insure that the populace remained aware of their wisdom, exploits, and piety, and of the favor in which they stood with the gods: they rewarded singers and musicians who wove their deeds into hymns and tales linking the ruler to the familiar heroes of tribal lore and to the gods, and sponsored festivals and competitions at which the songs were sung. They commissioned sculptors to fashion their likenesses, painters to decorate the walls of buildings with frescoes depicting their deeds, masons to raise commemorative stones, and carvers and scribes to incise upon them, in image and word, the record of their victories.

Thus there began to emerge, among the narratives of those times, a new of kind of tale, composed by praise-singers to celebrate the achievements of their king. Like the narratives of earlier times, it was a tale heard, not read; not written, but sung. It was not the manner of its telling that was new, but of what it told. For among the gods and ancestors of the sacred past now walked a different figure, living still: the person of the king.

The weaving of contemporary rulers and events into older, sacred tales had several important consequences. It provided a means of recounting current events—the experiences that people of diverse origins had in common—and thus fostered their sense of a common social and political identity that transcended tribal experience but was welded to it and to the sacred past. It promoted the idea that the gods took an interest in the ongoing social and political affairs of men. And it vastly magnified the special status, particularly in relation to the sacred, of the king. Through his association with the gods and the mythic figures of the past, and through the redaction and exaggeration that were features of oral narrative, the figure of the king took on superhuman proportions. As the tales were repeated and elaborated through generations of retelling, and the battles, exploits, and rulers of later times were conflated with the old, kings became quasi-mythic figures, not quite sacred themselves, but not quite human, either—set apart by their special relationship to the gods, and ruling by divine right.

The idea that kings ruled by divine right did not originate in the songs of praise-singers alone. It no doubt had its roots in the rituals through which the elders of earlier times had sought the guidance of the gods in the selection of a temporary leader and invoked their favor when the choice had been made. But there are important differences between how a process occurs and how it is represented. For no representation can be as complex as what it represents, and visual imagery and narrative in particular are characterized by a high degree of ellipsis: they leave out much of the mediating detail which would, in any case, be supplied by living memory of the original events and their context. In the matter of kings and the source of their authority, the ellipses of painting, sculpture, and narrative were of critical importance, for they often left out the intermediating role of the council in the selection of the ruler. In both image and song, the king was represented as receiving his commission to rule from the gods in person. To the living people involved in the events represented, such images and poetic ellipses may have been understood for what they were: artistic and dramatic conventions. But as living memory faded and contexts changed, the images and tales did not, and successive generations read them more literally—as evidence of the divine authority of their kings. Thus does human thinking follow forms of representation, and life come to imitate art.

Needless to say, the idea that kings ruled by divine authority immeasurably strengthened their power, for what the gods had granted, only the gods dared take away. Shielded from the power of mere mortals to act against them, some kings grew heedless of the needs of their people and of the complaints against them, and some so abused their power and privileges that the people groaned and wailed to the gods in their oppression. Of course, kings did fall—in battle, illness, and accident—and the sprawling palaces they constructed were all the more vulnerable, because of their size and extent, to the ravages of earthquake and fire. And an evil king is less able than a good one to rally the help of people in times of crisis, and more likely to face disaster. In the religious world-view of the times, however, the fall of kings was attributed to the wrath of the gods—so when a bad king fell, it seemed that his evil and the cries of his people for justice had moved the gods to act against him. Thus there grew up and spread, in song and story, an idea that is critical in the evolution of law, government, and religion: the idea that the gods are not disinterested in human affairs, or swayed this way and that merely by the lavishness of gifts, but are aligned firmly on the side of virtue, and particularly, of *justice*.

Ideas of justice and the means of attaining it, in the citystates of 3000 BCE, were not of course the same as our own. They had evolved out of tribal ways of adjudicating disputes among families and clans, and the codification of the most effective principles in memorable sayings that were repeated and invoked time and again until they were deeply ingrained in oral memory. By the time that kings and councils met to adjudicate disputes in the cities of Egypt and Sumer, there were hundreds of pithy proverbs and parables in which the accumulated social and psychological insights of some 60,000 years were distilled and stored.

These were made memorable by their vivid and concrete use of language and metaphor, by their plays on words, by the brevity and cadences of their saying, and, of course, by the frequency with which they were repeated. We have such proverbs still today: What's good for the goose is good for the gander; spare the rod and spoil the child; a bird in the hand is worth two in the bush; turnabout is fair play; let sleeping dogs lie. And modern parents well know how frequently some parental saying from their own childhood comes unbidden to their lips when their children quarrel: Take turns. He had it first; you can have it when he's done. You're older and should know better. Share and share alike. She can sit there on the way to Grandma's; you can sit there on the way back. Outside the still-oral world of childhood, we no longer much use such sayings and proverbs to adjudicate disputes. But the kings and councils of early citystates did. In part, judicial wisdom consisted of knowing a great many proverbs. Thus it was said of Solomon, in later times, that "he was wiser than all men... and he spake 3000 proverbs" (I Kings, 31–32). But wisdom also consisted of selecting the apt proverb for the right occasion, and of interpreting it so that the specifics of each decision would seem fair to all parties involved.

The transactions of trade became more central features of city life and writing permitted both exhanges and the idea of property to grow more complex. More of the disputes brought before the kings and their councils involved ownership, or quantitities or qualities of exchanges--of goods, services, lands. Since more and more transactions were recorded in writing, not only by the scribes of the temple but by others lured by better conditions into the service of increasingly prosperous landowners and tradesmen, the services of the scribes as readers of those records became essential at meetings to resolve disputes, and wary tradesmen also took care to have the decisions written down. Thus there began to accumulate hundreds of written records of specific decisions. Since consistency in the king's decisions was a major criterion of his even-handedness, and even-handedness the major evidence of his wisdom and justice, reference to the records of previous decisions came to play a central part in the adjudication of trade disputes. Property—again, through the instrument of writing—became not only transferable but cumulative and inheritable. As such, awards of property, would, for many, emerge as preferable to physical retribution in resolving disputes. After all, receiving the eye of another for the one of yours he put out may satisfy your rage, but it is not as useful in the long run as receiving his cattle or a part of his lands--and the choices given, too, were written down.

Initially, no doubt, written records of previous decisions were valuable aids in making the next. But as they accumulated, and the specifics of cases became more complex and varied, the chore of sorting through them to find parallels would have become increasingly unmanageable. Too much information, as we have already observed, is as useless as too little. Thus there originated in Sumer that process of reducing judicial decisions to a relatively small number of general rules, and—committing them to writing—the codification of law. The oldest evidence of such a written code dates to the reign of the Sumerian king Ur-Nammu, around 2100 BCE—some 300 years before the reign of the Babylonian king Hammurabi, and his later code in roughly 1750 BCE. It consists of a small clay tablet on which are inscribed both standards of weights and measures to be used in trade and the penalties for thefts and personal injuries of various kinds. These reveal the close connection of both writing and law to property and trade, and the preference for property rewards over the more vengeful "payment in kind" for assaults and injuries: a man must pay two-thirds of a mina for cutting off another's nose; 10 silver shekels for cutting off a foot. They also reveal the use of a form of coinage in the cities of the Second Millennium BCE, in the sense that uniform weights of precious metals might be exchanged for fixed amounts of goods. Coinage, in turn, is an indication of the growing sophistication of mathematics and calculation. These were applied not only to measurements of material objects but, far more important, to measurements of *time*.

The idea that time, which we experience directly simply as a continuous process of change in the world around and inside us, can be broken into units to be counted like material objects in a collection is one of the world's most peculiar and significant notions. Just how peculiar it is you may grasp by considering that no one has ever *seen* three "hours" standing together, like men on a street corner, or five "days" in a perceptible collection like chairs in a room. We can only see one changing of the sky from dark to light, or one passing of the moon across the sky, or one opening of the buds on trees, at a time. How is it, then, that we come to count them, just as we count objects we can see arrayed before us in a perceptible, "real" collection?

The key to that question, and to the "objectification" of time, lies in the observation that we *can* see as a "real" or perceptible group or collection, not "days" or "moons" or "springs," but the objects or marks we use to *represent* them. If you labor in my field from the rising of the sun to its setting, for example, and I give you a potsherd inscribed with a drawing of the sun to exchange at the market for bread, and do this as well on the next occasion and the next, you may collect the pieces of clay to exchange as a group. And when it became necessary, for purposes of dictation, reading, and drill, to assign a sound to those drawings of the sun, or the signs 1 and 11 and 111 and so on, there would seem no reason to use different sounds for cyclical phenomena (like successive risings of the sun) and objects collected in groups (like cows or chickens). They might all be represented, in speech and writing, alike: three cows; three suns (or days). Thus writing, we may guess, was deeply implicated in the notion that time, like material objects, might be broken up into units and counted.

That is not all. For just as it was discovered that new words could be generated by manipulating the object signs for them in different ways, so did it come to be discovered that new number relations could be arrived at by manipulating counting signs in different ways. And as simple counting gave way to calculation—addition and subtraction, multiplication and division—these processes were applied alike to units of physical and temporal measurement, giving rise to new ways to express and record the passage of time.

The objectification, recording, and calculation of time was significant for a host of reasons. But none was more important than its use in *dating*. The practice of attaching a discrete number to an event that recurred cyclically (e.g., a rising of the sun or its appearance in midwinter at the apex of a particular stone), then adding a number for each following recurrence, provided a way not only to record *counts* of days or years, as in a king's reign, but to tie other events recorded in writing to discrete moments in time. I do not mean, in saying this, that the Sumerians or Egyptians of the Third to the Second Millennium BCE had as yet arrived at the idea of a *beginning* of time from which to number years in succession. Their practice was to begin counting at the start of a ruler's reign, then begin anew at the start of the next. The idea of counting backward to a sacred tribal beginning, then numbering forward consecutively to arrive at a present year, would seem to be a later development, by peoples such as the Hebrews and the Mayans, who used genealogies, quasi-mythic oral accounts of past persons and events, and calculations based on assumptions about life spans and generations to arrive at a "year one" tied to the founding of their tribal world.

But the temporal "units" and counting systems established by the Egyptians and Sumerians provided nonetheless a basis for tying events to specific times, and thus gave rise to the idea of a non-repeating secular history of *human* events, as we understand that idea today. This is what it means to say, as does the title of one learned book, that "History begins at Sumer."

History also begins at Sumer in the sense that writing provided records that historians of times much closer to our own could use to reconstruct the life-world and thought-world of people and civilizations long gone. It does not mean that the people who first began to write used their styluses and clay tablets to chronicle their own experience for posterity, as modern peoples do. They used writing initially as an aid to memory—at first, in the limited contexts of trade, then to record more complex transactions, to document ownership and claims on property, to record agreements, disputes, and settlements, and to establish standards involving quantities, exchanges, and penalties.

As the need for scribes increased, the schools for training them grew. The opportunities for employment by those in positions of power—in the palaces of kings, the households of wealthy merchants, the splendid temples—attracted larger and larger numbers of young people eager to be trained. Thus there began to grow up a professional class of scribes—many of them, we may guess, the sons and younger kinsmen of an older generation of scribes, following in their fathers' footsteps. As their numbers grew, so did the diversity of the contexts and purposes for which their services were employed. Kings used them to inscribe on steles the record of their triumphs in battle; physicians used them to record the "formulas" for compounding herbs, oils, and other ingredients for poultices and potions for the treatment of various ailments, and thus speeded the training of their assistants; architects and builders used them to record building plans and perform the calculations required to ascertain the quantities of materials and laborers needed; praise-singers used them to make notes on the composition of new tributes to the king. And by 2500 BCE or so, in the temples of Sumer and Egypt, the priestly scribes began to commit to writing the genealogies, relations, special spheres of activity, and services required by the complex pantheon of Sumerian and Egyptian gods.

Around the same time, the use of writing took a new turn. In the hot and tiresome and often physically abusive scribal schools, the resentful and unhappy young began to use the strokes and shapes of cuneiform and the Egyptian hieroglyphics to speak to themselves of their own despair and unburden themselves of the grievances they dared not speak aloud to their masters. Thus there began to emerge, in the writings of the Third and Second Millennia BCE, a new form of *personal* expression. And what is most striking about it is that it is a literature almost invariably about stress and distress, a literature of lamentation and grievance.

The despairing tone of the world's first original and personal literature provides some confirmation of the hypothesis that citification and the scribal experience combined to produce just those conditions in which internal distress mounts, the "internalized other" of tribal experience fails as a basis for prediction and meaning, and the awareness of self as a lonely, autonomous, choosing "I" erupts into consciousness as a focus of attention. But what were those conditions? One was the intense and rigorous subordination of biological needs and impulses to self-discipline and control by the young in scribal schools. The demands of writing and reading, and of their masters, required that the young men who labored over their letters were to sit still for long periods of time; orient head and eyes in a single direction; coordinate eye and hand in fine muscle movements to produce the exact patterns of stylus marks required; bear the rap of the master's stick or the sudden sting of the whiplash on hand or back or head without flinching or rising to strike back; focus on the same repeated shapes and patterns without allowing attention to wander--while flies droned and settled or young women and more carefree lads passed chatting beyond the open porticos. Such rigorous control of impulse does not come naturally or easily to anyone, much less to healthy young men, and particularly at that stage in their biological lives. Indeed, it gives rise to fearsome inner struggles between impulse and will, struggles clamorous and painful enough to generate the kind of distress that focuses attention inward, to an internal battleground where those struggles take place and distress is most keenly felt.

But more important even than these psychobiological conditions were the social experiences of the young, and of the thousands of others who migrated in growing numbers from their close-knit agrarian villages to the promise of greater economic security in the cities. There they found themselves separated from the coherent tribal contexts and the relatively stable roles in which the "internalized other" of the tribe had provided a consistent basis for predicting the responses of others to words and deeds. However, in the cities they were thrust into interactions with others of vastly different ways, different languages, different gods, with those whose "meanings" and rules for behavior differed sharply from those of their own tribe. Such interactions would inevitably lead them to call into question the rules and predictions they had previously internalized as normal, thereby engendering internal conflict.

City life also involved membership in a far more diversified set of communities of others than did the more coherent structure of village life. It required one to function not only within the family, but also in the professional "guild" of those who performed similar kinds of work, in the military unit to which one was assigned for continuous drill and preparation for the battles to which one might be called, in the community of those who served a particular temple and god. In smaller, agricultural and tribal communities, work, family life, education, religion, and the arts are interwoven in such a way that the dictates of one are integrated with the others. But in city life, the demands of one's occupation often conflict with those of the family, and those of the family with those of the schools, and those of the schools with those of one's god, and so on. Each arena of activity demands, so to speak, a different self, with different values and rules for behavior, and different priorities for the use of one's time. Thus one is presented, over and again, with choices—and choices in which the internalized "voice" of the tribe provides little guidance.

These conditions, we may guess, were particularly intensified in the experience of the young sent to the scribal schools for training, for they were in many cases cut off not only from tribe but from family. They also found themselves among a bewildering array of strangers. The fragments of the notes that they inscribed to themselves tell us that they experienced their confusion and loneliness as deeply painful—not only because of the injustices they felt they were made to suffer, but because of a deeper failure of predictability, of *meaning*.

But why would they have committed these feelings, and the burgeoning sense of an isolated self that accompanied them, to writing? They did so, we may guess, because the conditions of schooling made it impossible to express such feelings in speech. Those close enough to hear—the priests and scribal masters—would scarcely have been disposed to listen; those who might be disposed to listen—family and friends—were not there to hear. Thus the unhappy young spoke to themselves of themselves, in writing. And the tablets on which they wrote held up to their eyes a new kind of mirror—a mirror of the internal life that made the lonely "I" visible at last to the eye. Thus writing provided the means through which the internal, isolated self could become an object of attention and interest to the self. By so doing, it greatly intensified and accelerated the dawning of a new kind of consciousness—consciousness of oneself as an autonomous, choosing individual, directed and motivated neither entirely by the gods nor entirely by the voice of one's tribe, but by some personal, separate "I" speaking somewhere within: a unique invisible spirit, *ka*, soul.

It may be that some of the personal accounts found among the fragments of scribal school tablets were in fact intended as the world's earliest "letters"—that is as communications to parents or friends to be given to others to carry home. This seems unlikely, because the fragments give no indication that someone else is being addressed. But by 2500 BCE the literate among Sumerians and Egyptians *were* using writing for personal letters—often addressed by fathers to their distant sons and consisting, for the most part, of instructions, maxims, and exhortations to study hard, live chastely, and fulfill the responsibilities of a respectful son to his father, family, and tribe. Like the earlier fragments of personal schoolboy writings, such letters give voice to the distress occasioned by a world undergoing revolutionary social and psychic change: a world where tribal and familial authority is breaking down, where sons live outside the spatial, social, and even psychic spheres of their fathers, where strangers are more frequently encountered than kinsmen, where the gods speak in a babble of competing voices. Or worse, where the gods fall silent, withdraw from human association, and even, like the shepherd-god Tammuz, die.

Our picture books and museums all celebrate the glories, the dazzling achievements of the Sumerians and Egyptians in that golden age some 5000 years ago, when, through the written word and the inscribed number, civilization and history, architecture and art, schools and "science," law and literature, and the self-reflective individual consciousness were being born. Perhaps we focus on the splendors of that birth beause it happened so long ago, and because in its outcome we recognize ourselves. And where we love the outcome, we remember in retrospect only the wonder, and forget the pain. But those in the throes of the second great cultural and communications revolution—from tribal to civil life, from speech to the inscribed word, from the communal to the individual self—did not have the advantage of hindsight. They had no futurists to tell them the great things being born. They had only the chaos of change and the fearful sense that a familiar and orderly way of life, for all its limitations and hardships, was passing away.

They lived, those people of the world's first writing cultures, at a moment not unlike our own. For we, too, stand at some unknown point in a process of extraordinary communication and cultural change—whether the beginning or the middle we cannot say, for the end is impossible to see. And it is impossible to say whether that end, when it comes, will bring forth something wonderful or just—an end. But we see all around us the disorder of upheaval and change, know its fear and feel our pain, and rightly grieve the loss of much that is good but passing away. And as in our time, so in theirs, there runs beneath the hustle and bustle of commerce and the thrill of invention and discovery, beneath the euphoric paeans of praise at the dedication of still another shining temple, a deep and throbbing threnody of grief and lamentation, a dirge on disorder and despair, on the death of meaning.

And indeed, the Sumerians and Egyptians who first began to write, some 5000 years ago, had reason to lament, and to fear. For with the breakdown of tribal life and the dawning of individual self-consciousness, not only disorder but death entered the world in a new way. I do not mean, in saying this, that before cities and writing and the coming to consciousness of the psychic "I" men and women did not know death, seek to avoid it, and grieve at its coming. Evidence of human awareness of death and its sorrow dates back to Neanderthal times and is often taken, in fact, as one of the first signs of a distinctively human and symbolic cognition. But it is one thing to feel and fear the pain of separation and loss when a cherished kinsman or companion is stilled forever, and quite another to contemplate the ultimate fate of one's own wishing, wanting, thinking, feeling "I."

It is one of the peculiarities of human self-consciousness that once we have become aware of our own thoughts and feelings, memories, pleasures and pains, we are all but incapable of imagining the extinction of that awareness. In fact, we cannot truly imagine it, because "imagining" is itself an activity of awareness. That is, we are always "there" somewhere when we attempt to summon up some sense of *not* being "there." We are perfectly capable of saying words like "I will simply cease to exist," but we cannot remember or imagine or approximate the sense of such a non-state because remembering, imagining, and sensing invoke a persisting "I" who am remembering, imagining, sensing. The result of this paradox is a profound and ineradicable sense that in some inarticulable way, some aspect of our awareness, our selves, however transformed, will always go on. Thus there arises, with the dawning of self-consciousness, a new concern with the fate of the individual "spirit," the internal "I," when the body dies.

As individual self-consciousness intensified in the Mesopotamian world of 2500–2000 BCE, so too did the idea of a personal after-life, different from the diffuse animism of earlier times in that the animating spirits of the human dead now maintained their personal identity, their individual character and awareness. But it was a grim and unhappy awareness, at least as the Mesopotamians construed it, for without their bodies, the dead were reduced to dim, powerless shades who wandered silent and disconsolate in the shadows of the Otherworld. Needless to say, such a fate was a dismal prospect, and it greatly intensified the dread of death, particularly among those who most delighted in the gusty life of the passions, of sensuous pleasures, of worldly power. Thus there entered into the tales of the Third Millennium BCE a new theme: the quest for immortality.

The concern with death, mortality, and immortality appears at roughly the same time in the great scribal cultures of Sumer and Egypt—around 2500 BCE—but in two quite different ways. In Egypt, the early deification of kings (i.e., the belief that they were offspring of the gods) led to the tradition that, after death, the king became one with Osiris, the god and ruler of the Otherworld. In this afterlife transformation, the king achieved not only immortality, but an eternal life of even greater physical power and pleasure than his earthly incarnation afforded. This outcome, however, depended on the incantation of magic spells inscribed on the walls of the king's tomb for his use during the perilous journey through the hazardous passageway between the worlds of the profane and the sacred. Those spells and incantations, the so-called "Pyramid Texts" of Fifth and Sixth Dynasty Egyptian kings (ca. 2400–2200 BCE), were in fact the medium through which the king's transformation was accomplished. Knowledge of their words and of the rituals they required, therefore, came to be seen as the key to immortality.

As the priestly class literate in hieroglyphics expanded, and as many entered the service of the powerful nobles now ruling the fragmented Egypt of the Intermediate and Early Middle Kingdoms (ca. 2200–1780 BCE), knowledge of the sacred spells spread to the larger class of local lords and barons. By 2000 BCE or so, they too had access to the "secrets" of immortality and thus attained, along with the king, identification after death with Osiris and the joys of eternal life. In later centuries, knowledge of the sacred texts, now many times revised, was disseminated even more widely, as scribal literacy spread and a burgeoning merchant class rose to wealth and power in the periods of the New Kingdom and of Empire. Thus by 1500 BCE, even the commonfolk of Egypt could attain joyous immortality in the Otherworld, aided by the sacred hymns, rituals, vows, and incantations inscribed on papyrus scrolls and buried with their preserved bodies to guide them on their after-life journey. These scrolls and the collections of sacred and magical writings they contain were inaptly, if understandably, called "books of the dead" by the 19th and 20th century tomb-raiders who found them, and the collation and recension of the various papyri by modern scholars has come to be called "The Book of the Dead." But, as many point out, this is a grievously misleading name, for the original scrolls refer to themselves as "The Chapters of the Coming Forth by Day"—a title that much more accurately reflects the optimistic and joyous Egyptian construction of the individual after-life.

The Sumerian concern with death, mortality, and immortality also began to be given expression around 2500 BCE, but in quite different form and ultimately with a quite different conclusion. The themes are sounded first in tales surrounding Gilgamesh, an historical king of Uruk in the Second Early Dynastic Period (ca. 2700–2500 BCE), later deified in Sumer as king and judge of the Netherworld. Perhaps because Sumerian kings were not originally viewed as descendants of the gods, they had no special claims on physical immortality, but were assumed to share the same dismal, disembodied fate of others who died. It may be that the historical Gilgamesh, who apparently lived a particularly sensuous and lusty life, was in fact obsessed by the prospect of death as he grew older; or perhaps the theme of death and the quest for immortality was a projection onto his figure of a more widespread cultural concern. In any case, tales about Gilgamesh and his quest for immortality began to circulate orally in Sumer not long after his death, and perhaps as early as 2500 BCE, they began to be written down.

The earliest dated written Sumerian accounts of Gilgamesh so far recovered (ca. 2100 BCE) are six separate tales, quite different in style and substance from the integrated epic into which they would later be woven by the Semitic Akkadians who dominated Mesopotamian culture from roughly 2300–2160 BCE. And the early Akkadian version differs in many details from the "late" form of the epic, as it evolved through centuries of Babylonian revisions into the twelve-tablet version found at Nineveh in the remains of the library of Ashurbanipal, king of Assyria around 668–627 BCE. Even in the earliest Gilgamesh tales, however, the concern with death, the quest for immortality, and the outcome of that quest are clear: only the gods are immortal, Gilgamesh is at last told. Man's fate is death.

Reduced to such a telling, the story of Gilgamesh sounds more like a pessimistic lament than a great heroic epic, and we would be hard-pressed to explain why such a gloomy tale so captured the hearts and imaginations of Mesopotamian women and men that it survived in countless retellings, in dozens of languages, for nearly 2000 years. The point is that for all its concern with death and the quest for immortality, *Gilgamesh* is not substantially about them, or about the world beyond the grave. It is instead a celebration of *life*. It tells of the intensity of human friendship, of the joy to be found in the deep bond between one man and another; of the pleasure and civilizing power of female sexuality; of the challenges and triumphs of physical hardship, struggle, and combat; of great achievements and great sorrows, and of great courage in bearing them. And in the end, it tells of the special immortality that humans may attain in the human world by devoting themselves to great works and deeds that will keep alive the honor and glory and perpetuation of their names. Perhaps most important, *Gilgamesh* moved to the center of the narrative stage, and lionized there, not the doings of the gods, but the deeds and struggles and accomplishments of humans. The gods, to be sure, provide the frame in which the story unfolds. But it is Gilgamesh's tale—*our* tale—not theirs. To a modern reader, this "point" of the epic seems clear: there is indeed an Otherworld, from which we mortals come and where the gods live forever, directing and moderating both their own and all worldly affairs. But the business of humans is *here*, not there.

In the Egyptian *Book of the Dead* and the Mesopotamian *Gilgamesh*, then, we find codified two different world-views and two different "solutions" to the problem of death. The Egyptian conception is more god-centered, in the 2nd Millennium BCE, and the Mesopotamian more human-centered. One sees mortal life as a preparation for an eternal life of potentially great pleasure, ease, and potency; the other sees mortal life as the only arena of human affairs, and the only venue for the attainment of spiritual immortality through fame and the perpetuation of one's name. One tilts the balance of human striving and significance toward the Otherworld and the after-life; the other tilts it toward the human life-world and history. In these respects, the first great written works of Egyptian and Mesopotamian culture offer two different answers to the question of meaning, in the face of death, that have echoed ever since in the philosophies and religions of Western men and women.

I say "Western," here, because for all their differences, the world-views codified in Gilgamesh and *The Book of the Dead* share an assumption that sets them apart from a third great world-tale that would later appear in the cultures of the East. For although they preserved the earlier cosmology of a universe divided into two realms, the sacred and the profane, and maintained the oral and tribal tradition of passageways between them that the gods might travel in either direction at will, the Egyptians and Mesopotamians closed the door that would have allowed mortals who entered the otherworld ever to return. In *Gilgamesh* and *The Book of the Dead*, human life is a one-way journey. The road or river we travel originate in the realm of the sacred and lead us back into the Otherworld when mortal life is done. But there, for the human traveler, the journey ends. We do not retrace our steps or cycle round to come into the mortal world again. That is a power reserved to the gods.

In constructing human life as a one-way path or journey, the peoples of early scribal cultures did not, of course, abandon the older idea of time and natural processes as a cycle—the conception that Mircea Eliade has called "the eternal return." Rather, they separated mortal human life and time from the worlds of both nature and the gods. The gods were, after all, the personification of natural forces—at least in their origins—and therefore came and went and returned again just as did the moon and the sun and the wheat fields in the spring. But writing, which allowed details of human events to be recorded and preserved over time; and numbering, which allowed them to be dated; and sculpting and drawing, which captured the distinctive features of individuals and personal self-consciousness, raising to attention the autonomous "I"—all these combined to make the uniqueness of human events and persons both significant and visible. They heightened the awareness of the differences between one battle and another, one ruler and another, one individual and another, and preserved these differences over generations of intervening time, in a way that the unaided human memory and the chanted account could not.

Thus it became harder to conflate one battle, one leader, one person with another so that they no longer seemed to exist over and again in a hazy sea of seamless time. It grew easier to see—and, in fact, hard to escape—that in their unique detail and individuality the persons and events of the human life-world came only once and did not return. In the mortal world, if not the world of nature and of the gods, time and life took on a direction, like the routes the trading caravans followed across the plains, or the great rivers of the Nile, the Tigris, the Euphrates, that flowed only one way down to the endless sea. Human time and life took on the metaphorical shape of the path and the river: the character of the line, not the circle; not of the loop, but of the pointed arrow.

Like the oral narratives of tribal and nomadic times, the great story of Gilgamesh and the tale implied in the *Book of the Dead* served many critical functions. Both contained passages that explained how the universe came to be—generated by the creator goddess Nammu out of the primordial sea, in the Sumerian cosmology, and out of nothingness by the creator god Ra-Atum Khepri (who himself emerged out of Nun, the primordial waters of chaos), in the Egyptian. And both tales served to explain how the universe worked. Like the social and architectural world of the Egyptians and Mesopotamians, the worlds of the sacred and the profane in their first literature were geometrically structured and hierarchically organized. They were realms in which both mortals and immortals occupied ranks that gave them different powers, privileges, and responsibilities, and both gods and humans played out specialized roles.

In the Sumerian sacred world, for example, An is the god of heaven, Enlil the god of air and the progenitor (with his mother Ki) of earth; Enki, the water god, is also the god of wisdom and the keeper of the water and food of life; Iananna (the later Babylonian Ishtar) is queen of heaven and goddess of light, love, and fertility, while her sister Ereshkigal is queen of the Nether World, goddess of darkness and death. In the Egyptian world, Shu (the ancient god of air) and Tefnut (god of moisture), both created by RaAtum-Khepri out of his own semen, in turn generate Geb (the god of earth) and Nut (goddess of the sky), and two of their offspring— Isis (goddess of fertility and secret knowledge) and Osiris (lord of life)—generate Horus, the god whose earthly incarnation is the king, the pharaoh who governs human affairs. Isis and Osiris, along with their siblings Set and Nephthys, also generate all the lesser gods of Egypt, as well as the powerful Thoth (god of writing, judgment, and magic) and Anubis (who presides over the ritual of embalming and guides the deceased to the Otherworld).

Both the gods and mortals, as represented in *Gilgamesh* and *The Book of the Dead*, have structures and rules of governance, procedures for adjudicating claims and disputes, and means of punishing those who disobey. In the Egyptian world-tale, for example, the god Thoth acts as "attorney" for Horus before the tribunal of gods who must judge between the competing claims of Horus and Set to be the rightful heir and incarnation of Osiris; and in the Sumerian tale, Enlil, powerful though he is, is banished by the other gods to the Nether World in punishment for his rape of the virgin Ninlil. Since the mortal world was construed, in both the Egyptian and Mesopotamian tales (as in the tribal tales they subsumed) to originate in the world of sacred space and time, the pyramidal structure of power and decision-making in the world of the gods served to explain and legitimate the social and political structure of the world of women and men.

Beyond this, the two tales, in their different ways, served the pressing psychological needs of peoples newly come to individual self-consciousness for a solution to the problem of meaninglessness that arose with the awareness of personal death. And most important, perhaps, the explicit and implied narratives of *Gilgamesh* and *The Book of the Dead* provided a sacred source of authority for the living of a just and ethical life. For in both tales, the gods are deeply involved in human affairs, and deeply committed to justice. Both narratives, therefore, have an intensely ethical and didactic bent: one must live responsibly, justly, honestly, and with courage and concern for others to attain either a joyous eternal life or the human immortality of fame.

By locating the source of human law, justice, ethics, and governance in the sacred, eternal world, the narratives of early scribal cultures gave them a potency that no appeal to "the survival of the group" or to "economic necessity" or to "simple human decency" could match. In effect, their linking of mortal to immortal life, of the profane to the sacred, perpetuated that psychological willingness to comply with the arrangements of human society that no civilization can survive without. For of all the "lessons" to be learned from human history, none can be clearer than this: that in the absence of a psychological acceptance of the social rules, ethical prescriptions, and cultural norms that allow humans to live in groups, there are no armies powerful enough, no police and courts and prisons numerous enough, no punishments severe enough to maintain civil order in any group larger than a tribe. This is not to say that the only means of perpetuating a willing acceptance of human law, ethics, and governance is to locate their authority in the realm of the sacred, although that is what women and men have done for some 30,000 years. Indeed, the most urgent question of our own time is whether we can find or construct some other narrative compelling enough, and meaningful enough, to allow a world civilization detached from the sacred to survive.

But that question would not arise in Western culture for some 4000 years. For in inventing writing and civilization and history, and in tying them to the world of the sacred, the Sumerians and Egyptians of 3000–2000 BCE laid the foundations of a new way of codifying and explaining the natural and social and psychological worlds. And it was a way that would persist, through extraordinary transformations, for centuries of generations still to come.

Selected Bibliography

Human Evolution

Rick Gore, "The Dawn of Humans: Neandertals," *National Geographic*, Vol. 189, No. 1 (January 1996).

Richard E. Leakey and Roger Lewin, *People of the Lake: Mankind and Its Origins*. Garden City, N.Y.: Anchor Press/Doubleday, 1978.

————, *Origins Reconsidered*. N.Y.: Doubleday, 1992.

C. Loring Brace and James Metress, *Man in Evolutionary Perspective*. N.Y.: John Wiley and Sons, Inc., 1973.

C. Loring Brace and Ashley Montagu, *Human Evolution* (Second Edition). N.Y.: Macmillan Publishing Company, Inc., 1977.

C. Stringer and C. Gamble, *In Search of the Neanderthals*. N.Y.: Thames and Hudson, Inc., 1993.

Geological Eras and Climatology

M. I. Budyko, *The Earth's Climate, Past and Future*. N.Y.: Academic Press, 1982.

Michael John Selby, *Earth's Changing Surface: An Introduction to Geomorphology*. N.Y.: Oxford University Press, 1985.

Prehistoric Art

Alexander Marshack, *The Roots of Civilization: The Cognitive Beginnings of Man's First Art, Symbol, and Notation* (Revised Edition). Mount Kisco, N.Y.: Moyer Bell, 1991.

John E. Pfeiffer, *The Creative Explosion: An Inquiry into the Origins of Art and Religion.* Ithaca: Cornell University Press, 1985.

The Nature of Language

Suzanne K. Langer, *Philosophy in a New Key: A Study in the Symbolism of Reason, Rite, and Art.* Cambridge, MA: Harvard University Press, 1957.

Edward Sapir, *Language.* N.Y.: Harcourt, Brace and Company, Inc., 1921.

Benjamin Lee Whorf, *Language, Thought, and Reality.* Cambridge, MA: The M.I.T. Press, 1956.

Children's Acquisition of Language

Jean Piaget, *The Language and Thought of the Child.* N.Y.: Humanities Press, 1959.

Standard texts on children's language acquisition from Roy Higginson, *An Annotated Bibliography of Child Language and Language Disorders*, 1992 and 1997 Supplement.

Self and Consciousness

Daniel C. Dennett, *Consciousness Explained.* Boston: Little, Brown and Co., 1991.

Bruce Gronbeck, Thomas J. Farrell, and Paul A. Soukup, eds., *Media, Consciousness, and Culture.* Newbury Park, CA: Sage Publications, 1991.

Nicholas Humphrey, *A History of the Mind: Evolution and the Birth of Consciousness.* N.Y.: Simon & Schuster, 1992.

Julian Jaynes, *The Origin of Consciousness in the Breakdown of the Bicameral Mind.* Boston: Houghton Mifflin, 1976.

George Herbert Mead, *Mind, Self and Society.* Chicago: University of Chicago Press, 1934.

Walter J. Ong, *Interfaces of the Word: Studies in the Evolution of Consciousness and Culture.* Ithaca: Cornell University Press, 1977.

Features of Oral Cultures

Bruce Chatwin, *The Songlines.* London: Jonathan Cape Ltd., 1987.

Mircea Eliade, *The Sacred and the Profane.* N.Y.: Harcourt, Brace & World, Inc., 1959.

———, *The Myth of the Eternal Return.* Princeton, N.J.: Princeton University Press, 1965.

John Miles Foley, *Oral-Formulaic Theory and Research.* New York: Garland Publishing, 1985.

John R. Goody, *The Domestication of the Savage Mind*. Cambridge: Cambridge University Press, 1977.

Eric Havelock, *Preface to Plato*. Cambridge, MA: Harvard University Press, 1963.

Albert B. Lord, *The Singer of Tales*. Cambridge, MA: Harvard University Press, 1960.

Walter J. Ong, *The Presence of the Word: Some Prolegomena for Cultural and Religious History*. New Haven: Yale University Press, 1967.

———, *Orality and Literacy: The Technologizing of the Word*. New York: Routledge, 1991.

Early Settlements/Cities

Jane Jacobs, *The Economy of Cities*. N.Y.: Random House, 1969.

Kathleen Kenyon, *Archaeology in the Holy Land*. N.Y.: Praeger, 1970.

———, *Digging Up Jericho*. London: Ernest Benn Ltd., 1957.

James Mellaart, *Earliest Civilizations of the Near East*. N.Y.: McGraw Hill, 1965.

———, *Catal Huyuk: A Neolithic Town in Anatolia*. N.Y.: McGraw Hill, 1967.

Peter Ucko, Ruth Tringham, and G. W. Dimbleby, *Man, Settlement, and Urbanism*. London: Duckworth Press, 1972.

Sumer and Egypt

John Gardner and John Maier, *Gilgamesh*. N.Y.: Alfred A. Knopf, 1984.

Christine Hobson, *The World of the Pharaohs: A Complete Guide to Ancient Egypt*. N.Y.: Thames and Hudson, 1987.

Joseph Kaster, *The Wisdom of Ancient Egypt: Writings from the Time of the Pharaohs*. N.Y.: Barnes and Noble Books, 1993.

Samuel Noah Kramer, *From the Tablets of Sumer*. Indian Hills, CO: Falcon's Wing Press, 1956.

———, *History Begins at Sumer*. Garden City, N.Y.: Doubleday, 1959.

———, *The Sumerians*. Chicago: University of Chicago Press, 1963.

John Romer, *Ancient Lives: Daily Life in Egypt of the Pharaohs*. N.Y.: Holt, Rinehart and Winston, 1984.

Jeffrey H. Tigay, *The Evolution of the Gilgamesh Epic*. Philadelphia: University of Pennsylvania Press, 1982.

Development of Writing Systems

Albertine Gaur, *A History of Writing*. N.Y.: Charles Scribner's Sons, 1985.

I. J. Gelb, *A Study of Writing*. Chicago: University of Chicago Press, Phoenix Edition, 1963.

PART II

TALES, TOOLS, TECHNOPOLY

(Jan. 1989). Lectures delivered at the Anglican Summer School, Perth, Western Australia

On Narrative

The U.S. is the world's best laboratory for studying change and its consequences for human life. No other culture has abandoned itself so joyfully—with so little hesitation or suspicion—to the march of technological progress. None has so willingly revised its traditional institutions and values—its schools, its families, its churches, its political traditions—to accommodate the new.

I cannot speak with much optimism about the kinds of changes that 50 years [now almost 100] of technological innovation have unloosed upon the cultures of the world. I suspect you have heard how children no longer read and, even worse, have trouble with logical reasoning and sensible speech. How schools are hopelessly floundering. How cities are decaying. How the homeless wander their streets, freezing in doorways on cold winter nights while the acquisitive young turn their backs. Surely, you have noticed how the quality of political leadership has deteriorated. And perhaps you have heard it rumored that politics has become via television merely another form of show business. The rumors are true.

Consider the recent national election centered almost exclusively around 30-second television ads and sound-bytes—the one or two sentence excerpts from longer commercials—in which the candidates deliver what were presumed to be especially witty or otherwise memorable lines. Perhaps that explains why the central issue of the campaigns, as far as anyone could tell, seemed to be the Pledge of Allegiance to the flag. Flag-waving has got to be the most efficient political use of expensive television time there is. One or two pictures, hardly any speech at all—the swell of patriotism, and out come the handkerchiefs (if not the voters) every time.

What I call the US laboratory of change is not self contained. Technologies and techniques have no nationalistic pride. Nor are the changes brought about by technology contained within national borders. And as new technologies and techniques spread out around the world, they carry with them the seeds of the same kinds of changes. These changes, or types of changes, are similar because technologies are not neutral. No tool is.

Let a man invent a hoe to ease his tilling of the ground, and he will change the surface of the earth and all that dwells therein, sometimes to his grief. But that is not all. The hoe will also change the shape of the hand that holds it and the muscles that work the hand. Let a man hoe long enough, and the hoe will bend his body to the shape its use requires. So it is with tools of doing. And so too with tools of *knowing*—with our means of information and communication. They change the knower as well as the known. Just as the body will bend to the shape of the hoe, so cultures will bend too in accommodation of their information technologies. But the process is gradual. We're usually unaware of the direction or degree of change until we are no longer able to straighten up again. By then we may not know what it is that has caused our pain. Unable to recognize its early signs, we don't name our disorder or diagnose its cause. And thus we fail to seek or prescribe an effective remedy.

Maybe there is time still where diagnosing the disease that's crippling our culture offers some possibility of changing its course. Perhaps, by providing a diagnosis of the malady that besets us—showing you how it arises and sketching some of its most recognizable symptoms—we can avert its worst consequences. So that together we can imagine some remedy.

First, to get a handle on the problem—to name it and make it visible—I want to offer a general point of view on human communication and, by applying it to the past, to generate some principles about media and culture change. What I talk about may seem, initially, very far removed from our present-day concerns. However, we have not arrived here overnight, and, in cases of cultural disorder no less than personal disease, the accuracy of diagnosis hinges on the care we give to the history.

So I start, then, with a point of view. I do this because what you can see about media and culture change depends on how you look at it. And it also depends on what you look at. Sometimes, students of change make the fundamental error of focusing primarily on technologies and on media as technologies. Clearly, this approach is indispensable for answering certain kinds of questions—such as what particular media are good for and what kinds of functions they will most likely serve. The structure of a garden hoe will tell you that it is not very useful for watering your flowers. And the structure of the instamatic camera tells you that its strong suit is the recording of images, not of sounds. But on the questions surrounding why media enter cultures when they do, whether they will have large-scale impacts, and how they will transform *us* over time—on these profound questions the technology tells us nothing. On these questions the media themselves are mute.

To understand media change you must start elsewhere. Not with technologies but with people, and what they are about, and why they do the things they do—including inventing technologies and discarding them. And to address those questions, you need an historian's point of view. And an anthropologist's point of view, and a psychologist's and even a philosopher's. More precisely, you need an ecologist's point of view. And since I consider myself an ecologist let me say briefly what that point of view entails.

The ecologist assumes to begin with that we humans are a species of responsive creatures, living in a set of environments characterized by change. Some of the changes humans respond to are the result of natural laws and phenomena, like the seasons, that seem to have little origin in our own behavior. But a far greater proportion of the change we have to cope with are changes that result from our own operations on our environment. In either case, change is inevitable, and it presents us with a continuous set of problems. Specifically, change creates problems of adjustment.

In other species, adjustment or adaptation is largely a biological process. But in humans, it's what we might call a technical process. By virtue of our capacity to manipulate symbols, to reason, imagine and create, we adjust our environments to ourselves and ourselves to our environments by developing or inventing new techniques and technologies. Sometimes our techniques involve new ways of doing, as when we establish a new form of government or modify our cultural habits to make new arrangements for the raising of children. Sometimes they involve new ways of thinking, as when we construct a set of new criteria for judging what we call "facts." And sometimes they involve new material creations, like digging sticks or wheels or money or computers.

But whether they involve new forms of economic and social organizations, new methods of thinking or new media, human techniques and technologies are always responses to something. And that something is problems—problems that result from change.

So, from the media ecologist's point of view, human history can be read as the history of our species' attempts to solve problems of adjustment to change.

Specifically, media ecologists read history as the record of our attempts to solve problems of information: how to get it, preserve it, interpret it, use it, disseminate it and control it. We also read history as the record of how our attempts at solutions have themselves introduced more change and therefore new problems, in an apparently infinite process. And since we do see this process as unending, it is also the way we read the present and the future. In fact, the point of view I've just outlined is so fundamental to any understanding of media change that I'd like to abstract it here in the form of three laws: the laws of media change.

The first law: Changes in communication are attempts to solve human information problems. The second law: Every attempt to solve information problems suffers from inadequacies. These inadequacies result in new problems which are the impetus for further change. And the third law: Every attempt to solve information problems itself introduces change into the state of our information and thus presents additional problems, which also generate further change.

The trouble with laws like this is that, once stated, they come across as either obvious (and uninteresting) or too abstract (therefore vague) to be useful. To demonstrate that this is not the case—to show you these laws are useful and how they work—I will apply them to a specific instance of media change in human history. I'll choose as my case language itself, because as the prototype of all human communication, language has a great deal to teach us.

So let me begin with the first law: that communications media are responses to human problems, especially problems of information. Language is so ubiquitous among people and so ancient in its origins that it is rightly regarded as the defining characteristic of our species. So, if the first law of media is correct, we ought to find behind language a problem of the most pressing urgency. And of course we do. To put it as simply as possible: Language was the solution of a very weak species in a hotly contested environmental niche to the problem of how to pass on survival-enhancing information to its offspring. Our ancestors were neither strong nor swift nor rapid reproducers, and they had neither the luxury of time nor the margin for error required to keep a species alive and adaptive in the face of change. Our survival required a means to store and transmit acquired information—and that information had to be in a form more subject to rapid revision and less perishable than DNA. Language is the most efficient solution to that problem our species has yet produced. And that is why it has survived everywhere as our primary communications technique.

But language is not a perfect solution. And that brings me to Law Number Two, which reminds us that every solution to information problems has inadequacies which themselves pose new problems and thus fuel the engine of change. In the case of language, these inadequacies are almost painfully apparent. Language is a wonderful code for storing and recording acquired information, but it must be stored in human minds. And the human mind is biological stuff housed in a soft and very vulnerable body which is, alas, all too perishable. Human memories are also limited in what they can hold and retrieve and, in turn, transmit to the young. So long as the amount of information we needed did not exceed our capacity for storing it collectively in the minds of fifty or so people banded together in tribes, these limitations did not constitute pressing problems.

Now we have to consider Law Number Three: New techniques of communication change the state of our information, and this becomes an additional source of new problems. In the case of language, two changes of enormous significance occurred. The first is that language introduced into the world a new kind of knowledge altogether. Before its development, our ancestors were, like all creatures before them, conscious of the world outside their skins. With the advent of the word, they became conscious of the world within. In a word, humans became *self-conscious*. And consciousness of self is the beginning of reflective thought.

Through reflective thought we become able to not merely record past experience but to reimagine our experiences. To imagine it differently and thus transform it. In other words, reflective thought allows us to represent alternative actions to ourselves—to imagine their various outcomes and to consider, revise and improve our plans without deadly risk. It also allows us to see new connections and combinations, and thus to invent new ideas and tools and ways of doing. Reflective thought allowed early humans to modify their environments. And when those environments could no longer sustain them, they were able to plan, and to move on to ever more diverse climes.

Thus the first major consequence of language for the state of our information was to increase by ever-larger exponents the quantity to be recorded, stored in memory, and transmitted to the young. The second consequence of language was also a result of self-awareness. For with the dawning of reflective thought and self-consciousness come curiosity about one's origins and, inevitably, awareness of one's own end. These created a new kind of information problem, not known on this planet before: the problem of *meaning*.

And the solution to that problem was the creation of an entirely new structure of information: the web of connected narrative we call a story or a tale. Among other things, narrative is a way of explaining oneself to oneself. Every waking moment—indeed, even in your sleep—you are telling yourself a story in which you are the central character. This need arises out of consciousness as inevitably as the need to breathe arises out of biology. That is why humans everywhere ask, as soon as their language is fully formed, "Where did I come from?" —and shortly after, "What will happen when I die?" They require a story in order to give meaning to their existence. Without air, the body dies. Without a tale, the self dies. Tribes and nations as well as people require tales, and may die for lack of a believable one. Perhaps, now living in a world made small by technology, we no longer believe in tribal and national tales.

However, tales do more than provide a person, a community, or a nation with a sense of identity. Narrative also provides the basic framework for organizing experience. Through narrative we select what is relevant and ignore what is not. Without tales, our ancestors would have been swamped by the volume of experience language permitted them to encode. Too much information, taken in the raw, would have been just as deadly as too little information. So narrative functions as a kind of information sieve, retaining only those chunks of information that fit its structure while allowing the rest to fall away. Thus by ignoring—in effect, destroying—some information, a tale makes experience manageable. Tales also provide the frame through which we assess our position and define our problems. They tell us what more we need to know and where to direct our efforts to acquire further information. In this way, narrative plays a central role in regulating the ecology of information and experience.

A quick run-through of some 150,000 years of history will show us how the cycle of media change with regard to language continued to play out. As we've seen, speech solved a problem in transmitting information by encoding it in a new form. But that form gave rise to enormous amounts of new information, which led to problems in how to select and organize it. Narrative solved that problem, but ultimately left an intolerable burden on our only means of storing that information: memory. Writing solved the problem of storing information, but created new problems in how to reproduce and disseminate it. Printing solved *that* problem, but also revealed gaps and inconsistencies in the narratives recorded from earlier times, now that people could study them and compare them in books. This created a problem in how to acquire more reliable information, to close those gaps and resolve those inconsistencies. And the solution to *that* was the development of a new set of tools and techniques for gathering and testing information, which we call science. Science in turn generated vast amounts of information at such a rapid rate that its efficient storage, revision and dissemination was beyond the means of our mechanical technologies. But technology solved these problems with a long string of engineering successes that have given us the complex of electronic media we have today.

And so we come at last to our own era. How are we to diagnose *our* problem? To begin with, let's not get distracted by the label the "Age of Information." Humans are understandably proud of themselves and their accomplishments, so we like to name our eras for what we are doing, and doing very well. The trouble with this mild form of self-congratulation is that it directs our attention to the wrong thing—to solutions, rather than problems. This blinds us to the driving forces underlying what moves us forward—and thus to the problems that lie ahead. In the case of the Age of Information, we have a particularly obtuse title. Every age is an age of information.

If we take the term to mean that ours is the age in which we learn how to acquire and generate information efficiently, well, that would certainly be worth remarking. But we would be wrong. It is science that solved the problem of generating reliable information, and science was the accomplishment of the past age, not our own. No, acquiring information is not the achievement of our age—and it is not our problem either.

The "Age of Information" tells us little except that we are generating, storing, transmitting and revising a great deal of information. To get a sense of the problem that does confront us, I offer you this advice: When everyone else is telling you what marvelous things communications technologies *can* do, you should nod and smile—and focus your own attention resolutely on what they *can't* do, because that is where our problems come from: not from what media have done, but from what they haven't. Even more important, ask what they have *un*done.

From the point of view of that question—what science and the technologies of our time have undone—the central problem of our age starts to become clear. Science and technology have unloosed a veritable deluge of information upon the world. At the same time, they have undone the vital regulator that we require to organize, manage and make it meaningful. For in solving the problem of acquiring information, science took apart narrative. It rendered toothless and untenable the prevailing religious tales of origins and endings. In its place, it gave us Darwin's tale, the tale of evolution, and—shortly after—what I call the Technopoly Tale. That is to say, the tale of technological progress with paradise to be restored, not in some misty hereafter, but here on earth, through the wonders of technology.

The Tale of Technopoly is proving dangerously inadequate. Like the sorcerer's apprentice, we are awash in a flood of information about an expanding world, and all the sorcerer has left us is a broom. From millions of sources all over the globe and beyond, through every possible channel, platform, and medium information pours in on a mounting tide. In every imaginable form of storage—on paper, in books and libraries, on video and audio tapes and discs, on film and silicon chips. And more is added—every minute, every hour, every second.

And we have no great problem in transmitting it or receiving information. No, getting it is not our problem. We are swamped by information. Drowning in it. Overwhelmed by it. And we don't know how to reduce it to manageable proportions, or organize it coherently. We are unable to sift the relevant from the irrelevant, or even to know what questions to ask. We have no sieve, no filter that might give a meaningful structure to all of this information.

In short, we face a crisis of narrative. In our personal lives, our lives as workers, as students and scholars, our lives as citizens of nations, members of cultures, humans on a fragile planet spinning somewhere in the void—people are suffering from a breakdown in meaningful narrative, of organizing and life-sustaining tales. The problem did not originate with us. It has been building for several centuries— from the time when improved communication techniques and technologies began to give us more information about a world larger than our old tribal or national tales could integrate. Certainly, the ascendency of science over the last five centuries has played a decisive role in our current narrative crisis. But it is our own communication technologies that have brought the problem to its present pitch—partly because they provide so much information about so large a world. And partly because they are incapable of generating a meaningful point of view, or reflecting on the need to do so.

This, then, is the problem our age must solve. Electronic information media are not addressing this problem, and there is no reason for us to think that they can or they will. A computer can answer the questions you put to it. It can even be programmed to generate its own questions. But it will not invite us on a quest for meaning. It cannot kindle compelling, creative curiosity, or point us toward transcendence. Television conveys many tales, but its commercial ones are all the same, in different guises: the Technopoly Tale or the tale of human life as consumption. At the moment, it's the only organizing tale we've got. That, and a handful of despairing short stories, encapsulated in one-liners on tee-shirts and bumper stickers.

The collapse of narrative, I think, is the problem of our era. And this means that the need for narrative is driving the engine of change.

I take it as confirmation of this point that many people who once abandoned religion as untenable or dangerously tribal are returning to it now—perhaps because some narrative, no matter how flawed, is better than none. We may be tempted to greet this turning with joy. But we might do well to temper our gladness with concern. Not all tales with a god at their center are life-giving or benign. And people who are driven to faith in despair of their lives do not always choose what to worship wisely or well. Too often their newfound faith cannot rest secure until everyone else has been sacrificed for their sins. And I think we are right to view the resurrection of old sorceries disguised as new—the retreat into unreason, into fantastic spiritisms, into the magic and mysteries of power associated with "New Age" thinking—as but one more symptom of the extremes to which our need for narrative is driving us.

I interpret the recent U.S. elections as another. It's by now a commonplace in the States to attribute presidential election results to the candidates' use of television. And there is much to be said for that observation. But I think the truth lies a little deeper. Not in that they used television, but in what they used it for. The Democratic candidate, Michael Dukakis, used his time to tell us about the nation's problems—pollution, drugs, infant mortality, the homeless, crime—and what he had already done and planned to do about them. The Republican, George Bush, used his time to paint with images and flags and songs a story of America the Beautiful—of Daybreak in America, of misty mornings on the farm, factory workers clasping hands, mothers rejoicing in the miracle of birth, children and immigrants saluting the flag, Americans lighting candles for the homeless, a thousand points of light. Dukakis gave us the federal deficit. Bush told us an achingly poignant, if totally mythic, tale. It is a measure of the depths of our narrative despair that knowing the facts we chose instead the deceitful tale.

People will have narratives. They must have them to survive. If they cannot find or construct new or better ones, they will seek meaning elsewhere, in the misty mornings of a vanished past or in a darker, uglier tribal tale. And I do not need to speak, I hope, of the kinds of solutions to which those kinds of tribal tales can lead.

So I think the problem before us now is clear. Somewhere our age must find new and more compelling ways to tell the human story. A story large enough to transcend personal boundaries and class interests, and tribal, racial and even national concerns. The information technologies of our world have made the world too small, and our interdependencies too great, for the older, narrower tales. Where and how we may find the notes to compose a new song—a song that sings of us all—it is too early to say.

On Technopoly

Our ability to represent, store and transform our experiences into symbols means that we humans do not live solely in a natural environment. Through our capacity to use language and other symbol systems, we also live in our symbolic environments. Which is to say, we live in a world of ideas and inventions, of social arrangements and values that are shaped by our ideas and our technologies.

Just as the natural environment can become polluted, so too can the environment of ideas—the world created by our symbols and technologies.

In fact, the diseases of the symbolic environment may be far more insidious. They develop slowly. They creep in. They're not recognized until it is too late to check their spread. In fact, more often than not, we welcome them with open arms, because they come disguised in delightful forms—like television sets and VCRs—and are usually wrapped in the glittering package labeled "progress." No nation and no culture is immune to the ravages they may wreak. Nor, in the electronic age, does distance provide protection. That's because a technology—whether a jet plane or a computer—does not simply transmit ideas. It is itself an expression of an idea, and quite capable of transforming our beliefs, our values, our relationships, and even the face of our planet.

Consider the automobile. When Mr. Ford introduced it on a mass scale early in the 20th century, he probably saw it as a relatively cheap and convenient way of getting around. He did not foresee that it also embodied a whole array of new ideas—ideas about the meaning of place and of home and of family and of community. The car dissolves the idea that shared space is the basis for defining our relationships, and instead sets us free to wander, rootless, wherever we might imagine things to be better. Certainly no one foresaw that in the service of this idea—the automobile—we would pave over our lands with tar, choke our cities, poison our air. That we would revise our notions of time—so that, for instance, we have redefined "good" as "fast" (not only in matters of transportation but even in our preferences for food). Well, the automobile has been with us for nearly a century and we're only just now beginning to see its consequences as an idea—even to grasp the fact that it *is* an idea and not just a machine.

We are even less aware of the ideas and consequences that lurk in other newer techniques and technologies—ideas that may be even more invisible and in the end perhaps more deadly. One such idea, or set of ideas, is a kind of infection of our symbolic environment that has already devastated much of the social landscape. I call this disease "Technopoly."

Tale of Technopoly has become our way of life. How that story began—the origins of "Technopoly"—will help explain what I mean by the term. It will give you a sense not only of how it arose but its symptoms, which should give you some idea of its power and its toxic consequences.

"Technopoly" describes a form of culture organized around a set of degrading and inhumane beliefs. To best explain what these are, I have to contrast Technopoly with two other kinds of cultures. The first we might call simply tool-using cultures. Until the 18th century, all cultures were simply tool-users. There was considerable variation both in the kinds of tools available to different peoples and from one culture to another. Some cultures had only spears and cooking utensils and some had crossbows and watermills and eyeglasses. But the main characteristic of all tool-using cultures is that their technologies were invented to solve specific and urgent problems of physical, material life. Tools were made to serve the social world of human relations and to fit within the symbolic world of art and myth and ritual and religion. No matter what new tools were introduced to make the material world more manageable, people could continue to believe in their traditions, in their gods, in their politics, in their methods of education, and in the legitimacy of their social organization. In fact, these beliefs directed the invention of tools and limited the uses to which they were put.

So, in a tool-using culture, technology is not hostile to other belief systems; it coexists serenely with the prevailing traditions that give a culture its distinctiveness and its meaning. There still exist on our planet a very few tool-using cultures, which we usually call primitive. We call them primitive, in part, because to us their tools seem crude and limited. But mostly because in any confrontation with a technocratic culture they are overwhelmed.

Now, a technocratic culture is entirely different—a more recent type of culture in which tools play a much more central role. Technocracy was born in the 18th century and came of age in the 19th and 20th, but its gestation period was quite long. Its seeds were sown in mediaeval times by three great technologies which ultimately brought into being the modern world. The first of these was the mechanical clock, which had its origins in the Benedictine monasteries of the 12th and 13th centuries. The clock was invented to solve a specific problem: namely, to provide regularity to the routines of the monasteries which, among other things, required seven periods of devotion during the course of the day. The bells of the monastery were rung to signal these periods of devotion, and the mechanical clock was a technology invented to give precision to the ringing of the bells. And so it did.

What the Benedictines did not foresee was that the clock is not merely a means of keeping track of the hours. It is also a means of synchronizing and controlling the actions of human beings. By the middle of the 14th century, the clock had moved outside the walls of the monastery and brought a new and precise regularity to the life of the working man and the merchant. The mechanical clock made possible the idea of regular production, regular working hours and a standardized product. Without the clock, it is no exaggeration to say, capitalism would have been impossible. Which, as Karl Marx noted, is a stunning irony: The clock was invented by men who wanted to devote themselves more rigorously to God, and ended up serving the men who devoted themselves to the accumulation of money. But more to the point, the clock undermined traditional notions of work, of economic relations and of social order.

The second great transforming technology was the printing press with movable type invented in the mid 15th century. And the third was the telescope, especially Galileo's, invented at the beginning of the 17th century. The printing press changed the form in which information was codified and preserved and transported. As a consequence, new methods of education and learning were developed, new forms of literature—including what we call prose—were created, and the beginnings of inductive science made possible. In other words, printing attacked the epistemology, the ways of knowing, of the oral tradition and put a new one in its place.

The telescope, the third transformative technology, for its part, attacked a fundamental proposition of Judeo-Christian theology: that the earth was the stable center of the universe and therefore of special interest to God. By proving that the Earth moves, Galileo and his followers ultimately placed the earth in an obscure galaxy, in some obscure corner of the universe, and left the Western world to wonder if God had any interest in us at all.

The clock, the press and the telescope: They attacked traditional conceptions of human relations, of economic systems, of learning and knowledge, of religious beliefs and practices. In subtle ways they set in motion a slow revolution in the relationship between humans and their tools. Where technologies had once played a subordinate role in the material, social and symbolic life of cultures, they began to move gradually to a position of central importance. The movement was slow. As late as the 17th century, even the greatest of Renaissance inventions—the assemblage of tools and techniques we call science—was seen merely as a means to social and religious ends. Newton himself conceived of his work as a hymn to the power and glory of God.

The great successes of the new technical means in dominating the material world came gradually to redefine and overwhelm their social and symbolic purposes. As a consequence, the social and symbolic worlds became more and more subject to the dominance of technology. By the end of the 18th century, and certainly by the beginning of the 19th, most western cultures were striving to become technocracies. The beliefs upholding traditional culture and institutions now competed with those of the dominating technologies—social mores, myth and religion had to fight for their lives.

As Alfred North Whitehead observed, the greatest invention of the 19th century was the idea of invention itself. Indeed, that idea left little room for the methods and beliefs of an earlier age. After learning how to invent things, the question of why we invented things appeared increasingly irrelevant. The idea that simply because something could be done it should be done was born in the 19th century. But this was not the only idea underlying technocratic culture. There also developed a profound belief in all the principles through which invention succeeds: measurement, objectivity, efficiency and standardization, expertise and progress. And it came to be believed, as well, that the engine of technological progress works best—most "efficiently"—when people are conceived of, not as children of God or as citizens, but as consumers. That is to say, as markets.

As I speak, not all nations have reached technocratic equality. China is now rapidly moving from a tool-using state of culture to technocracy. And I think that's true of most of the cultures we call the Third World.

Nor is technocracy universally admired. There are those who will become misty-eyed and romantic about the supposed superiority of the tool-using cultures of our more ancient past. And there is a powerful and compelling argument to be made for the integrity and cohesion and meaningfulness of early tool-using cultures, but it's not an argument I really care to make.

ON TECHNOPOLY | 189

For most of us, technocracies have so vastly improved the conditions of our material lives that their superiority over tool-using cultures is self-evident. (Think about electricity, or central heating.) Moreover, there is this to be said for technocracies: They do not entirely destroy the traditions of our social and symbolic worlds. They subordinate those worlds—they even belittle those worlds—but they do not destroy them. It is possible in a technocracy to still have holy men and to believe in sin. It is possible to have regional pride and to conform to the notions of family life. It is possible to respect tradition itself, and to find meaning in ritual. It is possible to believe in social responsibility and the practicality of individual political action. It is even possible to believe in common sense and the wisdom of the elderly. It is not easy, but it's possible.

Technocracies disdain such beliefs because holy men and sin and grandmothers and families and regional loyalties and 2000-year-old traditions are antagonistic to the technocratic way of life. They are criticisms of that way of life. They represent a thought-world that stands apart from technocracy and rebukes it—rebukes its language, its personality, its aspirations, its motivations and values, its entire belief structure. Technocracy disdains such thought-worlds, but it allows them to survive. The wiser technocracies in fact encourage them to survive even at the cost of tolerating that uncomfortable schism lamented by C.P. Snow in his 1960s book *The Two Cultures*. The condition that Snow described might very well serve as the definition of a technocracy: A technocracy is a culture in which two opposing worldviews—the technological and the humanistic—coexist in uneasy tension. The technological view is the stronger, of course, but the humanistic is kept alive.

Not so in Technopoly. Technopoly eliminates alternative thought-worlds in precisely the way Aldous Huxley outlined in *Brave New World*. It does not make them illegal. It does not make them immoral. It does not even make them unpopular. It makes them invisible and therefore irrelevant. And it does so by redefining what we mean by religion, by art, by family, by politics, by history, by truth, by privacy, by intelligence—so that our definitions fit the requirements of the technological thought-world. Technopoly, in other words, is totalitarian technocracy.

Perhaps the most characteristic example I can offer you at the start is a machine called HAGOTH, which was available to anyone in America a few years ago for $1,500. HAGOTH has 16 lights—eight green and eight red. If you connect HAGOTH to your telephone it lets you know whether the person talking to you is telling the truth. I'm not making this up. The way it does this is by measuring what is called the "stress content" of a human voice, which it does by recording its oscillations—how much it goes up and down. So here's how it works: You ask your caller some key questions like where did you go last Saturday night and HAGOTH goes to work on analyzing the replies. Red lights go on when there is much stress in the voice, green lights when there is little. As an advertisement for HAGOTH said "green indicates no stress, hence truthfulness." In other words, according to HAGOTH it is not possible to speak the truth in a quivering voice. Think about that. And I hope you agree: that's a very peculiar idea.

But no more peculiar than the idea of an intelligence test, which was invented by a Frenchman but has achieved its apotheosis in the U.S.. Actually, an intelligence test works exactly like HAGOTH. In an intelligence test, you connect a pencil to the fingers of a young person, address some key questions, and from the replies a computer will calculate exactly how much intelligence is in the young person's brain. There is no point in telling an intelligence test that intelligence can be expressed in a variety of ways, most of them having nothing to do with pencil and paper. The intelligence test, like HAGOTH, speaks with the authority of the Oracle at Delphi because the machinery of Technopoly is trusted implicitly.

While HAGOTH has mercifully disappeared from the market, at least for the moment, its idea lives on in the polygraph or "lie-detector test." In the U.S. these tests are taken very seriously not only by policemen and lawyers, but by corporate executives, who, increasingly, insist that employees be subjected to them. As for intelligence tests, they not only survive, but flourish. And they have been supplemented by vocational aptitude tests, creativity tests, mental health tests, sexual attraction tests and even marital compatibility tests. Now you might think that two people who live together for a number of years would know for themselves whether or not they get along. But in Technopoly such subjective forms of knowledge are not taken seriously. Individual judgements, after all, are notoriously unreliable—filled with ambiguity and plagued by doubt—and tests and machines are not.

Philosophers may agonize over questions like "what is truth?" and "what is intelligence?" But in Technopoly there is no need for such intellectual struggles. Machines eliminate complexity and doubt and ambiguity. They work quickly, they are standardized, and they provide us with numbers that you can see and calculate. They tell us when eight green lights go on, someone is speaking the truth. They tell us that a score of 136 means more brains than a score of 104. It's Technopoly's version of reality.

But why, you might ask, is *that* reality? The answer in part is that the machinery is designed and supervised by technical experts who in effect function as the high priests of Technopoly. Some of these priests are merely engineers. Some are called sociologists, some psychologists and some social psychologists. The god they serve does not speak of righteousness or goodness or mercy or grace. Their god speaks of efficiency, precision, objectivity, of health and normalcy and marketability. And that is why the concepts of sin and evil disappear from Technopoly.

Such concepts come from a moral universe that is irrelevant to the thought-world of technology. And so the priests of Technopoly have come to call sin "social deviance," which is a statistical concept. And they call evil "psychopathology," which is a medical concept. Sin and evil disappear because they cannot be standardized, objectified and measured—and therefore they cannot be treated by experts.

Expertise plays a great part in Technopoly's power to control people. Today, we have experts in how to raise children, in how to make love, in how to be lovable, in how to influence people, in how to make friends. There is no aspect of human relations that has not been technicalized and thereby relegated to the domain of experts, who share with the public the belief that their techniques, tests and numbers are superior to wisdom and common sense.

But I assume you know that there can be no experts in child-rearing and love-making and friend-making—that all of this is a figment of the technopolist's imagination. But it is what we end up with when we believe in the supreme authority of technology. And when we do that, we also allow our technologies to govern public life.

For a ready example, the university at which I teach computerized its operations about 10 years ago. Prior to that, the administration required from each of its faculty and staff members 17 pieces of information. These included your name, your address, your marital status, your Social Security number and a few other facts that we used to think were essential. After total computerization, the number of required facts increased rapidly. At the present time, the university requires more than 1200 pieces of information about each employee. Whether the university actually needs 1200 pieces of information has become irrelevant. The technical capacity is justification enough. That we no longer ask if this makes sense—indeed, that we hardly even notice—is powerful evidence that we are living in the Age of Technopoly.

A recent study in the United States revealed that nearly half the patients who have undergone heart bypass surgery in the last 10 years did not require it. Our hospitals have become places where illness is essentially defined as an engineering problem. With Technopoly, we do not use our technology for people, we use it *on* them—which is to say, people exist to accommodate technology, and not the other way around.

Examples abound. To accommodate the combustion engine we have allowed our air to be poisoned and our cities choked and turned natural landscape into pavement. We are not only allowing computer technology to redefine what we mean by privacy, but also to debase the status of human judgment. We now use computers to tell us who should be permitted to go to university, and who should be granted financial loans. We have allowed television to take charge of our national politics, discarding in the process an honorable tradition of intelligible and serious political debate. An American journalist recently observed that John F Kennedy was the first president who looked like a movie actor but that Ronald Reagan was the first movie actor who looks like a president. What he meant, of course, is that tele-politics does not require articulate language. It requires only the pleasing visual imagery of show business.

As politics has transformed to accommodate television, so too has religion. What unfolds as religion on the television screen is devoid of ritual, tradition, theology and continuity. In justifying his use of television to reach millions, Billy Graham said that he was sure that had television been available to Jesus when he delivered his Sermon on the Mount, Jesus would certainly have used it. Mr Graham says this of a man who declined to use even the written word, although it had been available for 1500 years before his coming. Unlike Mr. Graham, Jesus did not live in Technopoly. Jesus said, "For where two or three are gathered together in my name, there am I in the midst of them." Could it be that Jesus' meaning of "gathered together" is fundamentally different from Billy Graham's? That we do not "gather together" through television? Is it possible that Jesus would have no interest in his audience ratings? Is such a thing imaginable? To a technopolist like Billy Graham, that is inconceivable.

Machines and measurements redefine goals from what *ought* to be done to what *can* be done. If two or three are good, would not two or three thousand be better? And since television can reach two or three million, would that not be better still—and twenty or thirty million best of all? As for the *purpose* for which two or three might gather—well, that has been lost. Instead, the gathering itself becomes the end, and if it requires some changes in what you are doing to gather a bigger audience, so much the worse for religion.

Technopoly, you see, is the state of culture and the state of mind in which the only ends that survive are the ends technology can accomplish. The only questions worth asking are the questions technology can answer. The only problems worth solving are the problems technology and its experts can solve. It is a form of to-talitarianism centered not only on methods and machines, but on a handful of unquestioned assumptions about human beings and about knowledge. One is that humans are essentially consumers and groups of humans merely markets. A second is that the standardization—whether of things or behavior—is in all cases desir-able, that personal experience and individual judgments are sloppy and unreliable, that precision and measurement are the sole means of arriving at truth. Third is that the management of human affairs is the proper domain of technique and "ex-pertise"; that traditional sources of guidance—whether through ritual or intuition, common sense or a sense of morality, religion or art—are obstructions to be swept aside in the forward march of progress. And finally that in all things, fast is better than slow, new is better than old, more is better than less.

These are the principal elements of what I'm calling the Technopoly Tale. It is a large-scale, integrated belief system: A narrative that constitutes a way of explaining ourselves to ourselves, of selecting what we should attend to, of directing our behavior and judging its results. If it were one tale among many, perhaps we would have little to fear. But the Technopoly Tale is totalitarian. It exerts control over other tales, usurping how we understand and what we create. It crowds out alternative tales, rendering them inaudible, invisible, irrelevant, making them impossible to imagine. But in the end, the Technopoly Tale proves heartless and cruel, devoid of spiritual content and meaning. To the question "where did we come from?" Technopoly answers "an accident." To the question "how will it all end?" Technopoly replies "probably by accident." And to the question "how shall we live between accidents?" Technopoly replies "amuse yourselves—consume." And to the question "to what purpose?" Technopoly answers "to divert yourselves from noticing that life in Technopoly has no other purpose."

And that is why diversion becomes in Technopoly not just a side effect of media but its purpose. Amusement is the last refuge, you might say, of a people deprived of any more meaningful end. Or perhaps it is only the next to last refuge. Violence and drugs suggest that amusement no longer suffices to divert us from the emptiness of Technopoly.

There is nothing inevitable about the step from technocracy to Technopoly. But you have to see it, and you have to know where it will lead. You have some choice about the matter. There is no use in my pretending that it's an easy choice. To reject Technopoly you pay a price—in the loss of money and power and prestige and comforts. Moreover, the choice isn't all that is easy to see. Technopoly creeps up on us, so to speak, when we are looking the other way—at the bright benefits and the pretty packages marked "harmless" and "entertainment" and "progress." In the U.S., we did not notice that the marketers and the advertisers became the important storytellers of our age. We did not notice that television producers and anchormen had come to replace the poets and prophets and troubadours of earlier times. We did not notice that our social scientists had become gospel writers of a new and compelling kind. It is time for us to look seriously at the tales our technologies are telling and the lessons they teach.

Consider this set of questions. Are your children being taught to be consumers? Have they begun to believe that paradise is to be gained through technological progress? Do your popular stories teach that the only sin is ignorance of the newest and most efficient product? Do the stories suggest that all problems can be solved, and that they can be solved quickly through improved products and technology?

Do the stories repeat the glories of what is "new" and "fast" and "better"? Are you coming to believe that one should always look young? That to be old and to look old is to be ugly and contemptible? Is the purpose of your schools to prepare the young to market themselves? Is education an investment? Have your churches begun to talk more about how to raise attendance than about why people might attend? Do your social scientists tell you that their tests, instruments and measurements carry no agenda? That, like the technologies they use, they are speaking from a place of objective, neutral authority?

Are all your old tales fading from sight or getting harder to tell? Are the stories that were meaningful to you being nourished and cherished and kept visible? Or are they being swallowed up by the always-consuming Tale of Technopoly? I raise these questions. It is up to you to answer them.

Alternative Narratives

Of all the evils that torment the human spirit, there are two that are greater than all the others—more deadly than all the others—and from which most of the others grow. The first, I think, is a too-great certainty about the completeness of one's own knowledge. And the second is despair.

Of the two, I suspect that certainty is the greater evil, since it is only through certainty that we come to despair. For despair is not merely suffering, or a profound grief, or the intense confusion that accompanies a feeling that one has lost one's way. Despair is misery that's made final by the absolute certainty that the truth as you see it is the only truth there is. In this way, by denying possibilities greater than our own capacity even to imagine, certainty drives out hope.

The sights and sounds of mounting cultural distress, what I see happening with our frightened and floundering young—these things make me angry. They make me fearful and very much aggrieved. But they do not make me despair. The narrative crisis I have been talking about is marked by anguish, to be sure—and I do not want to trivialize or cheapen that anguish. People *are* suffering very greatly.

But it is also filled, this narrative crisis, with possibility—with hope for a new and better age guided by a new and better telling of the human tale. The task of finding it or forging it is all of ours to share. Here, I should like to offer you my own guidelines, my contribution, for such a tale.

Every tale is built on certain words that echo and re-echo throughout its telling. These words are like signposts, directing listeners to what is most important. It is impossible to tell the Technopoly Tale, for example, without using over and over such words as "opportunity," "potential," "ownership," "expertise," "profit." A different tale will call forth different words and there are four that I would place at the center of any new narrative that we might construct.

Where the Technopoly Tale hymns of human potential and power, mine would sing of limits. It is to me a sign of great hope that the word "limits" in all its forms has already begun to reappear gradually in the vocabulary after very long disfavor. Clearly, we don't much like the word "limits" as yet, perhaps because we're so unfamiliar with it. So we're inclined to disguise it, as in the acronym SALT, for the Strategic Arms Limitations Talks. But the idea is there nonetheless. And the attentive may pick it out more frequently now in discussions of such matters as earth's limited resources, or read it occasionally in the title of some major book, like the Club of Rome's major treatise, *The Limits to Growth*.

In most of these uses, though, the word "limits" is associated with the notion of restraint—of self restraint in the exercise of power. While that is, in itself, a very laudable ideal, what I mean by the idea of limits something both humbler and yet more profound. Not the surrender of power we think we have, for that can be merely the flipside of hubris, of overweening ego. But, instead, the recognition that we humans have claimed for ourselves powers and potentials we *cannot* restrain.

The fact of the matter is that we are crude, sensory creatures, living in a blink of time in an obscure corner of a universe so vast that our minds shy from too long a contemplation of it. Even at the sensory level, we are capable of detecting only the tiniest fraction of the change and complexity all around us, and we can attend to and remember even less. And we delude ourselves by thinking that our machines do more than extend by a tiny fraction the scope of our awareness. They change how much we know but not its limited structure. Our languages, our logics, our mathematics, even our machines conform to the patterns our peculiar biology suggests—and to laws of their own in ways that we have not begun to understand. And there is reason to believe that we never can.

In short, we do not know the world—only that very limited version that our biology and our symbols give us. We do not know ourselves—only those versions that our limited memories weave into patterns of half-told tales. We certainly do not know truth—only the shadows and the shards and the bright reflections of it, as of light diffused through dust, or as St Paul says, "through a glass, darkly." The glass of course is the prism of the fallible, the imperfect, the inescapably limited human sensibility and mind.

We need to remember that it is our ignorance that we must learn to restrain. Most of the power and potential we imagine ourselves surrendering is illusory. We have never had it, so it is not ours to give up.

The second word my story would sing is a word familiar to you: stewardship. It's a measure, I think, of the darkness of the glass through which we humans see that stewardship has come to be most closely associated with the idea of giving. In our new narrative, though, we must restore the word's original, opposite meaning. Stewardship is not giving. It is keeping, in the sense of tending, preserving, nourishing. In the sense we mean when we say, "The Lord bless you and keep you." The difference is no mere quibble, because too great an emphasis on what we have to give will lead us quickly back again to hubris and exaggerated self-esteem. And, just as bad, it will preserve the fundamental word in Technopoly: ownership. For we can only give what is ours by right to dispose of—what we think of as our own.

Part of the idea of limits, and the central meaning of stewardship, is that nothing we have is our own.

The plain fact is that none of us had the least part in shaping the land from which we take our daily bread or in designing these bodies that can sow and harvest and eat it. None of us earned our human talents, or created the social world that allows us to put our talents to use and reap their rewards. We are recipients, pure and simple, of a gift unearned by any of our kind. We may choose to say it is nature that endows us, but that does not diminish the gift. We would do well to remember that nature is only a shorthand, a word to sum up a thousand, thousand generations of creatures before us. We breathe because some earlier creature struggled up eons ago out of the sea. We stand because another, at the dawn of time, raised its head. We walk the streets of cities built by the sweat of others. Even such tiny knowledge as we do possess was gained by the labors of others, who sometimes died to achieve it.

We have a priceless inheritance and an awesome charge—to keep and tend; to nurture and enrich—and to pass on to others. Of course to pass it on. Not only to our own children, or the children of future generations, but to others who share our own time. We cannot enrich the gifts in our charge by hoarding—neither our resources, nor our knowledge. The products of our lands and our labors are not our own, any more than the lands themselves or the skills and knowledge that have been bestowed upon us. They must go to serve the common good, not by right but because there is no good that can endure except that held in common.

Stewardship calls into question a word that all of us love—I might almost say, adore. That word is "rights," as in human rights, inalienable rights. It is a word that breathes of such virtue and nobility that it is hard to conceive how a story based upon it could grow dark or evil—or how a good one could put it aside. Yet that is what I propose. Because a story founded on stewardship would not chant much of rights so much as sing instead of responsibilities.

We've grown so used to cherishing our rights that I want to pause to remind us all of the context in which the struggle for rights arose. It dates back to times when some, because they had superior force, justified their exercise of power over others by claiming a special covenant with God—a covenant that made them not stewards but rulers, lords of the earth, demi-gods, with powers to own and dispose below the heavens as God disposed above, by right divine. While the power of kings often served the people well, and confirmed the ancient original longing that men might themselves be gods, people accepted the claim of the divine right of kings to own and rule. When the rule of kings became intolerable, and the people discovered their own power, they did not reject the idea of divine rights and entitlements, but instead claimed them for themselves. Hence Jefferson's sweeping proclamation in the American Declaration of Independence: not that kings do not have rights, but that all men are endowed with equal rights. In its time, and for its time, it was a great and liberating statement, a grand solution to the tyranny of special privilege for a select few.

Today, perhaps, we are ready to consider another, humbler solution to such claims, and one more harmonious with the idea of stewardship: We may be ready to relinquish the position that humans have special rights at all, and to embrace the idea that neither god nor nature endows us with entitlements—only responsibilities. That it is responsibility—not rights—that fall equally on all.

In the Technopoly Tale, the idea of rights becomes that of entitlements, in a shrill, insistent and ever-expanding set of competing claims. We speak not only of straight rights and gay rights, women's rights and men's rights, but the right to life and the right to die, the right to work and the right not to work, the right to information and the right to privacy, the right to education and the right to reject education. Advertisers, of course, long ago incorporated the idea of rights into a simple and powerful mantra of greed. Promoting self-indulgence and an infantile disregard for consequences, they have trivialized what it means to want, to deserve, the claim to a right. We've grown accustomed to hearing about our right to be thin, the right to have the hair color you always wanted, the right to look and feel young, the right to a vacation, and the right to instant credit. We *deserve* a break today (at, of all places, McDonald's). Advertisers will always find ways to merchandise their products. But were such phrases as "you have a right" and "you deserve" and "you are entitled" replaced by phrases that talked of new responsibilities, you'd begin to hear a difference—in how we tell the story of our world and therefore act upon it.

I do not believe that if we banished claims to rights that disputes would cease and that courts and the law would no longer be needed. Responsibilities may come into conflict just as rights do, and we would always need some way to adjudicate which human responsibilities have the greater claim on us. But think how different the arguments would be with each of the parties claiming greater responsibility instead of offended rights.

Of course, I would not argue for banning the word "rights"—or any word for that matter. That would run counter to the fourth theme of the tale I propose, a theme that I cannot find the right word for—or not, at least, in English. I'll settle for "humility," though even that is not quite large enough, to hold all of what I mean.

What I'm trying to get at concerns the surrender of our will to control: To have humility is to relinquish the profound illusion that we have the wisdom or the power or the right to manage nature or the social order or the lives of those we live with—or even our own lives—according to some final plan, some ultimate good, we are certain we see. The humility I'm speaking of goes far beyond mere tolerance of uncertainty and of other's views. Tolerance, I'm afraid, is too often tainted by hubris. Too often it suggests that, in the certainty of *our* truth, we deign to grant to others the right to pursue *their* wrongs. As though we have nothing to learn from those who do not share our beliefs.

Humility does more than admit the incompleteness of our knowledge. It welcomes it! It delights in ambiguity, relishes inconsistency in different tellings of the human tale, cherishes the coexistence of different versions of the truth, and of different ways of knowing it. Humility does not require, or even permit, us to believe that new truths abolish older ones. Or that a vision that helps one people lead their lives must be the final vision—or the vision best for all. Humility finds—in the infinite expanse of knowledge and truth, and in the diversity of human perceptions—the courage to change with change. And the hope that forbids despair.

Well, those are my four words: limits, stewardship, responsibility, humility. Of themselves they are only words, and as words they do not make a connected tale. A tale is more than words. It is a coherent account we give ourselves about ourselves and about the world, that speaks of where we have come from, and how things have been, and where we are going, and why. To be a useful story, it must be large enough to accommodate what we have learned of our past and what our technologies let us know of our expanding world. And to be life-giving, it must allow us to nurture all whose lives are entwined with ours on this small and fragile planet whirling somewhere amidst the stars.

Where shall we find such a tale? The answer I think is where we have always found new tales: in the older ones we have already been telling. We do not need to invent a story for our times out of nothing. Humans never do. Since language and thought and consciousness began, we have been weaving together accounts of our experiences, our worlds, our gods. And every generation has passed on its ways of accounting and its stories. As new generations have encountered more and more of the world and its complexities, and by their own actions complicated the physical and social world, each generation has had to re-read the stories of the past—not rejecting them, but revising and expanding their meaning to accommodate the new. The great revolutions and revelations of the human past have all been great retellings, new ways of narrating ancient truths to encompass a larger world.

For instance, we are inheritors of two great and different tales. The more ancient is the one that begins, "In the beginning, God." And the newer is the account of the world as science and reason give it. One is the tale of Genesis. The other is Euclid's tale, and Galileo's, Newton's, Darwin's. Both are great and stirring accounts of the universe, and the human struggle within it. Both speak of human frailty and error, and of limits. Both may be told in such a way as to invoke our sense of stewardship, to sing of responsibility. Both contain the seeds of a narrative more hopeful than the tale Technopoly tells. And both embrace the complexity, diversity, and interdependency of the world we now encounter through our new technologies.

But both also contain the potential to lead us to monstrous error. And that is why both have, in some measure, failed us. Or, rather, we have failed them. Science and religion can provide us with hopeful, useful and life-giving narratives if we learn to re-read them. To read them with new humility *as* tales—as limited human renderings of a far greater truth that we can never fully know. If we read them—either science or scripture—with pride and arrogance, if we claim that either gives us truth, direct and final, then all their hope and promise turn to dust.

Science read as universal truth, rather than a human tale, is easily made to serve Technopoly. Scripture read as universal truth, not a human tale, degenerates to Inquisition, to Jihad, to Holocaust. In either case, it is certainty that abolishes hope and robs us of renewal.

I believe we are living just now at a special moment in time—at one of those darkening moments when all around us is change, and we cannot yet discern the way to go. Our old ways of explaining ourselves to ourselves are not large enough to accommodate a world made paradoxically small by our technologies yet also larger than we can grasp. Yet we need a way to navigate through the more complex and incomprehensible without being overwhelmed. We cannot go back to simpler times and simpler tales—to a time when the tales made by tribes and nations allowed for each to pursue its separate path. For in a world of electronic technologies there are no places to hide or withdraw—or not for long. We cannot make the world accept one tale, and that our own, by chanting it louder than the rest or by silencing those who are singing a different song. We need a larger reading that encompasses many truths and that lets us grow with change.

We can only make the human tale larger by making ourselves a little smaller—by seeing that the vision that each of us is granted is but a tiny fragment of a much greater truth not given to mortals to know.

Final Tidbit: "Nystrom's Nuggets of Wisdom"

[These are part of a speech Neil Postman used to deliver every year or so to students at NYU, "How to live the rest of your life." The speech consisted of 22 rules along with Nystrom's "Nuggets." This bit was excerpted from *Neil Postman's Advice on How to Live the Rest of Your Life*, which Janet Sternberg published in ETC: A Review of General Semantics, Vol. 63, No. 2 (April 2006), pp. 152–160. Published By: Institute of General Semantics.]

Nystrom's Nugget #1

Reserve the word "friend" for someone who knew you when you still wore braces on your teeth, who has on at least one occasion spent the night with you in a hospital emergency room or police station, and who will without hesitation commit perjury for you in a court of law. Other people may rightly be called "acquaintances."

Nystrom's Nugget #2

Think regularly and deeply about your inevitable end. As Samuel Johnson reminds us, the prospect of one's death wonderfully concentrates the mind.

Nystrom's Nugget #3

When you arise each morning, remind yourself that today you do not have to go to a gas oven with your sisters, brothers, children, and friends. This thought may help you to deal more courageously with the fact that it is raining and your paper is late.

Nystrom's Nugget #4

Cherish your parents, your aging relatives, and all the elderly, wherever you meet them. They may not be smarter than you, but they have suffered longer than you, and you may learn from that.

Nystrom's Nugget #5

Do not place too high a value on honesty and plain speaking. You are not wise enough to know what is the truth, and what seems plain to you may only bring pain to others.

Reading List

Editor's note: Few of these works are directly referenced in Nystrom's published work. However, these are some of the titles that we know she read and discussed, and to that extent appear to have had a significant impact on her ideas. Along with the bibliography from Part I, they help give us a sense of her thinking. And to the extent that media ecology can be said to have a corpus, these foundational texts are its embryo.

Ames, A. (1960). *The morning notes of Adelbert Ames* (H. Cantril, Ed.). Rutgers University Press.

Auerbach, E. (1953). *Mimesis: The representation of reality in western literature.* Princeton University Press.

Bateson, G. (1972). *Steps to an ecology of mind.* Ballantine Books.

Berger, P & Luckmann, T. (1966). *The social construction of reality: A treatise in the sociology of knowledge.* Anchor Books.

Bertalanffy, L. (1968). *General system theory: Foundations, development, Applications.* George Braziller.

Birdwhistell, R. L. (1970). *Kinesics and context.* University of Pennsylvania Press.

Boorstin, D. J. (1987). *The image: A guide to pseudo-events in America.* Atheneum.

Boulding, K. E. (1956). *The image: Knowledge in life and society.* University of Michigan Press.

Burke, K. (1945). *A Grammar of Motives.* Prentice-Hall Inc.

Campbell, J. (1982). *Grammatical man: Information, entropy, language, and life.* Simon & Schuster, Inc.

Carey, J. W. (1989). *Communication as culture: Essays on media and society.* Unwin Hyman.

Carpenter, E. & McLuhan, M. (Eds.). (1966). *Explorations in communication*. Beacon Press.

Cassirer, E. (1946). *Language and myth*. Harper & Brothers.

Chomsky, N. (1972). *Language and mind* (Enlarged edition.) Harcourt, Brace, Jovanovich.

Douglas, M. (1966). *Purity and danger*. Routledge and Kegan Paul.

Douglas, S. (1987). *Inventing American broadcasting, 1899-1922*. John Hopkins.

Eagleton, T. (1983). *Literary theory: An introduction*. University of Minnesota Press

Eisenstein, E. L. (1979). *The printing press as an agent of change: Communications and cultural transformations in early modern Europe* (Vols. I and II). Cambridge University Press.

Ellul, J. (1965). *Propaganda: The formation of men's attitudes* (K. Kellen & J. Lerner, Trans.). Knopf.

Ellul, J. (1964). *The technological society* (J. Wilkinson, Trans.). Knopf.

Ewen, S. (1988). *All consuming images: The politics of style in contemporary culture*. Basic Books.

Foucault, M. (1977). *Discipline and Punish: The birth of the prison* (A. Sheridan trans.). Pantheon Books.

Geertz, Clifford. (1983). *Local knowledge: Further essays in interpretive anthropology*. Basic Books.

Ginzburg, C. (1980). *The cheese and the worms*. (J.&A. Tedeschi, Trans.) John Hopkins

Goffman, E. (1959). *The presentation of self in everyday life*. Doubleday & Company.

Goody, J. R. (1977). *The domestication of the savage mind*. Cambridge University Press.

Hall, E. T. (1966). *The hidden dimension*. Doubleday.

Hall, E. T. (1973). *The silent language*. Anchor.

Havelock, E. (1976). *Origins of western literacy*. Ontario Institute for Studies in Education.

Hayakawa, S. I. (1947). *Language in thought and action*. Harcourt, Brace & Company.

Heisenberg, W. (1962). *Physics and philosophy: The revolution in modern science*. Harper & Row.

Innis, H. (1950). *Empire and communications*. Clarendon Press.

Innis, H. (1951). *The bias of communication*. University of Toronto Press.

Jaynes, J. (1976). *The origin of consciousness in the breakdown of the bicameral mind*. Houghton Mifflin.

Johnson, W. (1946). *People in quandaries: The semantics of personal adjustment*. Harper & Brothers.

Korzybski, A. (1933). *Science and sanity*. International Non-Aristotelian Library Publishing Company.

Kuhn, T. S. (1970). *The structure of scientific revolutions* (2nd ed.). University of Chicago Press.

Lakoff, G. & Johnsom, M. (1980). *Metaphors we live by*. University of Chicago Press.

Langer, S. K. (1957). *Philosophy in a new key: A study of the symbolism of reason, rite, and art*. (3rd edition). Harvard University Press.

Langer, S. K. (1953). *Feeling and form*. Charles Scribner & Sons.

Langer, S. K. (1968). *Language and mind*. Harcourt, Brace & World.

Marvin, C. (1988). *When old technologies were new: Thinking about electric communication in the late nineteenth century*. Oxford University Press.

McLuhan, M. (1962). *The Gutenberg galaxy: The making of typographic man*. University of Toronto Press.

McLuhan, M. (1964). *Understanding media: The extensions of man*. McGraw-Hill.

Mead, G. H. (1934). *Mind, self and society*. University of Chicago Press.

Meyrowitz, J. (1985). *No sense of place: The impact of electronic media on social behavior*. Oxford University Press.

Mumford, L. (1963). *Technics and civilization*. Revised Edition. Harcourt, Brace & World.

Mumford, L. (1967). *The myth of the machine, Vol. 1: Technics and human development*. Harcourt, Brace & World.

Mumford, L. (1970). *The myth of the machine, Vol. 2: The pentagon of power*. Harcourt, Brace, Jovanovich.

Nystrom, C. L. (1973). *Towards a science of media ecology: The formulation of integrated conceptual paradigms for the study of human communication systems*. (UMI No. 7412855) [Doctoral dissertation, New York University].

Ong, W. J. (1967). *The presence of the word: Some prolegomena for cultural and religious history*. Yale University Press.

Ong, W. J. (1977). *Interfaces of the word: Studies in the evolution of consciousness and culture*. Cornell University Press.

Ong, W. J. (1982). *Orality and literacy: The technologizing of the word*. Methuen.

Perkinson, H. (1991). *Getting better: Television and moral progress* (2nd ed). Transaction/Routledge.

Perkinson, H. (1995). *The imperfect panacea: American faith in education* (4th ed). McGraw Hill.

Perkinson, H (1996). *No safety in numbers: How the computer quantified everything and made people risk-aversive*. Hampton Press.

Pfeiffer, J. (1982. *The creative explosion: An inquiry into the origins of art and religion*. Harper and Row.

Popper, K. R. (1966). *The open society and its enemies, Vol. 1: The spell of Plato* (5th ed.). Princeton University Press.

Postman, N. & Weingartner, C. (1969). *Teaching as a subversive activity*. Delacorte.

Postman, N. (1985). *Amusing ourselves to death: Public discourse in the age of show business*. Viking.

Postman, N. (1976). *Crazy talk/stupid talk*. Dell Publishing.

Postman, N. (1994). *The disappearance of childhood*. (2nd ed.) Vintage.

Postman, N. (1979). *Teaching as a conserving activity*. Delacorte

Postman, N. (1992). *Technopoly: The surrender of culture to technology*. Knopf.

Radway, J. (1991). *Reading the romance: Women, patriarchy, and popular literature*. (2nd ed.) University of North Carolina Press.

Richards, I. A. (1929). *Practical Criticism: A study of Literary Judgement*. Harcourt, Brace, Jovanovich

Rosenblatt, L. (1978). *The reader, the text, the poem: The transactional theory of the literary work*, Carbondale, IL: Southern Illinois University Press.

Sapir, E. (1921). *Language*. Harcourt, Brace and Company.

Schmandt-Besserat, D. (1992). *Before writing*. University of Texas Press.

Schudson, M. (1978). *Discovering the news: A social history of American newspapers.* Basic Books, Inc.

Shannon, C. E. & Weaver, W. (1949). *The mathematical theory of communication.* University of Illinois Press.

Sontag, S. (1977). *On photography.* Farrar, Straus and Giroux.

Tuchmann, B. (1978). *A distant mirror: The calamitous 14th century.* Knopf.

Turkle, S. (1995). *Life on the screen: Identity in the age of the internet.* Simon & Schuster.

Watt, I. (1967). *The rise of the novel: Studies in Defoe, Richardson and Fielding.* University of California Press.

Watzlawick, P., Bavelas, J. B. & Jackson, D. D. (1967). *The pragmatics of human communication: A study of interactional patterns, pathologies, and paradoxes.* WW Norton and Company.

Weaver, W. (1949). The mathematics of communication. *Scientific American, 181*(1), 11–15.

Weizenbaum, J. (1976). *Computer power and human reason: From judgment to calculation.* W.H. Freeman.

White, Jr., L. (1962). *Medieval Technology and Social Change.* Oxford University Press.

Whitehead, A. N. (1927). *Symbolism, its meaning and effect.* The Macmillan Company.

Whitehead, A. N. (1948). *Science and the modern world.* Mentor Books.

Whorf, B. L. (1956). *Language, thought, and reality: Selected writings of Benjamin Lee Whorf* (ed. John B. Carroll). M.I.T. Press.

Wiener, N. (1948). *Cybernetics.* John Wiley & Sons.

Wiener, N. (1967). *The human use of human beings; cybernetics and society.* Avon Books.

Williams, R. (1975). *Television: Technology and cultural form.* Knopf.

Wittgenstein, L. (1963). *Philosophical Investigations.* (G.E.M. Anscombe, Trans.) Oxford: Basil Blackwell.

Addendum:
Remembrances

A thinker's published works endure over time and space. But what of the legacy that lies beyond the merely bibliographical? For so many brilliant minds—Nystrom's very definitely among them—to restrict the definition of 'contribution to the field' to the written word is woefully inadequate. Chris Nystrom was enormously and quietly generous. Her scholarly career was devoted to the personal and more evanescent contributions: officially, in classroom lectures, in her office and at conferences, helping with dissertations, officiating on commitee, and participating in the many oral examinations; but unofficially, and perhaps more remarkably, in the conversations she shared with colleagues and students—over lunch in the faculty dining room at Bobst Library, after class, perhaps over a glass of wine in a pub, or having coffee while seated in a cafeteria at some seminar, or meeting up at the local coffee shop.

In a very real sense, Chris's most important legacy is a living one: the students she challenged and inspired and sent out into the world to challenge and inspire others. Which is why, in preparation for this volume, we contacted a number of Nystrom alumni and asked them to share their own reflections and remembrances. Here are some of the responses we received.

"Chris had such a profound influence on both me and media ecology. When I was lost in my dissertation project, Chris helped me plan my course; she gave me a map and the belief that I could do this thing. She didn't have an obvious public presence, but anyone who passed through Media Ecology at NYU knows she had a pivotal influence with the department. Unlike many academics, Chris didn't seek fame or status but knowledge and clarity in thought. Chris wouldn't hesitate to challenge ideas. In the classes she team taught with Neil, we learned from the way she would wince in disagreement at some of his statements.

Chris helped to significantly shape the curriculum, choose the books and plan the conferences. She was that rare professor who is both an individual and a team player. She helped make the department more than a parade of students seeking degrees, jobs and status—into something of a family or, if family is too strong a word, a collective. Even now, years after I graduated, years after her death, media ecology is not just my degree: more importantly it is a part of my identity, my place in the world.

I really miss Chris and often think of things I wish I had said to her...."

Robert Albrecht, Ph.D., NYU, 1991, New Jersey City University, author of *The Arts and Play as Educational Media in the Digital Age*

"I went back to school for my PhD later in life, in my mid-fifties. Chris Nystrom was my academic advisor and chaired my dissertation committee. She was able to honor and to help me draw upon my professional experience while teaching me key ideas in media ecology and the fundamentals of scholarly research. She demanded quality, but gave me very free rein to explore far-ranging disciplines, ideas, and methods. I continue to be grateful for the time I spent with Chris, which was full of the joy of learning."

Mary Ann Allison, Ph.D., NYU, 2005, Professor Emeritus Hofstra University, co-author of *The Complexity Advantage*

"Chris Nystrom was my role model—first as my professor and mentor, and then also as my friend. She embodied a wonderful combination of rigorous scholarship and humanity. She was deeply self-critical but also funny, and fun to be around. And she could be really tough at times. But only because she expected of her students what she expected of herself: depth, thoroughness, and constant self-doubt—all qualities that at least partly explain why her work was published post-humously by her students. We are all so lucky they did."

Eva Berger, Ph.D., NYU, 1991, co-author of *The Communication Panacea: Pediatrics and General Semantics*

"Building on some of Marshall McLuhan's insights about the impacts of com-munication media on cultures and even human evolution, we early '70's students thought of ourselves as engaged in giving birth to a new pre-paradigmatic communications discipline. When I joined the program as a Masters Candidate in 1972, Christine Nystrom was one of a team of scholars Postman had helping guide our studies. Chris, who agreed to be my doctoral chair, had herself been a foundational contributor. Her own doctoral dissertation attempted to systematize the various approaches and theories swirling around in our nascent communications program into a coherent set of theorems about media and the proper questions we should be asking ourselves as we practiced this new Media Ecology approach. We thought Media Ecology would become THE academic communications paradigm.

If Neil was the resident public intellectual of the Media Ecology program, Chris was its heart and soul. Guiding my own dissertation research, she was always supportive, insightful and patient. As I rambled on about myths, television advertising and Claude Levi-Strauss, she encouraged my intellectual curiosity while helping me overcome roadblocks.

Decades after, Chris and I met for lunch to talk about old times. Though it was taught as part of communication programs worldwide, media ecology had not become THE academic communications paradigm. I asked Chris how she felt about that.

'We have sown our seeds.' was her reply, 'That is good enough.'

And that's true. For the cadre of Neil and Chris's students, the disciplined study of and teaching about our media ecosystems continues."

Robert K. Blechman, Ph.D., NYU, 1978, author of *Executive Severance* (a comic mystery novel composed entirely on Twitter)

"What can I say about Dr Christine Nystrom? She was a friend, a confidant, a role model, and a polymath. Her ability to render the most difficult or abstruse subjects into plain English was remarkable. I studied with all the greats—Postman, Gerbner, Birdwhistell—but there was something special and just plain cool about Chris. Her insight, wit, and sensitivity set her apart. Example: When we met once to discuss an issue in communication theory, Chris veered off- topic into an analysis of Yeats' poetry. I was fascinated but a little confused—til the light dawned, and I realized that the tangent was an unexpected and completely brilliant way to illuminate my question. Chris could do that: juggling multiple, complex ideas at once, yet never to the detriment of clarity.

This book is a testament to her, but a live interaction was the best way to see the rose in her extraordinary mind."

Moshe Botwinick, Ph.D., NYU, 1980, Director of Research at Sesame Street 1980–1990, aka Marc Salem of *Mind Games*

"Chris Nystrom was a woman of intelligence and commitment with a sly sense of humor and a researcher's instinct for truth. She was a wonderful colleague as we pondered in the first year of the program what "media ecology" could possibly mean, even though we had both signed up to be in the first year of an untested, esoteric but exciting field. I remember Chris sitting in a meeting we all held in someone's apartment once more parsing media ecology's meaning where she sat on the couch next to me listening with what I still recall as almost extrasensory intensity. What Chris then did with that listening was help create with Neil and Terry and the rest of the faculty and the students the nucleus of what would become the deepest insights into the program. We knew then that we were prescient, that we were on the cusp of the future of the way people would begin to think about communication. Chris took her passion and curiosity and became an anchor for this new type of investigation.

I honor her depth, her curiosity, her ability to translate clues into a whole field of endeavor. I remember her wry laughter and the camaraderie we all had in the early years of the program. She contributed her rich perspective into a program that influenced hundreds of students and through them hundreds perhaps thousands of others. I am glad to have begun to pioneer this field with Chris as a companion."

Renee Cherow-O'Leary, Ph.D., NYU, 1977, President, Education for the 21st Century and Adjunct Professor, Arts, Culture and Media Program, Rutgers University

"I knew Christine Nystrom very well from my time in the Media Ecology master's and doctoral programs at NYU. She was a pain in the ass, albeit one that was far more brilliant than you were. She could go over a single sentence in a paper for twenty minutes. WHY language was important was the point. And if you couldn't handle the small details, you would never see the big picture. Sure, Nystrom was a pain, but she knew hundreds of books inside and out. We were constantly given excerpts of detailed drafts, "laws" and outlines of things she was writing. They didn't just help me in my classes with her, they helped me be a more involved and better teacher.

The works of Christine Nystrom will not only provide insights into her brilliant analytic mind, but also into the field of media ecology. I like to think of her in the afterlife, looking down at my writing and sadly shaking her head. Probably deservedly."

Brian Cogan, Ph.D., NYU, 2002, Molloy College, author of *Encyclopedia of Punk*

"There were few who knew her that did not love her: for her work in our Media Ecology program, for her selfless dedication to our work and our projects, for those pointed questions that sharpened our thinking, our writing, or our presentations. For generations of doctoral students at NYU, Chris Nystrom—part of the trinity that was Neil, Terry and Chris—was a voice in our heads, a primary audience as we wrote or spoke, a significant part of our conversations with the world. One of the questions that would inevitably be part of our work would always be, 'So, what do you think Chris would say?'"

Salvatore Fallica, Ph.D., NYU, 1991, NYU

"Perhaps more than any other person in the Media Ecology program at NYU, Christine Nystrom touched my life in a way I will never forget. She was a brilliant scholar, a passionate scholar, a disciplined scholar. With great tact and sensitivity she helped me bring out the best in my writing by bringing out the best in my thinking. I will always be grateful to Chris for role-modeling deeply intellectual scholarship, but at the same time for encouraging me to allow compassion and empathy for others to inform my work."

Peter K Fallon, Ph.D. NYU, 1996, Roosevelt University, author of *The Metaphysics of Media*

"Christine was my mentor and my dissertation advisor. And I would not have it any other way.

She had the most supremely linear and incisive mind I have ever encountered. And working with her could be…daunting. But her measured, always spot-on response to your thinking, your ideas, your writing always led you so much further and deeper than you would have gone on your own, which was right on track to where you needed to be.

When I think back on how I ended up in the Media Ecology program at that time, I realize how lucky I am. Christine will always be my intellectual mother, and the greatest influence on how I think: a gift for which I could never adequately and appropriately thank her. All I can do is ensure that her influence lives on in my work. Like the rest of us, I am that much the richer for knowing her, for having worked with her, and for having her imprint live on in the ways, and to the extent it has shaped all that I do.

If it was Neil who took McLuhan's passing use of the term 'media ecology' and built upon and ran with the metaphor for all it was worth, it was Christine who truly followed through on it to create the fully-realized conceptual ground we now recognize as the field of media ecology. We must recognize her for this—not just those who learned from her, but those who we continue to tell."

Thom Gencarelli, Ph.D., NYU, 1993, Manhattan College, co-author of *Baby Boomers and Popular Culture*

"Sharper than a surgeon's scalpel, intellectually generous, profoundly analytical, brilliantly inquisitive, a master of connecting disciplines…and able to leap tall buildings in a single bound. These were Chris Nystrom's contributions to Media Ecology, her students, and her colleagues throughout her career. Chris's was not a search for answers so much as it was the call to create a structure through which sense could be made of the connecting strands of the universe.

Once, deep in a classroom conversation about the power of language she challenged any student to write the words 'I sell Chris Nystrom my soul in exchange for an A in this course.' I still have the notebook where I penned those words. This small blurb of praise cannot in any way compensate for the wonder, awe, knowledge, and joy that Dr. Nystrom brought to my life and the lives of so many others. These writings will shape and guide the research of students and faculty for years to come."

Stephanie Gibson, Ph.D., NYU, 1991, University of Baltimore, author of *The Emerging Cyberculture*

"Christine Nystrom prepared generations of scholars and teachers to think critically about media, culture, and the human relationship with their symbolic environment. She knew how to ask questions that precisely identified weaknesses in arguments and strengthened them, and she taught her students how to formulate these questions themselves. I still use my notes from her courses to hone my thinking, and I am grateful that her writing and notes have been collected into these volumes so that subsequent generations of students can benefit from them."

Michael Grabowski, Ph.D. NYU, 2006, Manhattan College

"Chris Nystrom was that rare combination as a teacher of a voice of clear reason and a source of emotional support. Years after completing my doctorate, I went down to NYU after my first major book was published to have lunch with Neil and Chris. After lunch, Chris insisted on taking me to a local bookstore, where she introduced me and the book to the store owner. She was a champion of her students long after they had graduated, for the rest of their lives."

Paul Levinson, Ph.D., NYU, 1979, Fordham, author of *New New Media*

"Chris deserves far more credit for the thinking that went to the creation of the Media Ecology program at NYU than she has received.

She was my dissertation advisor and I think of her as a friend. We'd been to each other's apartments for social encounters. One of the best involved organizing small groups of friends to attend performances of Shakespeare productions, mostly at the Public Theater. I did this for a few years—a week or so before the date of the play, we'd get together for dinner and to read an edited version of the play that I put together. We'd take turns with parts and discuss what we thought of the characters. It was a great way to prepare for the performances. Chris was as enthusiastic, articulate, and insightful about Shakespeare as she was about our dissertations. She covered all the bases."

David Linton, Ph.D., NYU, 1982, Professor Emeritus Marymount Manhattan College, author of *Men and Menstruation*

"Chris was much more than a brilliant writer, an original thinker, and a professor who never cut corners when it came to teaching her students. Among the treasures in my family albums are several pictures taken in Chris' place in downtown Manhattan late in the summer of 1989, when she invited me and my family for a small gathering to help celebrate the recent arrival of our first child. I can never forget how Chris played with Xuanmin, made him laugh, and helped him burp after the bottle. You should see the carefree joy and genuine curiosity on her face then. To us in the family, Chris was also a kind, fun, and loving 'auntie.'"

Casey Man-Kong Lum, Ph.D., NYU, 1989, William Paterson University, author and editor of *Perspectives in Media Ecology*

"For me, Chris Nystrom set inspiring examples of theoretical daring and skill, systemized thinking, and precision."

Joshua Meyrowitz, Ph.D., NYU, 1979, University of New Hampshire, author of *No Sense of Place*

"As a teacher Chris prepared for every class as if teaching it for the first time; she would consult the readings and create her handwritten notes for the evening, no matter how many times she taught that course. When teaching, Chris would take a comment from a student and stop and consider it, sometimes for the better part of a minute. She was not afraid of the silence, although it's possible it made some students uncomfortable.

As wonderful as it is to be immersed in the energy and thoughts that arise in Greenwich Village, a definite myopia can emerge. Chris never let you forget to think more broadly and inclusively. No one's sensibilities should be dismissed without investigation. Goodness knows we need that lesson now more than ever.

Neil Postman used to joke that as long as he waited long enough, Chris would forget that some idea or other was hers and he could then write his next book.... I actually saw that in action when we were somewhere—I think Amsterdam—and Chris was talking about some idea and Neil was writing things down saying 'slow down, slow down.'"

Bill Petkanas, Ph.D., NYU, 1990, Professor & Co-Chair, Western Connecticut State University
Missy Alexander, Ph.D., NYU, 2000, Provost and Vice President of Academic Affairs, WCSU

"Chris Nystrom had a question she was famous for asking: 'So what?' It was never enough for your work to be interesting only to you—it had to do something bigger, had to have a purpose, had to feel necessary. 'So what?' was an invitation to be a better thinker and scholar, and to be ready for whatever criticism might come your way.

So many years later, I still keep a piece of paper with the words 'So what?' printed on it, in enormous font. Today, I pose this question to my own graduate students."

Devon Powers, Ph.D., NYU, 2008, Temple University, author of *On Trend: The Business of Forecasting the Future*, and co-author *Blowing Up the Brand*

"I have never met anyone as dedicated to and enthusiastic about the life of the mind as Christine Nystrom. While presenting in Dissertation Proposal Seminar or the monthly colloquia, you could feel the intensity with which Chris was listening and trying to 'get' what you were saying—the big and small ideas, the sources of the inquiry, the meaning of that topic to you as an investigator—even if the larger import of the project was as yet unclear. This was, of course, summed up in Chris's perennial question—'So what?' She meant this not as a dismissal but instead thought-provoking preparation for rigorous challenges that we would face throughout our careers as scholars, consultants and teachers. If we couldn't artic- ulate how and why what we were exploring connected to the world outside the academy... then why were we doing it?

Chris taught me that scholarship needed to intervene in what existed, but also be relevant to what would or could be—to contribute to a larger conception of how people think about media environments and the cultures they create. Chris's scholarly work evidences this continual striving to connect, expand, explore and make explicit media ecology's relevance to the human endeavor.

Beyond the seriousness with which Chris took her mentorship role was her generosity of self. She took the time to get to know us as people and shared our personal and professional trials and successes. I miss her and I am grateful that Chris Nystrom's work is being brought to the larger audience it so richly deserves."

M.J. Robinson, Ph.D., NYU, 2008, Brooklyn College, author of *Television on Demand*

"The Media Ecology program showed me that big ideas could be immense fun—for me, it was the first time being smart was something to be encouraged, even expected—and Chris was a wonderful dissertation advisor. Where else could I have done a dissertation on 'acoustic environments' and who else would have encouraged me to stick with it? The eclecticism of the program prepared me for a career I had never even heard of—executive coaching and mediation. I use what I learned every single day.

Chris was a good friend as well as a mentor and educator. She came to the rescue one night when I had been attacked in my apartment building. After a day or two of forcing myself to go home each night, she told me to stop being so brave and dragged me off to her apartment for some sleep. I am grateful for the guidance and friendship I found with Chris. She is greatly missed."

Maria Simpson, Ph.D., NYU, 1980, executive coach, consultant, trainer and mediator, author of *But How Do I Say That?*

"Christine influenced my thinking in a manner few other people during my adult life have been able to imitate. Her critical judgment and well-honed skepticism have become an integral part of my intellectual and ethical reasoning. Her erudition was what I would describe as 'isotopic.' For instance, when an element gains a neutron, that's sufficient to change the whole nature of the atom. The added particle shifts the entire behavior of the element. Chris had an analogous effect upon me. She would utter something concisely—often in a rather benign manner, but which would have such force of intellect—that I could never perceive the universe in the same fashion again upon grasping the truth and significance of her utterance."

Jonathan Slater, Ph.D., NYU, 1987, Chair and Professor of Journalism and Public Relations, and director, Institute for Ethics in Public Life, SUNY College at Plattsburgh

"Chris had a brilliant mind, and she was the first true theorist of media ecology, developing hypotheses, models, and methodologies. Chris brought structure, order, and coherence to the Media Ecology program because that was the kind of person she was,—structured, orderly, and coherent—but also because that was what the program needed, and Chris was the kind of person who did what needed to be done.

Chris was a dedicated and demanding teacher, insisting on scholarly rigor, unwilling to accept anything less than our best efforts. And she always gave us her best efforts. She paid attention to what we had to say, really read what we wrote, and critiqued both form and content in fine detail. She could be intimidating, and she didn't win any popularity contests, but she pushed us to be better, to be the best that we could be. Chris was my teacher, mentor, and advisor, and I credit her with making me a better writer, and teaching me how to be a scholar."

Lance Strate, Ph.D., NYU, 1991, Fordham, *author of Media Ecology: An Approach to Understanding the Human Condition*

"Christine Nystrom had a profound impact on my career. Her approach to media studies combined both curiosity and intellectual rigor that encouraged me to dig deep below the surface. As a mentor, she was encouraging, but never coddling, which pushed me to deliver my best. To this day, her work and words influence my approach to media criticism and content creation."

Toni Urbano, M.A, NYU, 1997, Director, NYU-TV and the Television Center

Lance Strate
General Editor

This series is devoted to scholarship relating to media ecology, a field of inquiry defined as the study of media as environments. Within this field, the term "medium" can be defined broadly to refer to any human technology or technique, code or symbol system, invention or innovation, system or environment. Media ecology scholarship typically focuses on how technology, media, and symbolic form relate to communication, consciousness, and culture, past, present and future. This series is looking to publish research that furthers the formal development of media ecology as a field; that brings a media ecology approach to bear on specific topics of interest, including research and theoretical or philosophical investigations concerning the nature and effects of media or a specific medium; that includes studies of new and emerging technologies and the contemporary media environment as well as historical studies of media, technology, and modes and codes of communication; scholarship regarding technique and the technological society; scholarship on specific types of media and culture (e.g., oral and literate cultures, image, etc.), or of specific aspects of culture such as religion, politics, education, journalism, etc.; critical analyses of art and popular culture; and studies of how physical and symbolic environments function as media.

For additional information about this series or for the submission of manuscripts, please contact:
Lance Strate, Series Editor | *strate@fordham.edu*

To order other books in this series, please contact our Customer Service Department:
peterlang@presswarehouse.com (within the U.S.)
orders@peterlang.com (outside the U.S.)

Or browse online by series:
www.peterlang.com